Unraveling Time

Joe R. and Teresa Lozano Long Series
in Latin American and Latino Art and Culture

Unraveling Time

Thirty Years of Ethnography in Cuenca, Ecuador

ANN MILES

University of Texas Press ⌄⌄ *Austin*

Requests for permission to reproduce material from this work should be sent to:
Permissions
University of Texas Press
P.O. Box 7819
Austin, TX 78713-7819
utpress.utexas.edu/rp-form

∞ The paper used in this book meets the minimum requirements of
ANSI/NISO Z39.48-1992 (R1997) (Permanence of Paper).

Library of Congress Cataloging-in-Publication Data

Names: Miles, Ann (Ann M.), author.
Title: Unraveling time : thirty years of ethnography in Cuenca, Ecuador / Ann Miles.
Description: First edition. | Austin : University of Texas Press, 2022. | Includes
bibliographical references and index.
Identifiers:
LCCN 2022007998
ISBN 978-1-4773-2618-3 (cloth)
ISBN 978-1-4773-2619-0 (paperback)
ISBN 978-1-4773-2620-6 (pdf)
ISBN 978-1-4773-2621-3 (epub)
Subjects: LCSH: Ethnology—Ecuador—Cuenca—History. | Social change—
Ecuador—Cuenca—History. | Ecuadorians—Ecuador—Cuenca—Biography. |
Overtourism—Ecuador—Cuenca—History. | Americans—Ecuador—Cuenca—History.
Classification: LCC GN564.E2 M45 2022 | DDC 305.800946/47—dc23/eng/20220304
LC record available at https://lccn.loc.gov/2022007998

doi:10.7560/326183

Contents

Acknowledgments

A project that is as embedded in time as this one is necessarily involves a world of others who have helped and inspired in both big and small ways. The debts have mounted as the years have accrued. A number of colleagues in Ecuador have been there from the start of my career more than thirty years ago, providing friendship and conversation and lending me their *palanca* when needed. In the early years, when communication technology was limited and Ecuador seemed much farther away, these people helped tether me to the place. Most important among them are Ana Luz Borrero and Jaime Astudillo from the University of Cuenca and Lynn Hirschkind, an independent scholar whose knowledge of Cuenca is as deep as it is long. Over the years, my time in Cuenca was enriched by long conversations and collaborations with many other scholars and friends in Ecuador, including Debbie Truhan, Leonor and Bolivar Crespo, María del Carmen Ochoa, Claudio Galarza, José Cardenas, Kay Wilson, Anne Carr, Patricio Carpio, Juan Pablo Vanegas, Juan Martínez Borrero, Pablo Parra, Israel Isidro, and Mateo Estrella.

Several colleagues read parts of this book or listened to my plans for it, in some cases well before any of us knew exactly where it might be headed. Among those whose comments found their way into my thinking and writing or whose interest and support have buoyed me along are Hans Buechler, Frank Salomon, Kristina Wirtz, Maria Amelia Viteri, Alisa Perkins, Sarah Hill, Jim Butterfield, and Todd Kuchta. In recent years, conversations and email exchanges with Matthew Hayes have provoked me to think about lifestyle migration to Cuenca in ways that I was otherwise disinclined to do. His insightful yet compassionate interpretations challenge me to do better. I am exceedingly appreciative for Kathleen Skoczen's enthusiasm and tough love early on, Robert Ulin's embrace of friendship and careful and gentle critique, and David Hartmann's unfailing trueheartedness. I also wish to acknowledge my colleagues on the advisory board of the University Center for the Humanities at Western Michigan University for our lively conversations and their warmth and support. I am indebted to my dear friend Irma Lopez for always caring.

This book was substantially improved because of the hard work and combined wisdom of the three scholarly reviewers, O. Hugo Benavides, Rudi Colloredo-Mansfeld, and Walter Little. Each brought a fresh perspective to the manuscript, helping me to see it, or the potential for it, in ways I did not anticipate. Working through their circumspect and sage advice and commentaries has expanded my thinking and helped me write a better book by far. The peer-review process, when it works well, helps writers build on their strengths and attend to their weaknesses. I am grateful to these three reviewers for their honesty and for helping me to do both of these things.

Casey Kittrell at the University of Texas Press saw an early version of this manuscript, and it is only because of his careful reading, insightful commentary, and persistent vetting that it developed in the way that it has. I am thankful for his thoughtful yet firm recommendations and his patience, and I am much appreciative of his enduring commitment to this project. He is a writer's editor.

I have been asked from time to time how I have been able to keep up the connections and relationships I have in Ecuador over such a long time. The answer to this question is fairly simple. I never had to choose between my family in Michigan and my friends, family, and ethnographic work in Ecuador. My husband, Rich, and my daughter, Isabel, have always been steadfast, ready, and enthusiastic companions in fieldwork. They too see the families I work with as our own extended family, and I am fairly convinced that Rich and Isabel are dearer to people in Ecuador than I am. I know my friends in Cuenca share my hope that the connections between our families will live beyond us; in 2018, as Lucho drove my daughter and me to his house, built from earnings from his hard work in New York, he kept pointing out landmarks to Isabel. "See here, Chavela [a nickname for Isabel], you have to look for this building, . . . and this is where you turn right. Some day, when we old folks are gone, you'll need to find your way here."

This leaves me with the biggest debt, the one I cannot ever repay and the one that remains largely nameless. While most of the people described in this book have told me to use their real names, I am hesitant to do that or to thank them publicly here by those names. This digital world can be an unexpected one. But this much I know is true: my career and my life are unthinkable without the Quitasacas and their extended kin and without Blanca and Jessica and all the others named and unnamed here. It is their *cariño* that has made Ecuador a place my family is happy to visit, and it is their patience, affection, and trust that is at the heart of every word I write.

Unraveling Time

CHAPTER 1

The Ethnography of Accrual
1988–2020

When I first met Rosa Quitasaca, in 1988, she was living in the city of Cuenca, Ecuador, raising her five children in two rooms. A rural-to-urban migrant from the surrounding countryside, Rosa and her husband had come to the city a few years earlier to make a better life for their children. Rosa did not dress like an urban woman but displayed her rural heritage by wearing the clothing of a *chola cuencana*. The *chola cuencana* is known regionally as a rural woman usually engaged in agriculture or the marketing of agricultural products and identifiable because of her distinctive clothing. The *chola* is distinguished by her two long braids, locally produced straw Panama hat, richly colored ikat-dyed shawl, and *pollera*, a thick, wool, usually embroidered, gathered skirt. Some rural-to-urban migrant women tried to disguise their country backgrounds and the associated stigma by wearing western-style clothing, perhaps a simple skirt or, less likely, pants, but Rosa told me she would never abandon the *pollera*. Changing her clothing, she said, would be like wearing a carnival costume; it would be a kind of performance of an identity that was not her own. At the time, I interpreted this as a clear example of identity politics; Rosa was resisting hegemonic ideals of proper city comportment and openly refusing to deny or devalue her rural heritage.

Then my certainty about Rosa's plucky resistance to urban pressures slowly unraveled as I watched her year by year shed the *chola cuencana* clothing if not wholly the identity. Encouraged by her teenage son, who was embarrassed by his mother's *chola* dress and the rural lifeways it signified, Rosa's transformation came bit by bit. First she stopped wearing the hat, then she replaced the shawl with a sweater, and by the late 1990s her two braids turned into a ponytail, and she abandoned the iconic *pollera* in favor of a common, western-style skirt. Her skirts were conservative, falling well past the knee, and I thought she wore them self-consciously and a bit awkwardly. Even then she told me that pants were most certainly out of the question for her; she was far too old to make that kind of radical move. But that resolution did not last either, and by the early 2000s she was wearing pants, only around the house "for the cold," she said. In high altitudes the nights can be chilly, and when there is no sun, homes often remain dank throughout the day. By 2011, when her youngest son graduated from high school, Rosa accompanied him to the ceremony wearing tight pants and high heels. Today her hair is in a short bob, she never thinks of putting on a skirt, and her *polleras* lie in a dusty box under her bed. She now considers them "antiques."

This book is about changes, ones that come incrementally and those that are radical or strategically planned, and about the ethnographic process of documenting and interpreting them. Change can come slowly, fitfully, and by degrees, like Rosa's progression away from the *chola* identity, and sometimes, like the chic restaurants that accompany tourism and gentrification, they may seem to appear overnight. Occasionally, changes, like a mother quietly accepting and loving her openly gay son in New York, are noteworthy to me only because I know things were not always this way. The arc of human lives and the pace and shape of the worlds people navigate collide in myriad ways to reinforce the essential or shift something in another direction. My goal in this book is to present an ethnographic portrait of a city, Cuenca, Ecuador, and the people who live there over a time of rapid social and cultural change. I strive to portray a place in motion but also to highlight the intimate details of people's lives, in some cases over three decades. As time passes and lives unfold, children grow up, renovations displace families, people get sick, streetlights make neighborhoods safer, remittances from overseas build new homes and sometimes tear families apart, roads connect people who once were far away, cafés and bars offer nightlife, and cell phones replace hanging out at the corner store as a space for meeting friends. I aim to make sense of the disparate experiences and perspectives of a culture over time, how people experience the changes they seek and the ones that are forced upon them, and how ethnographic writing can capture some of this.

While I examine change over time and rely on thirty years of ethnographic observations, this book is not a contemporary reexamination and updating of earlier research themes (Babb 2018), nor is it what has come to be known in anthropology as a restudy or revisit. In a restudy, an anthropologist returns to a location, usually a small, remote village, perhaps after decades have passed, to follow up on previous work, either theirs or someone else's (Knauft 2002; Pace 1998; Pendelton 2002). Bruce Knauft returned to New Guinea fifteen years after his original research to document "a world before and after" (2002, 11). Because restudies are usually conducted many years after the original fieldwork and in some cases several decades later, they are exceedingly useful for documenting, as Knauft does, how things have changed, especially after new and usually disruptive encounters with global capitalism. The Gebusi are no longer the relatively "traditional" and isolated group they were in 1980 when Knauft first met them, and among the numerous alterations he found was the awareness that they were now marginal and subordinate in a state that sees their lifeways as backward and dispensable. A revisit of this type, usually characterized by a long absence, allows differences to stand out in sharp relief—people once did that, and now they do this.

In contrast, this book does not represent a revisit to a past, estranged (Scheper-Hughes 2001),[1] or temporarily inaccessible (Price and Price 2017)[2] field site; instead it is an attempt to describe what it is like to maintain connections and record culture over the long term. I have been going to Ecuador every year or every other year for three decades, staying always in the same city and reconnecting with many of the same people whom I met in 1988–1989. The regularity of my engagement can make it difficult for me to recollect what things were like when I was first there because those understandings have been layered over, year after year, with new impressions as I revisit Cuenca annually or biannually.

It is possible that my frequent visits may have made identifying changes harder, not easier. So, for example, one year someone might tell me that they are thinking about buying land to build a home. The next time I come, I might be driven to see the plot and hear a description of what they have in mind. The following year they may share with me some sketches for the layout of the house; the year after I might see that a foundation has been laid, then a concrete skeleton takes shape, and pretty soon having a house of one's own seems like something that was somehow always in the works (Lobo 1982). So much of change builds on itself, as first one small thing happens, then another, so that the point when something becomes different is not all that clear. I attempt here to describe change as it occurs in the small moments over the long course without relying on a before and after as a central organizing idea. One way I do this is to focus on individual biographies and the important and ordinary moments of everyday lives. This is the best way that I know to animate the abstract or ambiguous and begin to understand the significance of cultural practices, continuities, and changes. The past, it seems to me, can be found in a life story in which what was and what is are blended in memory and experience.

To complicate matters, I tackle understanding culture and change in an urban environment, a city of nearly a half million people. Cities have change knit into the very fabric of daily life, and difference, cultural and otherwise, is usually just around the next corner. Cities attract innovators and change makers like Rosa, who moved to the city so things would be different for her family, and development is integral to the urban ethos. As cities position themselves for the future, they plan and implement all kinds of projects that resonate not just locally but globally, as the recent influx of North American expats to Cuenca shows. Cities are complex and diverse places, and it can be challenging to delineate ethnographic or analytic boundaries when studying them. The ways and means by which people and ideas circulate and are expressed in a city are endless.

Doing ethnographic work in urban settings often means having to narrow one's lens or risk becoming overwhelmed by the possibilities and discontinuities; it means accepting that modernity and globalization are a constant presence and not an identifiable or partial incursion. To contain the intersecting and overlapping possibilities inherent in city life, as urban anthropologists we often limit our work to a specific topic, much as I did when I studied women suffering from lupus, or to a neighborhood or defined geographic area. Doing so constructs some practical and conceptual boundaries around what can often seem too fluid or diverse to pin down. Often, those boundaries are more apparent than real. In my case, while my early work with rural-to-urban migrants was geographically bounded in the central historical district, since then I have mostly followed people, taking me throughout the city and its various neighborhoods, sometimes to rural homes and even to New York City.

When I began my ethnographic research in 1988, the small village study was still the gold standard in anthropology, but that was soon to change as we confronted an increasingly dynamic world and a shifting set of disciplinary expectations. The 1980s brought a radical, postmodern critique of classic, objective, realist ethnographies, usually conducted among small, remote groups, igniting a disciplinary reckoning. Most of the critiques were concerned with examining and coming to terms with the postcolonial power dynamics inherent in the anthropological endeavor, including who we study and how, how we write, how we make claims to authoritative knowledge of other cultures and peoples, and how we might reflect on our own subjectivities as they come to bear on our ethnographic work.

Today, ethnography has come unbound from the village; multisited ethnography is the norm, and that early postmodern variation of sincere self-reflexivity seems to be beside the point. Our reflexive concerns today are far less self-referential, and they primarily concern anthropologists' responsibilities as ethical and sympathetic actors and writers. Sympathy entails responsibility, if not for righting wrongs, then for at least getting the story right. Michael Jackson considers the idea of "fidelity," that is, how ethnographic writing can do justice to others' experiences and the difficulties of balancing the empathetic and personal with the neutral and general in writing. Jackson observes, "Judging when to define one's task as one of creating order, identifying causes, and connecting facts (i.e., knowing, explaining, or interpreting the world) or as one of describing, narrating, and communicating the experience of life as lived becomes a crucial issue" (2017, 60). I share Jackson's concern here and want my writing to both say something and *mean* something, that is, to inform, enlighten, and also move the reader. For Jackson, this means the writer cannot always close the gap between "what can be described and what can be explained" and that "sound" writing "involves a resistance to closure, a resolve to *suggest* meaning rather than spell it out" (59). Jackson is not arguing against objectivity but rather recognizing that writing about the human condition requires one to allow for uncertainty. When writing about people, understanding may be more important than explanation, and ambiguity is itself a kind of realism.

As globalization and media technology have ramped up the pace of travel and expanded the venues for exchange, ethnography too has embraced a rangy kind of methodological, textual, and experiential eclecticism. The field has expanded to include online spaces and media, and so, in recent years, I have kept up with the goings-on in Cuenca by reading the local paper online and streaming news radio, and I follow the growth of the expat population through their online newsletters, blogs, and forums. To be sure, open access to media resources goes in several directions, and although it is easier for me to keep up with what people in Ecuador are doing, they too can read what others and I write about them. Our writing and therefore our presentations of others are far more available and more subject to scrutiny than ever before, and this too is worth considering (J. Jackson 2015). Indeed, in 2015 the expat community in Cuenca exploded in online fury when an analysis of their racial privilege written by the Canadian sociologist Matthew Hayes came to their attention. The online responses to an abridged version of his article were quick and harsh, and the commenters berated and belittled Hayes for pointing out the white privilege that expats often unknowingly exercise. Completing the circle, these posts, then, became yet another source of information and insight into the feelings and thinking of the gringo community in Cuenca.[3] I ended up writing a conference paper about expat privilege and anger and the cultural inabilities of North Americans to face their racism and privilege.

Long-term ethnographic engagement of the type I write about here is a kind of ethnography of accrual. By accrual I mean to draw attention to both circumstances on the ground that appear to be different as time passes and the means by which we come to know, experience, and interpret those changes. I do not simply mean that visible changes add up, although quite often they do, but also that the processes of knowing, interpreting, representing, and writing are constituted on multiple accruals of experiences, interactions, observations, and ideas. Accruals can come slowly or quickly; they can be obvious or hidden, single stranded or multidirectional. Moreover, the meaning of accruals is always subject to the moment at hand. My field notes have accrued over the decades, yet they have meaning only through an ever-moving set of "head notes"—the shifts in thinking or in prominent theories or the general swirl of ideas that influence our perspectives at any given moment (Sanjek 1990).

In this book I examine ethnographic accruals from multiple perspectives. Most simply, we will see the accrual of time in the lives of individuals and how the biography of a life is an enactment and a representation of multiple accruals. Thirty years is a goodly amount of time in a life; children grow to adulthood, young people's dreams are shattered or fulfilled, and mothers find their hectic lives caring for children have slowed and they stare down loneliness. Sometimes people now tell me things because the years have accrued and I look older, and that somehow changes their perceptions of me, or more commonly because I have been in and out of their lives for so long now that they no longer worry about saving face.

Some interpretations of what I have observed come to me only after many years have passed and I learn more, put ideas together in a different way, or understand the difference between something of importance in the moment and something with deeper resonance. In other words, accruals open the door to different understandings. For example, it took me nearly twenty years of hearing the term *sufrimiento*, suffering, first among the poor, then among the wealthy, and finally among the chronically ill, for me to understand it as far more meaningful than my first interpretation of it, as a sign of peasant women's resistance, would suggest. It was the accrual of years, of changing circumstances, of experiences, and of anthropological theories that led me to see women's *sufrimiento* as a far more profound expression of women's social and moral conditions (Miles 2013).

While accruals can sometimes help fill in knowledge gaps and extend and enrich interpretive powers, they also can seemingly complicate understandings as more information and further examples can easily serve to whittle away at surety. Accrual brings to mind the old adage of the more you see the less you know, or as David Parkin writes more particularly about ethnography, "The closer we get to our field through prolonged involvement, the more fuzzy the categories by which we know it" (2000, 265). I am challenged to offer conclusive statements about trends that I have witnessed, to explain their origins or their effects. Instead, I often turn to descriptions of the various elements—structural changes, political dynamics, interpersonal experiences, and cultural flows—to suggest possibilities for what might be consequential and to contribute to the reader's understanding of the meaning of accruals for those who experience them.

Ethnography over Time

In the past, that is to say, when I started doing ethnography in the late 1980s, anthropologists could clearly delineate their fieldwork time and place; one was "in the field" or not. Travel was expensive and often difficult, and there were few mechanisms to stay in touch across the distance. Laptops and portable computers were not common then, and the internet was in its infancy. Most serious writing about one's fieldwork occurred upon one's return home, and it involved, at least in part, what Catherine Allen has called "memory work." Allen returned frequently to the small Peruvian village of Sonq'o in a cycle of "traveling, visiting, and remembering" that formed the substance of her ethnographic writing (Allen 2002, 8). Memory work is vital to anthropological descriptions because field notes, photographs, and tape recordings capture only so much, and memory fills in the details. Reflecting on something is not the same as being immersed in it, however, and the process of remembering brings some things to the surface and not others. But that is only a small part of the value or meaning of memory work. Memories are not just about remembering facts or events; they are social and emotional constructions created through interactions and understandings with people and places. As Allen points out, memories are revisited and reworked every time we return to the field or increasingly now, when the field comes to us.

Although anthropologists have long agreed that culture is enacted in everyday life, nothing brings this idea to life more completely than going back to the same place and seeing what you thought was true dissipate, disappear, or be flatly denied. Elizabeth Colson writes that long-term fieldwork helps researchers see how people are "in the stream of time," and time, as we know, changes everything (1984, 1). Our participants very often do not do what they tell us they are going to do, confounding our expectations and theories, and then our own interpretive frames shift too. Those of us who do long-term ethnography in the same place no doubt have written things that now appear to be naïve or, to put the best spin on it, have not stood the test of time. There were times I thought something was far more consequential, resonant, and durable than it turned out to be, throwing into doubt the explanatory power of my interpretations. Rosa's shift from the *pollera* is a clear example of this.

Moreover, long-term ethnographic engagement with a single individual or a small group of people can create sympathies of mind that are difficult if not impossible to unravel. Much of my early work was centered on families adjusting to rural-to-urban and transnational migration, and I spent many years going back and forth visiting with a very small group of families. At a certain point, however, I came to wonder if my presence in the lives of the families I worked with no longer made them typical examples of how life was changing for the poor. Some of my interventions over the years were big, like helping to pay for children's schooling, and sometimes, as I have learned, even the smallest things I have said or done were taken into some account. To wit, Rosa's daughter is sure that her mother's favorite ice cream flavor is blackberry not because she loves blackberries but because I do. "She likes anything you like," she told me. I don't know how to truly take into account what I have meant in the lives of my closest friends in Ecuador and how I might have changed things both big and small for them. At a certain point I had to confront the realization that I might be seeing something that is to some extent a product of my own creation, and I don't mean theoretically. Would they be who they are today without my influence? After years of conversations and watching our children grow up and seeing one another through good times and bad, have we co-constructed one another to such an extent that we are unreliable witnesses of each other's lives?

I do think, however, that the advantages of long-term engagement in one place for truly understanding cultural concepts and change are incalculable and far outweigh the disadvantages. While much has changed over the years in our anthropological orientations, the truth is that what we as anthropologists strive to understand is still as simple as a "native's" point of view (Malinowski 1961, 25; Howell and Talle 2012, 3). Yet, so much of the cultural is unknowable, even or perhaps especially for those deeply enmeshed in its every nuance. Nothing should be taken at face value.

Still, anthropologists do that all the time. Sometimes we take what we see and hear at face value because our interlocutors manage to convince us to do that. Sometimes we take them at face value because they fit with our own schematic understandings of how culture is negotiated or enacted and sometimes because that is all we can know and it appears to be better than knowing nothing. It is here that time spent in the same place might afford some advantages. That back-and-forth movement from field to home and back again, flawed as it is, is a crucial means of revealing our own interpretive positions.

The practice of long-term ethnography obviously provides the ethnographer with a view of how people's lives move chronologically through time, and it presents opportunities to move between the past and the present. This works on several dimensions. Sharing memories of times spent together is a source of relationship building and an important way for me to gauge how people see the trajectories of their own lives. Often when I talk with Ecuadorians about our shared past, they are reminded of some awful place they lived or how difficult their circumstances were. "Remember when we didn't even have a bathroom?" or "Who can say *how* many families lived in that building!" Or, more nostalgically, "Remember, Anita, when we made those *humitas* at my mother's house?"[4] Comments like these allow me to see how people understand their lives today in comparison to the past and to get a feel for what and who matters to them. These reminiscences often lead to longer conversations, and not infrequently I learn things I did not previously know. While anthropologists regularly recognize that the people who inhabit our field sites become a part of our past, Johannes Fabiano argues that ethnography is enhanced when we also become part of the pasts of those with whom we work (2014, 90).

Anthropological fieldwork, by its very nature, dabbles in the personal, and anthropologists linger at least partially "in the shadows" where the "border between personal life and formal ethnography begin to blur" (Goslinga and Frank 2007, xi). These relationships can tug at our emotions in uncomfortable ways, as closeness leads inevitably to responsibility and then too often to self-recrimination when our expectations for ourselves come up short, or our understandings of responsibility do not match those of others (High 2011; Mintz 2000). Close relationships in the field often develop serendipitously, perhaps over a shared meal or a mutual need, or they may come about slowly when two people find they have a kind of rapport. They are incredibly important not just for the collection of data but also for the well-being of the anthropologist, or at least they were for me in a time before Skype and email. Fieldwork in Ecuador in the late 1980s, even in a city, could be lonely business. My communication with home during my year and a half of initial fieldwork came via snail mail, and that was when the Ecuadorian postal workers were not on strike. The need for companionship and company would sometimes be as strong a motivation for me as collecting data for getting out and visiting people.

Time also changes how we feel about events and relationships, sometimes making things easier to talk about and sometimes offering a significant revision of a previous interpretation. As I return to events in the past with people, I find a certain degree of solace in the consistency of the stories and impressions that are retold, providing me with some assurance that I got some of them right. But then, I am also surprised from time to time when events are recounted differently or have been given alternate meanings. I cannot always know what to make of these discrepancies. It is unlikely that one version is truer than another, and we all change how we feel and understand events over time. A slight that threatened a relationship is repaired by a single gesture, or an evolving family crisis reconfigures how an earlier event is understood. Given the transnational migration from the region and the remittances sent back, there are constantly shifting alliances of who is sharing, who is not, and what that says about them. Often it is not the singular instance that matters but the patterns of instances that accrue over time.

Over the years, my status in life has changed, and that too has affected my relationships in Ecuador. Every time I return, there are subtle and not-so-subtle shifts in how Ecuadorians see me, how they treat me, and the expectations they have for my behavior. I have gone from being a *señorita* to a *comadre* and *madrina* (co-mother and godmother) to a *señora* and a *madre* (wife and mother), and each of these statuses has different expectations and privileges. The most difficult status for me was certainly that of *señorita*, in part because I was new to Ecuador and my relations were still tenuous, but also because there was little cultural precedence in 1988 for a young, single woman to travel and live on her own in Cuenca. While most people understood that I was from a different culture with different standards of behavior, I still received plenty of comments about how my parents must be *descuidados*, careless, to let me travel on my own. People also held plenty of stereotypes about the promiscuity of American women gleaned no doubt from movies, television, pin-up calendars, and even tourists. In 1989 the movie *Fatal Attraction* reached Ecuador and, referencing that movie, one Ecuadorian asked me whether it was common for a man and a woman to meet at a business meeting and have torrid sex in the elevator afterward, as happened in that film. In the United States, viewers likely interpreted this scene as a plausible but highly dubious plot development, but in Ecuador it was seemingly taken at face value.

Stereotypes about American women surely influenced the interactions I had with some Ecuadorians early on, and I have written elsewhere about the awkward relationships I had with many of my friends' husbands (Miles 2004). Men in particular did not know what to make of me, as there were no behavioral models for how to interact with a young, white, female foreigner. I found that Rosa's husband, Lucho, was often aggressive and vaguely rude to me, and he frequently made off-color remarks about the American tourists he encountered in his job as a long-distance bus attendant. I found myself avoiding him by trying to time my visits when I knew he would be out. His behavior, however, changed overnight when I became his daughter's godmother. Once we became compadres, he had a clear code of respect and reciprocity to follow, and our relationship improved considerably. He still jokes, but his humor is now self-deprecating, and I find it charming rather than insulting. When he was living in New York in 2001–2011, he and I talked on the phone regularly, establishing a relationship unmediated by Rosa and the rest of the family.

And then, the passing of time has changed how others see me. It is now much easier for me to start conversations with strangers in Cuenca than it was thirty years ago. As an older woman, I garner an immediate respect that I did not when I was younger, and it is not considered terribly inappropriate for a woman my age to strike up a conversation with a male stranger. People are no longer taken aback at the impropriety of my assertiveness. More to the point, no one flirts with me anymore, no one thinks I might be flirting with them, and I do not have to worry about what impression I am creating by engaging strange men. My graying hair ages me in Cuenca far more than it does in the States, as most people in Ecuador do not begin to go gray until well into their seventies. In 2018, at a public assembly about mining, I was chatting with a campesino who asked me if I was retired, like so many other expats in town. When I responded that I still had ten more years before I could retire, he asked my age. Looking closely at the white hair on my temples, he said, "You must have worked really hard in your life!" I burst out laughing at this and replied, looking at his work-worn and weather-beaten hands, "Not really!" Finally, *cuencanos* too have changed some, and they are now far more used to seeing foreigners in their city; the novelty of it has worn away, and I no longer have to explain how I found my way there.

Sometimes making a connection with someone depends on the circumstances of our lives that invariably change over time. People can open up in different ways at different times, or you may find that you both moved in a direction that brings you closer or further apart. Take Carolina. Since the 1990s, I occasionally ran into Carolina, the daughter-in-law of one of my closest friends, Blanca, when she visited her mother-in-law. Carolina always struck me as an outgoing and sociable young woman, but frankly, I did not like her very much when we were younger. She has always been very interested in American popular culture, and she had the habit of peppering me with rapid-fire questions about singers or actors or models or beauty products. She always seemed simultaneously overly curious and disappointed in me. She frequently asked the kinds of questions that are, at best, considered inappropriate in the United States, such as why I did not wear more makeup, how much money I made, and why I had only one child. She was full of unsolicited advice about how I might improve my appearance or how many children I should have. Her husband, Blanca's son, migrated to work in the United States in the late 1990s, leaving Carolina with a small son to raise on her own. They divorced several years later. I did not see much of Carolina after 2005, but then, in 2016, I spent three months in Ecuador without my family, and the dynamic changed between us. Our children were grown, we were middle-aged women, and much to my surprise, Carolina became one of my steady companions during that time. We spent nearly every Sunday together putting gas in her beat-up little car and touring around together with Blanca. Carolina was game for anything, even if it was cleaning the farmhouse of Blanca's aging father. As I watched Carolina roll up her sleeves and mop out the filthy house of her now ex-grandfather-in-law or listened as she talked about how, when she is troubled, she goes to the hill overlooking Cuenca and thinks about all the worse suffering of all the people down below her, it struck me that I had given Carolina far too little credit all along.

People's lives unfold in bits and pieces, in moments of reflection or *confianza* that are impossible to plan for or to orchestrate. This is, of course, one of the advantages of being there, so we can capture those elusive, unplannable moments when something is revealed (Geertz 1988). In 1989 I asked Rosa to explain *envidia*, envy illness, to me. As we sat in her humble kitchen shucking peas, she glanced at her eldest son and told me that *envidia* was something only old people believed in anymore and that she, a rural-to-urban migrant and aspiring modern woman, really did not know much about it. I had run into this kind of response frequently in Cuenca. People did not wish to appear old-fashioned or superstitious, and they often dismissed my questions about folklore as things only the old people knew. To be sure, her response signaled something about social impression making, but I was nonetheless disappointed in it, not only because it did not help me learn about *envidia*, but because I thought that we had established enough *confianza* between us that she would trust I would not judge her. I pushed her a bit to tell me something more, but she would not budge; that was to be her answer. Then, a few weeks later, as she and I sat on a crowded, noisy bus on our way to her childhood home, she told me about a bout of *envidia* she experienced years before that was so severe that she almost died. Who can predict when someone will open up or when a seed planted earlier will bear fruit? Many years later, when she was diagnosed with lupus, an ambiguous autoimmune disorder, I brought a different lens to understanding her earlier *envidia* experience. Was this her first serious lupus flare? It took another woman almost twenty years to tell me about how painful her relationship with her migrant son had been for her. I could see it and sense it, but she never spoke of it. All of that, by the way, the telling and the not telling, forms a part of what I think I know.

Each time I return to Ecuador I find families in different positions economically and interpersonally. As families move through time, children grow up, parents age, family dynamics evolve, and relationships ebb and flow. But there is a certain precarity to many people's lives there that exposes them to insecurity. For those who are on the margins of the informal economy, fortunes rise and fall over time as business ventures fail or employment shifts. Someone who was once steadily employed working for the city may find himself unemployed when the government changes. One young man I know was trained as a police officer, but he lost his job when the city elections brought a different party to power. Now he sells sandwiches on the street. Often family members borrow money from one another, and this can cause strain when the borrowers cannot pay it back. Family members do not have the means to strike out on their own, and many young married couples and unmarried young adults live with their parents. When things go well, this can be a source of emotional comfort and support, but sometimes young people chafe under the surveillance of their parents. There have been times when I arrived to find families fighting among themselves, and I may see very little of one person or another. Often, by the next time I come, no one remembers why they were fighting the time before, although occasionally a rift can last for years. I try to pay attention to what causes the tensions in families; at the same time, I now know the particular emotions they evoke, although important, might be transitory.

Ecuador 1989–2019

I spend some time in this book describing the city of Cuenca, the capital of the southern highland province of Azuay, and Ecuador as a whole in an effort to contextualize how lives unfold and to demonstrate the ways ideas linger and are transformed through time. Small and insignificant compared to its neighbors, the country has always been precarious economically, with a small elite commandeering much of the wealth. Plagued by the boom-and-bust cycles inherent in export economies, Ecuador has historically been at the mercy of global markets as prices for commodities shift unexpectedly. In 1987 a powerful earthquake ruptured Ecuador's oil pipeline, catapulting the country into an economic crisis that lasted years. The 1990s were an especially tumultuous time in Ecuador, and I could see the effects of the political and economic instability in everyday lives as families struggled to put food on the table or pay health care expenses. Indeed, more people migrated to the United States at the close of the decade than at any other time in history, most looking for some way to circumvent the lack of opportunity at home (Jacome H. 2004; ONU Mujeres 2015, 50).

In the 1990s Ecuador maintained a mostly free-market, neoliberal, trickle-down agenda, borrowing heavily from international lenders and racking up enormous debt while cutting social services. Poverty rates rose astoundingly, from 34 percent in 1995 to 56 percent in 1999 (Fretes-Ciblis, Giugale, and López-Cálix 2003, xxxiv), as the rich became richer and the poor became poorer. Health care and education costs rose, as did food prices, at the same time that wages fell. Most of the families I knew made slow and steady progress over the decade, such as a better apartment or a child graduating from high school, only because they had remittances from kin in the United States to supplement local wages.

The late 1990s also brought extensive political instability, which reached a zenith with the very short-lived, scandal-ridden, corruption-filled presidency of Abdala Bucaram in 1996–1997. Bucaram, popularly nicknamed El Loco, the crazy one, was thrown out of office after a year for mental incompetence, to be followed by two interim presidents.[5] The decade culminated in the financial crisis of 1998–1999 and the meltdown of the banking system. The crisis was so severe that in 1998, 15 percent of Ecuadorians were unemployed and 56 percent were underemployed in the informal sector (Gerlach 2003, 157). There was record-high inflation and a plummeting GDP (Jacome H. 2004). With government coffers empty, public workers were only sporadically paid, resulting in daily protests by those workers and frequent service interruptions in health care and education. Everyone felt the pinch in those days as prices outstripped wages and strikes at hospitals and schools made daily life difficult. All over town, taxi drivers turned off their engines at stoplights to save a few drops of gasoline.

In 2000, despite widespread protests, Ecuador abandoned its currency, the sucre, and dollarized the economy in a chaotic and difficult transition. Many economists agree that dollarization stabilized the monetary system over the long term, but the initial shock was brutal. The exchange rate for the Ecuadorian sucre fell dramatically just prior to dollarization, making the transition appear to be a net loss for most people as their sucres were suddenly worth far less than before (Beckerman and Solimano 2002, 12). Prices for goods rose dramatically right after the dollarization, yet salaries were still pegged to the devalued sucre, creating a disconnection between the prices for goods and the amount of money people were taking home. Even middle-class families were stretched to their limits. One woman told me that, oddly, coins were hard to come by early on, so market vendors who normally jingle a pocketful of coins in their aprons could not easily make change for customers. The solution was to round prices up, and everyone paid more for everything. Some argue that the shift to the dollar helped facilitate the retirement migration of Americans a decade later.

Soon after dollarization and the removal of Jamal Mahuad, the president who oversaw the messy transition, Ecuador began to turn away from neoliberalism, and move toward slowly increasing the government's role in guiding the economy (ONU Mujeres 2015). Interest in incremental change soon gave away to more radical positions as staggering inequality led to the rise in 2007 of Rafael Correa, a self-declared twenty-first-century socialist, to the presidency. Those were heady times in Ecuador; a new approach to inclusive governing seemed to be taking shape. My university friends were skeptical of some of Correa's more lofty promises, and the very rich, whom I do not know, no doubt hated him, but Correa sparked something in people that gave them hope. Although openly critical of neoliberalism, Correa was not anticapitalist; he argued for incorporating all citizens into the benefits of capitalism rather than seeking to dismantle it. His goal was to move Ecuador away from neoliberalism and toward a policy of *sumak kawsay* (in Quichua)[6] or *buen vivir* (in Spanish), both meaning "to live well," a concept that originated in Indigenous communities in the Andes. *Sumak kawsay* promotes harmonious living with the environment and one's community and advocates for social justice and equality (Hidalgo-Capitán and Cubillo-Guevara 2014). Correa oversaw the adoption of a new constitution ostensibly oriented around *sumac kawsay* that gave the natural environment rights and provided the means for a "citizen's revolution" aimed at redistributing wealth (Becker 2011).

Correa embarked on an ambitious agenda of debt restructuring, earning the ire of the United States when he refused to pay back loans. He promoted national industries by heavily taxing imports, and he reinforced the infrastructure by building roads and airports, among other projects. Bolstered by high oil prices in his first year as president, Correa plowed money into social services, especially health care, transforming Ecuador from a country with one of the lowest investments in health care in Latin America to one of the highest. In a few years' time, life expectancy increased and malnutrition decreased (De Paepe et al. 2012). His government provided free college educations for those who scored well on entrance exams, promoted tourism, made it easy for expats to import their personal property and access health care, and provided incentives for Ecuadorians abroad to come home and start businesses. Under the Correa-backed constitution of 2008, those with disabilities were given rights to employment and benefits that they had been customarily denied. Finally, Correa is credited by some with improving primary and secondary education by reforming and standardizing curricula and monitoring teachers. Teachers were required to sign in electronically every day, thus assuring that they showed up and did not leave early, and to post their lesson plans and complete online assessment rubrics regularly. Some chafed under this kind of scrutiny, while others welcomed the oversight it brought.

Under Correa, it seemed to me that for the first time Ecuadorians were proud of their country. Stores had signs that said, "I am Ecuadorian and I pay my taxes," and "It's better if it's made in Ecuador!" There were antilittering billboards that read, "It's your country. Love it!" In his weekly national addresses, called *sabatinas*, Correa celebrated different locations, cultures, and cuisines from around the country, and radio and television stations were required to air a certain percentage of Ecuadorian content and have public-service spots extolling cultural and artistic diversity. Correa systematically and successfully countered what Ecuadorians call their national "inferiority complex." I had long noted that Ecuadorians considered imported products, from lollipops to refrigerators, to be better than Ecuadorian ones; that a professional such as a doctor must be superior if she has studied abroad; and that whatever Ecuador might have to offer tourists, it could not compete with Peru (Masi de Casanova 2011). Correa's public campaigns to "love Ecuador," to keep Ecuador clean, and to buy Ecuadorian products succeeded in changing Ecuadorians' perceptions about their own country. The new roads that Correa built using Chinese money made moving around the country much easier, and more Ecuadorians were traveling for leisure and getting to know their own country in new ways.

However, as Correa's agenda unfolded over his two terms as president, he became increasingly unwilling to accept criticism or allow transparency. Early on in his first term, he severed ties with the Indigenous movements that helped bring him to power, breaking promises to preserve Indigenous lands. By 2013 Correa sought to tighten his control by limiting free speech, and he established a surveillance apparatus, Supercom (Superintendencia de Información y Comunicación), that monitored the communication of political rivals, the press, and some argue the social media accounts of everyday citizens. A friend reported to me that she wrote something critical of Correa on Facebook, and the next week received a notice from the government that she was remiss in paying her taxes. Correa purchased surveillance technology from China, and hundreds of cameras were mounted in cities, including outside the home of a known political rival. Reporters were jailed for writing critical analyses of his presidency, and newspapers were forced to print retractions of uncomplimentary articles. Correa went so far as to urge citizens to take it upon themselves to report and stop critics of the government, effectively turning Ecuadorians against one another, and he squelched critical social movements by outlawing public protests. In one truly ridiculous and completely brazen public incident, Correa stopped his motorcade in Quito to accost a teenage boy who had made an obscene gesture at him. The boy was arrested and given twenty days of community service for giving the president the finger. In the days before Donald Trump and the normalization of Twitter as a means for politicians to get back at their critics, Correa was mocked by the HBO comedian John Oliver for his thin skin, and much to Oliver's delight, he weighed in and insulted Oliver on Twitter. At the time, this seemed incredibly outrageous behavior for a head of state.

When I was in Cuenca in 2016, Correa was on everyone's minds. He was nearing the completion of his two terms and was attempting to run again by blocking a constitutional amendment imposing a two-term limit. The discussions I had with people about Correa were weighted heavily toward the negative at this point. Some noted his suppression of the press, calling him a dictator. Others were unhappy with the concessions made to China that allowed Chinese goods to flood the market and disrupt local producers, the mounting debt to China, and the lack of transparency at the top. Several people argued that he moved too fast in some cases and the unexpected consequences of the changes he made had hurt them. Correa's government provided free college tuition at the public universities, replacing the sliding scale that was used previously, without building capacity at the universities first. Soon there were more students asking to enroll than the universities could accommodate. The solution was to impose more difficult entrance exams, which privileged those who went to better, usually private high schools. Previously, the elites often chose to attend private universities because the cost differentials between public and private, for them, were minimal. Now, the elites were lining up for free tuition in the public universities, taking the seats that were once filled by students from less prestigious backgrounds who invariably do not do as well on the standardized exams. One of the most unsettling comments I heard about Correa was from a once-poor family whose children had slowly entered the middle class. They were upset about being taxed at higher rates to support the social spending on the poor. Fully adopting the language of neoliberalism, they encapsulated their position by asking, "Why should we pay for their poor decisions?"

In 2017 Rafael Correa was replaced by Lenín Moreno, a one-term vice president under Correa who many thought would be a placeholder for Correa's eventual return. Moreno turned out to be anything but a puppet of Correa and became a harsh critic of him and his policies. Moreno vowed to dismantle the surveillance apparatus, examine the financial dealings and lavish spending of the Correa government, and prosecute corruption by his administration, including his second vice president, Jorge Glas, who was found guilty of accepting bribes from the Brazilian construction company Oderbrecht (Ruales 2017). By 2018 the corruption allegations against now ex-president Correa filled the press, and few people in Cuenca had anything good left to say about him. When I talked with store owners and taxi drivers and others about politics in 2018, they were universally disheartened and cynical. Correa left them with the impression that everyone in government is corrupt; although they were glad that he was gone, they had no love for Moreno, either, and they fully expected that he too would disappoint them, probably sooner rather than later.[7]

Experiencing Cuenca 1988–2018

My recollections of Cuenca in the 1990s generally center on three themes: how ubiquitous transnational migration from the region had become, how regularly government services seemed to shut down, and how each time I returned the city seemed more sprawling. By the end of the 1990s, nearly every family I knew had sent someone to New York, their best chance to hold things together at home as the local economy faltered. The prices of food and gas rose steadily throughout the decade, and strikes by health care workers, bus drivers, and municipal workers periodically made it impossible to access health care, go to work, or have garbage collected. Students took to the streets demanding an end to the neoliberal policies that threatened to privatize schools and clinics. Graffiti appeared on the walls of the Universidad de Cuenca declaring, "The heroic destiny of our youth is to defend the university for the people!"—not an empty platitude, given the frequent strikes by students who roamed through neighborhoods turning over cars and blocking traffic. Yet despite the turmoil, conditions were worse in rural areas, and the city continued to grow from a smallish place of 180,000 inhabitants in 1989 to more than 400,000 in 2001 (INEC 2002). The city experienced significant population growth as people migrated from rural areas to urban ones; its geographic area has expanded as well, with once-rural neighborhoods being incorporated into the city. Since 2008, expats from North America and Europe and refugees from Venezuela have been the most obvious new immigrants to the city.

The experience of being in the city is now very different than it was before. It is decidedly more cosmopolitan and far less distinctive. When I started going to Cuenca in the late 1980s, city buses were old school buses painted bright colors that huffed and puffed through the town, sometimes with patches of daylight visible through the floors and almost always with brakes squealing. Back then the buses were two-man operations, with a driver and an attendant who was often a boisterous and scrappy boy or teenager who hung outside the door shouting the route destinations, collecting the fares, and generally keeping passengers orderly. Bus stops were approximations, and most buses only came to a full stop for women and children. Shouts of "Sube, sube, sube" (Step up) echoed down the streets of town, as men were expected to "step up" when a bus slowed down, making a graceful hop with a leading foot. By the mid-1990s, used transit buses brought from Argentina had replaced those old school buses, and bus stops were clearly marked and attended. A few years later, turnstiles were installed, and the assistants all but disappeared as fares were collected by drivers or by automated collection tills at the front of the bus. By the late 2000s, electronic transit cards made finding change unnecessary, and in 2018, city buses went completely electronic and now take no cash. That latter transition did not go terribly smoothly, and the early days saw plenty of disgruntled passengers. I know this not because I was there at the time but because I read the newspaper and heard it discussed on La Voz del Tomebamba radio station that I stream in my kitchen while making dinner in Kalamazoo, Michigan. By the end of 2018, a fleet of new electric buses was delivered to the city, and the first test runs of an electric tram system, the *tranvia*, were conducted. The tram was engineered and built by a French multinational company and funded in part with Chinese loans.

In 1999 the city's historic center joined a growing list of Latin American places deemed UNESCO World Heritage Sites, inaugurating a flurry of renovations, public works projects, and infrastructure improvements such as the *tranvia*. These projects were aimed at attracting outsiders to the city, including tourists and a bit later North American retirees. The expat community in Cuenca really became a noticeable group in 2009 after the city was named a "retirement haven" by *International Living* magazine and the story was picked up by Yahoo News. Soon news stories appeared on ABC News, the *Miami Herald, Huffington Post*, and other media extolling the virtues of Cuenca as an affordable, safe, and culturally rich expat destination. While it is difficult to pin down the number of expats because they are an unusually mobile population, Milton García Álvarez, Pablo Osorio Guerrero, and Luis Pasot Herrera report that in 2010 there were 9,700 foreigners living in Cuenca, up from 3,500 in 2001 (2017, 17); about a third of those expats were retirees, the vast majority of whom (93 percent) came from North America (21). The authors found that new immigrants began to alter the real estate market in Cuenca, accelerating the redevelopment of the historical center and contributing to the increase in real estate prices.

In 2016 I spent three months talking with shopkeepers and residents in the *centro histórico* and heard just how unsure so many people were about the changes they experienced. Market vendors and even small bodega owners all complained about how hard it was to make a living since supermarkets opened up all over the city, cutting into the profits of the small merchants. Prices are generally lower in the supermarkets, where everything is conveniently located under one roof. Some merchants lamented the growing nightlife in Cuenca and the crime and delinquency they thought it had brought. They blamed both the children of transnational migrants, who they said have too much money and too little supervision, and the tourists and expats for the growth of the restaurant and bar scene. One woman objected to seeing two women holding hands, noting, "Lesbianism has never been a part of our culture!"[8] A man remarked that he just couldn't get used to seeing tourists wearing shorts and flip-flops. Indeed, no *cuencano* would have ventured out of the house in short sleeves in 1988 except to play sports. It is, in other words, both big and small changes that worry people.

At the same time that many more people have been coming to Cuenca from outside of Ecuador, *cuencanos* are now traveling. I have watched as once-poor Ecuadorians travel outside of Ecuador not just as labor migrants but also as tourists. This may well be the development that has most surprised me; I never thought the poor women I knew in the 1980s would have enough money to travel or be able to do the essential culture work of getting tourist visas (Berg 2015).[9] I remember clearly how distinct the worlds I once traveled in seemed. My first departure from Ecuador in 1989 was on the now-defunct Eastern Airlines, back when international flights were still relatively classy affairs, complete with warm towels for freshening up before a meal was served on ceramic dishes—in coach. As I sat on the plane thinking about the ease of travel my privilege allowed me and how far away I seemed to be from the streets of Cuenca, my breakfast tray arrived. On it were those little, single-serving packages of jelly with colorful images of fruit on them. I remember holding them in my hands and getting teary-eyed because they were just so delightful, and I thought the children I met in Cuenca would have loved them and been enchanted by the cleverness of it all. At the time I remember thinking that the children would never get the chance to see these wholly unimportant jelly packets, never mind the world from 30,000 feet.

Now some of the people I know have been able to amass capital or wealth mostly because of the undocumented immigration of their family members, and they have been able to secure tourist visas to the United States, something that was once considered an utter impossibility if not a ludicrous aspiration. Blanca has three sons in the United States who helped fund the purchase of her nice working-class home. She has gone to New York to visit her sons on a tourist visa several times now, always with a roasted *cuy*, guinea pig, in her luggage. Rosa, the daughter of rural peasants and the granddaughter of *huasipungos* (indentured servants on a hacienda), was raised tending cows in the countryside, yet she went to visit her son in New York in the spring of 2017. Vicente posted pictures on Facebook of Rosa with the Empire State Building in the background. She was able to secure a visa because of the house she owns, paid for by remittances sent by her husband, who stayed ten years in the United States. Her well-educated daughters coached her on how to answer questions at the US consulate in Guayaquil, such as mentioning her legally documented brother in the United States but not her undocumented son.

Comings and Goings: No Me Olvide

In his beautifully written ethnography *Lines in the Water* about life in small villages around Lake Titicaca, Ben Orlove ponders the meaning of remembering and forgetting in the Andes. He first noticed the theme as he said his goodbyes to people after completing his initial fieldwork in the late 1970s. Even those with whom he worked closely for a long time exhorted him upon leaving not to forget them. Although it was admittedly a somewhat formulaic leave-taking refrain, Orlove was touched, but he also was puzzled by the intensity of the requests not to forget them. At the time he figured the comment was a reflection of the status differences that are so deeply ingrained in Andean society. The poor just do not think they are worthy of being remembered, and humility is an important mode of public presentation for them.

It was not until several years later, while discussing his work in a class, that he was reminded of the villagers' exhortations and thought more about the emotional content of the comment. What were Peruvians saying and feeling when they asked not to be forgotten? Home in California he found answers in an unlikely place. As a DJ on the campus radio station, Orlove was playing recordings from the Andes when he noticed that the theme of forgetting came up in many of the songs. Most of the references were about lovers, but he found it particularly interesting that the laments of the singers were not about abandonment or infidelity by a lover but about being forgotten. Examining the Quechua lyrics more closely, Orlove noticed that forgetting was not seen as an unfortunate lapse of memory but a reflection of a betrayal of intimacy and equality. In the Andes, the powerful can forget the powerless, and when they do, they render them socially meaningless. This sense of being forgotten and even more so betrayed has its roots in structural forces and extends ideas about the worthiness of persons into personal relationships. Orlove writes, "These people had been told, directly or indirectly, how inferior they were as peasants, as Indians, as uneducated boors, as residents of Peru's backward hinterlands. How easily these inferior people could be forgotten, even by the people they most trusted—even by lovers" (2002, 8).

When I first read Orlove's work in 2005, I was struck by the truth of how easy it is to hear something as Orlove did, pause over it for a time, and then forget about it until something brings it back and puts it into different relief. Like Orlove, I also was told repeatedly when I left the field in 1989, "No me olvide" (Don't forget me). I too remember finding it strange at the time. How could I forget the people I spent so much time with over the year and a half? I remember wondering at the time whether Ecuadorians really did think me so shallow that I would forget them so easily. But once I left, I did not think much more about it; indeed, I forgot about it entirely until I read Orlove's book years later. Only then did the refrain come back to me. Like Orlove, I interpreted "No me olvide" as an expression of the kind of humility expected of the poorer classes that they figured I might not find them worthy of being remembered. But in contrast to Orlove, I also understood it to be something like an admonishment; I saw more agency in the request than Orlove does. While certainly noting the inequality between us, I *could* forget them because I was the powerful leave-taker who was moving on to a different life, they were also expressing a clear directive for what they expected of me. I *ought not* to forget them.

Inspired, in part, by their admonition, this book reflects more than thirty years of engagement with people and a place. I recount ethnographic experiences and individual lives as well as describe the historical and social circumstances that frame my understandings of life in the city. During the period this book encompasses, some distinctive developments have occurred in Cuenca that have altered much. Among those big changes is the UNESCO World Heritage designation and the global promotion of the city and its culture, the increasing independence of younger women like Rosa's daughters whom I watched grow, the continued transnational migration predominantly of men to the United States, and the arrival of a significant North American expat population. In four main chapters of this book, I explore each of these themes, respectively, from multiple perspectives that document their impacts, rationales, and influences.

Each of those chapters is followed by a shorter "Dateline" segment to draw attention to the range of ideas, people, events, and processes that have enlightened my ethnographic work and filled in my understandings. The dateline segments suggest rather than imply meanings and offer a sense of the stories, biographies, observations, and situations from which an anthropologist working over the long term might draw to form interpretations and impressions. Some dateline segments describe a singular event or occurrence such as the appearance of the Virgin or the renovation of a plaza; others present a longer view and document the lives of particular individuals over thirty years. Their variation and specificity reflect how ethnography can occur simultaneously in the short term and long term as certain compelling events rivet our attention on one thing or another, even as individual lives continue to unfold in all their particularity. An ethnography of accrual moves continually from public to private worlds and from describing something in the here and now to putting together the pieces of a lifetime. All this is done in a context of continually shifting modes of interpretation.

While the stories I present here are embedded in the details of a particular place—Cuenca, Ecuador—the processes I describe can be found throughout Latin America's provincial cities. Rural-to-urban migration fueled the growth of most Latin American cities through the 1980s, and then in the 1990s transnational migration to the United States or Europe accelerated, shifting the focus from the regional to the global. Historic areas in cities of similar size, such as Sucre in Bolivia and Arequipa in Peru, also became UNESCO World Heritage Sites in recent decades, adding to the list of Latin American cities that are promoting heritage tourism as a primary economic strategy and cementing their status not as regional centers of commerce or education but as cosmopolitan, international cultural destinations. I arrived in Cuenca in 1988, on the cusp of the transformation from migration directed primarily into the city to migration moving outward to the United States and before the UNESCO World Heritage designation figuratively and metaphorically transformed the landscape.

Remembering and Forgetting

This first "Dateline" is composed of a series of letters I received from Rosa's family in 1990, the year I returned to the United States after my first fieldwork visit. At the time, postal mail was the only means of communication, at least at the beginning of our separation. The Quitasacas did not have a phone until about midway through 1990 when they moved to a new apartment and were permitted to receive calls on their landlord's phone. The mail system was not very reliable, and letters seemed to take a very long time to be delivered, if at all, contributing to the overall sense of loss and distance.

The letters were usually written by the eldest son, Vicente, on behalf of his mother, who never learned to write beyond a few words. These letters touched me considerably at the time for their poignant depictions of the experience of absence; I felt pinpricks of responsibility when I read them, and I understood that there were expectations of me. I remember noting the formality of the letters, a sign I interpreted much like Orlove does "No me olvide," as an indicator of serious concern about status differences and maintaining a position of humility. The letters reflect the broader Andean sensibilities about loss and betrayal that Orlove describes, but with a twist. By this time, Rosa was already experienced with navigating transnational relationships since her brother had been in New York for years. She knew how difficult it was to maintain transnational ties but also how important they are. While it is easy to see in these letters the sorrow over loss and absence, I also interpret them as an attempt by Rosa to wrest control of a situation she seemingly had no control over. These letters employ affection, attention to the rules of politeness, gift giving, expressions of emotional distress, and plaintive requests as means to build and maintain our relationship over the distance between us and to stave off what might otherwise seem like the inevitability of my betrayal by forgetting.

Cuenca 15 de enero 1990

To Miss Anita Miles

Today we greet you with love and affection and wish you a Happy New Year.[1] Here in Ecuador we miss you very much. Christmas was very sad for us, since you left Ecuador we cannot forget how you used to spend time with us. Your departure was a real blow, especially to Mama and all my siblings. We all became sick and we are worried because we don't know if you have arrived home or not. It's hard to forget you and we are always with tears in our eyes, we feel your shadow when we go out on the street. Write to us and tell us what is going on there. Forgive us, Anita, for not writing right away but Mama was sad and the post office changed hours.

Here's what happened since you left. When you left it was summer and now it has been raining

So, we say goodbye and please excuse the poor handwriting.

Vicente

Anita: Do me a favor and send some *Sports Illustrated* magazines

Cuenca 2 de marzo de 1990

Many greetings from all of us in Cuenca. Everyone is well after so much worry about your trip and we are happy to have gotten your letter because we heard nothing from you. The day we picked up the letter my mother cried listening to what you wrote. We also had a good time at Carnaval and we apologize for not writing sooner but we were with our grandparents in Cumbe with the whole family and then we went to our other grandparents.

We are sorry to hear that you do not have your boyfriend any longer and hope that you are not suffering too much. Don't be sad, you must make yourself tough. With all your work you will be sure to succeed [*seguir adelante*].

Our uncle who was lost for a while has arrived back in Ecuador and we spent Carnaval with him.[2] We are sending a cassette so you can remember us—send one of your voice in Spanish so that we can remember your voice. Or if you want you can send a cassette with music from Syracuse.

Forgive my poor handwriting. And, in the last letter we said that Mami was sick, but she went to the doctor and now she is better.

So with this we say goodbye Anita. The cassette that we sent is of *música antigua* the music of Mom and Dad's youth. It's sentimental music. I hope you don't forget how to speak Spanish.

A big hug from Ecuador.

Vicente

Cuenca 20 marzo del año de 1990
Greetings with affection and love from all the family.

Let us know when you are coming back to Ecuador, now that you don't have a boyfriend there is no barrier to coming. But, if you get another romance it will be impossible for you to come to Ecuador and we all want you to come back. It makes everyone happy that Anita will return to Ecuador.

From all of us,
Rosa (dictated to Vicente)

Cuenca 10 de abril del año de 1990
We are writing this letter today a bit sad remembering all the good times we had when you were here. We hope you are happy and in good health.

This week in Ecuador we are celebrating Holy Week and we are remembering that last year when we first knew you and you visited us on Good Friday with flowers. It's sad to remember. It's also cold and rainy. Also, Anita, we thank you for the money you sent, and we now know you are a godmother to all of us. God will pay you. We are here with arms open when you return to Ecuador.

We just got three letters from you so please excuse us for not writing but we were very preoccupied with moving apartments. We are now on Pio Bravo and Vargas Machuca and we are all very happy because the house is big and new and we are on the third floor. You asked for a phone number for us and here we will have one. You can call after 7 p.m. Monday through Friday.[3] You also asked for the phone number of our uncle in Manjantan [Manhattan]. His number is———.

We sent you a scarf that Mami knit, we hope that you like it. We now also have the maize to make *humitas* that you like so much and that you made with us, but you are very far away.

Anita we want you to write us very soon to see if you got the scarf so that we can send you a sweater—we are not sure if it will arrive by mail. Write us right away when you get the scarf.

With a big hug from the great distance that we find ourselves in.
Vicente

Cuenca 6 de junio de 1990
Greetings to you Anita, and all of your family. We have not heard anything from you—the last letter we got was from 14 March when you sent the magazines and since then we've sent three letters in March and April. In May we didn't send a letter because we were hoping to get one from you. We pray we'll get one soon.

Monday the 4th of June and today Wednesday the 6th Mami has had very sad dreams and she dreams she is talking to you Anita. Since you left Ecuador she has had lots of bad dreams, we also have to tell you that Alejandra did not complete her first communion the first of June but we put it off to the 10th of June. This is all very sad. Our Uncle Manuel in New York spoke to you but please pardon him—it really seems to us that he is RUDE.

All we ask is that you send us a letter. We know you have a lot of work and that's why we do not write to you more. In the next letter we'll send pictures of Alejandra's communion.

Don't forget to write us soon.

Vicente

Cuenca 7 de septiembre de 1990

Greetings from all of the family. We want to tell you that vacations are about to end and we are about to start our classes again. We all passed into the next grade and now Marisol will start school.

We are all well here and everyone remembers you, my grandparents and aunts and uncles too. Cecilia likes to look at the pictures and Beto, always a brat, says whenever he's told to do something that he is going to go live with you. Alejandra will write you her own letter with her bad handwriting.

Anita, in your letter you said you might visit our uncle Manuel in New York. Anita, it's really better that you don't visit him. He has turned into a tyrant and he doesn't want to know anything even about his own sister. He doesn't want to know anything about here because there is so much money there and he has started to talk *muy costeño*,[4] so please excuse the ignoramus. He was not like this before, he left here sad, bitter, and humble. When he left he said he would help my uncle Miguel and my father go to the U.S. but now he does not want to know anything about us. My uncle Miguel and Papi wanted to go to the U.S. because there is money there, but instead Uncle Manuel bought property. Life is hard here with very high prices.

Before I say goodbye, I, Vicente, am going to ask a really big favor. Could you buy me a secondhand camera because I would like to work and become something in the world. It would help me in high school and the one that you gave me before is serving me but it is always breaking and I have to fix it. With this I can earn a living and that's why I am asking the favor because I know the cameras there are really good. You could mail it. I beg your pardon, Anita, for asking favors from you. I'll send you a picture taken by me.

My Mami says goodbye with a tear in her eye. She sends a doily for the table.

Vicente

Cuenca a 28 de octubre de 1990

Greetings from Ecuador to Miss Anita Miles. Thank you for the gift you sent, we will never forget you. When you left we never thought that you would call us, but when you called it was such a surprise to hear your voice. It made us all happy. You also said you would come to Ecuador. When are you coming so that we can prepare something good for you?

Forgive the poor writing of Alejandra, for Rosa.

Cuenca, 19 de diciembre de 1990

Greetings with much affection to you Anita from the family. We are all in good health. Cecilia remembers you when she looks at your picture.

It seems to us, Anita, that you are not getting our letters and have forgotten us. We always pass by the post office to ask but there aren't any letters. Sometimes we are afraid to write. Are you getting our letters? We are really worried because we are not getting any responses.

Beto still remembers you and whenever we are on the Avenida de las Americas he always says he's going to get on an airplane and go to find you.

We sent you a small present, there is no way to send something more. We hope you like the sweater.

Goodbye from Ecuador.

CHAPTER 2

Making a Cosmopolitan City

Since 1990, city planners and the governing elites of Cuenca have been endeavoring to find a path to the future almost exclusively by "recuperating" and commodifying the past. It is a very particular past at that. The 1999 UNESCO World Heritage Site designation has accelerated and more clearly defined this project as one that celebrates Cuenca's colonial rather than its Indigenous heritage. While the most important archaeological site in town, Pumapungo, acknowledges the Cañari and Inca histories in the region, the city as a whole has built its cultural identity almost exclusively on imaginaries about the colonial period and nostalgia for a lost time and heritage.[1] Spanish and French architecture, traditions such as the Paso del Niño parade at Christmas to welcome the Christ child, and the iconic living symbol of Cuenca, the *chola cuencana*, are the most potent symbols and sellable images of the city. These are all colonial creations. The marketing of Cuenca that occurred since the UNESCO designation has brought with it tourists and expats in numbers, most of whom see in Cuenca exactly what the elites want them to see: a modern place of clean streets, Wi-Fi–equipped plazas, and manicured walkways where time has stood still, in all the right ways. It is this juxtaposition of a path to a modern future and a nostalgic penchant for an idealized, colonial past that has long framed Cuenca's promotion of the city.

Since the UNESCO designation and in an effort to advance tourism, the city has set forth to beautify its material heritage, including the renovation of markets, plazas, and colonial-era buildings, refurbishment of cobblestone streets, and construction of a walking path along the Tomebamba River, which demarcates the southern border of the *centro histórico*. Along the way, municipal market vendors were first temporarily displaced and then permanently downsized, multifamily housing has been converted into hotels and language schools, and scores of foreigners have bought properties that they now rent on Airbnb.

The UNESCO designation cites the "intangible" value of Cuenca's patrimonial center, which lies in the nonmaterial resources in what Rodrigo López Monsalve calls the "human spirit, mind, and collective sensibilities" of the city (2003, 13),[2] that is, culture. The notion of an idealized culture has always mattered in Cuenca but not like it does now. While the city has long claimed historical significance as a commercial center, since the 1990s Cuenca has transformed its historical center from a place where people primarily lived and worked to one that other people visit and experience.

After the UNESCO World Heritage designation, Cuenca began the process of displaying its culture as a marketable commodity to tourists and expats. Cuenca is not alone in taking this tack to promoting development; it is a common enough strategy. Critiquing the ways that tourism affects localities, Bella Dicks argues that "places today have become exhibitions of themselves," as they employ agreed-upon sets of ideas about the value and meaning of local or regional culture to create a sense of authenticity (2007, 1).[3] Cuenca's *centro histórico* in 1989 was primarily a geographic point of orientation, like "downtown." Now, *centro histórico* is a symbolically loaded term resonant with ideas about identity, civic values, and shared patrimony. "Cultural patrimony," a concept once reserved for the highbrows at the university, is now in the common parlance, and every *cuencano* knows the city has some.

I explore Cuenca's cultural identity from various perspectives. My own early fieldwork was marked by the class relations and hierarchies constructed in the colonial period and stubbornly held onto for centuries. The system of elite privilege was beginning to be tested in the 1980s by the transnational migration of poor Ecuadorians as a means to circumvent the local barriers to upward mobility, but it was still a salient organizing principle. This changed somewhat over time, but white privilege still figures into why expats in 2010 found Cuenca so utterly charming. The longer historical record of Cuenca offers a view into how the past works to configure current understandings of Cuenca's cultural value. The city's elites, many of whom trace their descent to Spain, tell a very particular story of the past and the present, one that romanticizes the past, whitewashes inequalities, and places the elites front and center in the creation of what and who matters. There is some nostalgia here, no doubt, for a time when elite authority over public decision making went unquestioned. Those in power have embarked on renovating the city's historical center to suit their vision of how the past should be incorporated into the present, and in the process, they have made the city more hospitable to moneyed outsiders and less welcoming to local merchants and residents.

Performing Class

In 1988 Cuenca had a population of about 180,000, and I was only one of a handful of white foreigners living in the city center. There have long been expats in Cuenca, but their numbers were small in the late 1980s; they had little obvious commercial impact, and most were fully integrated into Cuenca's social life through marriage or work. The North American expat migration was still decades away, and the transnational migration of real importance in the city was that of poor Ecuadorians to the United States. This migration started in rural areas at least a decade earlier but had reached levels that were starting to get the attention of *cuencanos*. Large stores were opening, filled with shiny appliances meant for the new homes built from the remittances of workers in New York. Tourism was still relatively undeveloped in Cuenca, however, and aside from a few tourist agencies, there was not much obvious promotion of the city or nearby places such as Cajas National Park and Ingapirca, the most important Inca site in the country.

Doing urban anthropology differs somewhat from small-village studies because it is usually not readily apparent that the researcher is there, and the anthropologist cannot rely on gossip or word of mouth that spreads news to the rest of the community.[4] I was, like other recent arrivals to town, a bit anonymous. I have assumed that in smaller places it would be easier to get to know people since the anthropologist's presence is more remarkable. Mary Weismantel's (1989) description of the ruckus she caused merely by walking down a lane with her great big feet in the rural Ecuadorian town of Zumbagua comes to mind. There is none of that in the city, even one as provincial as Cuenca was in the late 1980s. While this was certainly a time, unlike the present, when the extended presence of a *gringa* was noteworthy and earned me more than a second look, Cuenca was also a big enough place that while I might be watched by my neighbors, in a city known for its studied politeness people were unlikely to strike up conversations with me.

My initial research focused on the changing family lives of rural-to-urban migrants. Much of the literature at the time about Latin American cities focused on these migrants, describing the importance of ethnic identity and how kin and regionally based social networks helped people transition to modern city life. Extended families and neighbors from rural homes often banded together in the city, living near one another and helping out with childcare, housing, and employment (Altimirano 1984; Lobo 1982). In places with little public investment in infrastructure and services, these networks functioned as social safety nets for migrants in the city. In many places, migrants formed regional village associations that connected their city networks back home to their rural villages (Lobo 1982; Hirabayashi 1986). These more formal associations offered personal and financial assistance to new migrants in the city and a ready social life hosting saint's day celebrations and other events.

These studies, typical for the time, described migrants as entrepreneurial, forward-thinking cultural brokers who moved between separate cultural spaces; they stood in stark contrast to works of a decade or so earlier that portrayed migrants as wallowing in a culture of poverty that impeded progress. Migrants were now seen in a new light, one in which they became agentive actors in a modernizing process. In this model, a fundamental contrast was made between core locations, modernizing cities usually, and peripheries, which were occupied by ethnically differentiated peasants (Middleton 1981); the two were seen as incompatible spaces. Soon, however, as the pace of global exchange accelerated in the 1990s, it became increasingly difficult for anthropologists to identify distinctions they once supposed were real between rural and urban, modern and peasant, and local and global (Glick Schiller and Salazar 2013).

In Cuenca, a smaller, regional city, I looked for but never found any evidence of regional village associations, nor did I find migrants generally enjoying the company and comforts of close kin in the urban setting. Perhaps the nearness of their home villages made this unnecessary, or perhaps the mestizoization of the region decades earlier weakened localized ethnic identity. Rural residents in areas surrounding Cuenca were uniformly Spanish-speaking, and despite having Quichua surnames, they identified as *cholos* or mestizos, not as Indians. What I did find was that migrants were scattered all over the city center and that nuclear families generally managed the day-to-day concerns of city life on their own, with little sense of a regional or ethnic identity derived from their rural heritage (Altimirano and Hirabayashi 1997; Paerregaard 1997). More often than not, migrants adopted urban pretensions such as changing from a *pollera* to a skirt, dismissed rural lifeways, and tried to minimize their rural origins and affiliations. Transnational emigration only exacerbated the detachment of extended family ties as concerns over sharing remittances drove people to minimize, not maximize, connections.

Rural-to-urban migrants in Cuenca mostly lived in the historic district of downtown, where old colonial-era mansions were partitioned into one- or two-room apartments. My initial research plan was to start by going door to door in the *conventillos*, as these building were called, to conduct semistructured interviews with migrant women. The interviews gave me a glimpse of where people came from, how long they had been living in the city, and how many children they had, among other details, but in reality, the interviews were mostly a pretext to meet migrants. Talking to women was not always straightforward, however, and I often found them fairly hesitant and suspicious of me when I knocked on their doors. And really, who could blame them? Whites, foreign or domestic, had never done much to help them and usually wanted something from them. And, of course, I did too.

Cuenca is often portrayed as a place of conservative values that privileges a class of "nobles" who use their social leverage as a means of controlling access to wealth. In her 1980 dissertation Lynn Hirschkind describes Cuenca's elite class as "self-designated" nobles who took advantage of the historic isolation of the region to consolidate wealth and status. While agrarian in origin, by the 1950s they had begun to shift the locus of their wealth to the city and occupied white-collar, bureaucratic, and business positions. The nobles were in charge of city government and filled the ranks of the clergy and university faculty. They maintained their exclusive status through in-group marriage with other nobles, although marriages between nobles and the rising nouveau riche mercantile class had become increasingly common. Hirschkind notes that the nobles' style of comportment was distinctive with an effort to display "gentility and refinement" in their interactions and presentation (1980, 132). Two decades later, David Kyle describes the closed nature of the class system in Cuenca as "a conservative, complex social hierarchy based on kinship and closely maintained by ideological, legal and economic means" (2000, 51). Cuenca's paternalism is fostered by a system of *palanca* (leverage), in which knowing the right people eases social constraints and greases the wheels. Everything from registering a child in the right school to getting a job or having a telephone installed in the 1980s was made easier by *palanca*.

Performing class is a crucial part of social interactions in Cuenca, and it can be accomplished through dress, tone of voice, and demeanor. In general, there is a certain formality to how people interact with one another, both within and between status categories. I was taken aback when poor family members stoically shook hands and awkwardly patted each other's arms after a long, sad absence, and I was equally disconcerted by how seriously those in the upper classes took themselves. When rich met poor, the rich were aloof and formal if not condescending, and the poor, especially women, assumed a humble demeanor, trying to appear compliant by saying as little as possible. My relationships with poor migrants probably benefited from the formality and condescension of the elites because my more informal comportment was unexpected for a white person, and it was therefore disarming. Gringos were still a curiosity in Cuenca in the late 1980s, something I think helped rather than hindered my research.

Like many anthropologists, my differentness allowed me to move between social spaces and social class positions that often were not open to members of Cuencan society or that they were generally unwilling to explore. It was and remains a unique sort of privilege. In 1988, mutual stereotypes as well as embedded historical inequalities segregated *cuencanos* physically and socially. There was really no good reason for an elite woman to find herself in a *conventillo*, and relations between the poor and elites were marked by studied reserve and pro forma expressions of politeness that disguised the mutual suspicion about who would have the upper hand with whom. Each assumed the other wanted something from them. As an educated American, I was accepted into the homes of the elites, and as an anthropologist, I was able to work my way into the kitchens of the poor. I might be invited on Monday to a three-course family lunch with fine china and a hovering maid, where I sat awkwardly in my best clothing discussing art history, and on Tuesday find myself sitting in the dark kitchen of a two room *conventillo* chatting about the outrageous price of rice in the market. This flexibility to move between usually more discrete social realms can feel dissembling at times, but it also allowed me to see the vast social class differences and how seriously these differences constrained people.

In recent decades the city has grown tremendously, and today the urban population is about a half million. Those formerly poor rural-to-urban migrant families are now often the families of transnational migrants to the United States, and they are more likely to be homebuilders and home-owners and not renters of squalid rooms. The children I met and teased in 1988 are adults with children of their own and sometimes pretty good careers. Far better educated and more socially savvy, they demonstrate little of the aching humility their parents displayed in the face of urban elites. Increasingly, the children of once-poor rural-to-urban migrants find themselves in the same college classrooms and offices as the children of the elites. Yet, the city still is seen as a place where the old and new worlds meet in a kind of inspired harmony, where art and culture are valued and promoted, and where civic pride, community, and tradition are preserved.

Especially as one moves a few blocks away from the city core of Parque Calderón, where stores are shiny and any worldly, the neighborhoods of the *centro histórico* still have small artisan shops of bakers, cobblers, tailors, and tin workers. And family name still matters, as I was reminded in 2016. On a sunny afternoon I found myself on a nearly abandoned street in the center of town, a street closed to traffic for months on end because of tram construction. The businesses had all fled, tired of waiting out the endless delays in the project. I ended up chatting with an elderly gentleman sitting in his doorway who was hard of hearing just enough to not be able to hear me all that well and therefore identify an accent. Over the course of our fifteen-minute conversation, he asked me several times, "What family did you say you are from?"—mistaking me, no doubt because of my whiteness, for someone from an elite family with a good name.

Cuencans display a profound interest in personal identities, and although perhaps not nearly as vital as they once were, surnames still carry with them an acknowledgment of class and social status; there are noble names, good names, and there are Indian names. Everyone knows the difference. But more than this, intellectuals have an obsession with exploring ideas about their collective memory and local or regional identity. Newspaper articles, coffee-table books, and university conferences explore Cuencan history, memory, and identity with almost fanatic zeal. Most historical, anthropological, and sociological research at the local universities is focused on the local context of the city or the surrounding countryside. Having an internationally designated "patrimonial" center has authenticated this discourse and institutionalized it; now most everyone understands, or they should, the potency of Cuenca's historical legacy and the value, both real and symbolic, of their cultural patrimony.

The tendency for *cuencanos* to look outside of themselves for convincing representations of themselves, as the UNESCO designation seemingly prompted, is not a new one for the city or exclusive to Cuenca. Indeed, Sarah Radcliffe and Sally Westwood (1996) argue that since the French Geodesic Mission in the eighteenth century, Ecuadorians have seen themselves through the eyes of Europeans. In fact, the name of the country, Ecuador, comes from that expedition, whose aim was to map the equator. One of the most-visited pubic monuments in the country is Mitad del Mundo (Middle of the World), which celebrates the French expedition and marks where Europeans identified the equator, although it turns out they were off by a few meters. Reports about their city from the French expedition and later those of Alexander von Humboldt, the famed German naturalist, present interesting tropes as well as challenges to the development of a regional identity. For hundreds of years, *cuencanos* have tried to enhance some descriptions and worked to rewrite others.

Cuenca: A Nest of Vipers?

The city of Cuenca was founded by the Spanish in 1557 by nineteen original *vecinos*, a legal definition that allowed a Spanish person or family to own land and participate in government. Among the original *vecinos* is one woman, María López. This original group outlined the geographic plan for the city, including the central plaza, today called Parque Calderón, that is still the heart of the *centro histórico* (López Monsalve 2003, 28). From very early on, all buildings in the city, public and private, had to conform to the specifications outlined by the administrative council. Contrary to Cuenca's later reputation as a city of intellectuals and scholars, the early colonists were uninterested in writing and devoted themselves to economic activities including agriculture, mining, and artisanry, for which they actively exploited the local Indian population to do the hard labor (López Monsalve 2003). Throughout the sixteenth and seventeenth centuries the city continued to grow, as did the control of the Catholic Church; its members who were educated in Quito and elsewhere remained the only men of letters in Cuenca. The members of the French Geodesic Mission resided in Cuenca from 1737 to 1740 and found the city to be a rough place, filled with uncultured inhabitants. Because few residents were themselves writing about the city, some of the first written descriptions of the culture come from outsiders such as those in the expedition. Decades later, the famed German explorer and naturalist Alexander von Humboldt provided the most thoroughgoing descriptions of the city, social relations, and natural environment.

In 1802 Humboldt sojourned for twelve days in Cuenca as part of his five-year exploration of the New World. He had been traveling in South America for years before he reached the city, then in the Real Audiencia de Quito jurisdiction. His intentions for the expedition were to document the flora and natural features of the New World, and in Ecuador he climbed Chimborazo Mountain near Quito to an altitude of 19,000 feet, higher than any European had gone before. From that vista he formulated a theory about the interconnectedness of the natural world (Wulf 2015, 20). One can easily imagine how such thinking might arise in the Andes, where scrubby versions of lower-altitude plants struggle to survive the harsh temperatures, microclimates abound at various altitudes, and a few kilometers downslope in any direction can lead to rainforests on one side and tropical lowlands on the other. Humboldt also commented in his diaries about the human life he observed in Ecuador and seemed somewhat less impressed by what he witnessed. In particular, Humboldt was taken aback at the racism of the Spanish in the Americas, commenting, "In America, fair skin is what decides the rank that a man holds in society" (in Hurtado 2010, 5). He further noted that renting a horse was more costly than hiring an Indian to carry goods. Humboldt found Ecuadorians, in particular the whites he encountered, to be "especially lazy," avoiding work or finding others to do it for them (in Iñiguez 2012, 169).

Humboldt's descriptions of Cuenca in 1802 include commentary on its location nestled among arid mountains with a pleasant green valley to the south and rivers of different turbidities and colors that frame the city's limits (Iñiguez 2012). Indeed, Cuenca's official name, Santa Ana de los Cuatro Rios de Cuenca, is a reference to its geographical location in a valley (*cuenca*) surrounded by four rivers (*cuatro rios*). Humboldt identified plants that had yet to be officially classified and noted that although the city was planned in an orderly fashion, its buildings were not very impressive, calling them "less than mediocre" (in Iñiguez 2012, 169). Humboldt made mention of a large sum of pesos held by the Church to build a new cathedral; he called the funds "dead money" since the inhabitants had too little "industry" to see to the completion of the work (Humboldt 2005, 219). Indigenous people in the area had recovered somewhat from the devastation of disease and conquest, but labor remained scarce. Humboldt generalized his dim view of townspeople as lazy but wrote about one man of intelligence and learning he encountered in Cuenca. The wealthy resident Spaniard Pedro García had constructed a solar telescope that Humboldt admired and used, and far from being indolent, García had established a press, made porcelain, distilled chemicals, and printed cotton cloth (Iñiguez 2012, 169).

Cuenca reached its peak population of the colonial period around the time of Humboldt's visit. The 1778 census showed Cuenca to be the most populous city in the Real Audiencia de Quito, with a population of 18,919 (Cordero Espinoza, Achig Subía, and Carrasco Vintimilla 1989, 18), and it was in many ways better connected to the port of Lima than it was to Quito or Guayaquil. Cuenca was a center of textile production; cotton from the central valley of Peru was processed and woven in Cuenca by artisans in the city and across the rural countryside. As wealth grew locally, the city's architecture and organization took shape. However, with Ecuador's independence from Spain, granted in 1820, the textile industry withered, as did Cuenca's population, which by 1826 had dropped to some 9,000 residents (Cordero Espinoza, Achig Subía, and Carrasco Vintimilla 1989, 20). Textile entrepreneurs moved to Guayaquil, the newest center of production and an easy trading port. Cuenca then took on the character of a conservative backwater, and its roads deteriorated, isolating it from the rest of the country. Rural agriculture for local consumption dominated the economy.

The public Universidad de Cuenca was founded in 1867, and the city slowly earned a reputation as a place of learning and culture. Architecture in particular became an important feature of Cuenca's intellectual, civic, and artistic profile. While Spanish architecture dominated the early development of the city, in the nineteenth century buildings in the *centro histórico* took on the form of French neoclassicism. European-inspired architecture remains central to Cuenca's artistic image and has remained a guiding force behind the politics of urban development through the twentieth and early twenty-first centuries. The architect Fernando Cordero, who was the mayor of Cuenca from 1996 to 2005, presided over the initiation of the city's early days as a UNESCO World Heritage Site. Cordero supervised the restoration of markets and buildings around town, setting the stage for its long-term development as a tourist destination.

It is clear that the contrasts that Humboldt drew between the natural surroundings and the city are themes that historians of Cuenca, very often *cuencanos* themselves, have been elaborating on since. Victor Manuel Albornoz begins his description of Cuenca by discussing the landscape where "spacious valleys," forests, and rivers provide a "play of lights and colors, of notes and harmony, all of which produce a spectacle of magnificent beauty" (1950, 9, translation in original). The city had grown to 60,000 by 1950, and perhaps writing against Humboldt's description of laziness, Albornoz calls the population "exceptionally industrious" (11). He notes that Cuenca is a city that "believes in God and loves hard work" and "has everything one needs for a noble culture," including universities, newspapers, literary magazines, museums, and other cultural institutions (109). In a 1965 work the historian Ricardo Márquez Tapia notes, "Few cities in America have consolidated an identity as vigorously and profoundly as Cuenca" (1995, 7). Márquez Tapia then spends a good portion of the history identifying individuals, the "illustrious" names behind the city's artistic, entrepreneurial, and commercial progress. Writing in 2012 about the colonial period, Juan Cordero Iñiguez notes that Cuenca is known as a place inspired by nature and beauty, profoundly invested in poetry and literature, quick to challenge national authority, and "modest in demeanor but arrogant as a city" (209). Similarly, Mónica Mancero Acosta (2012) describes Cuencan culture as displaying an affinity for aristocratic values of patronage and respect; she states that elite *cuencanos* have historically demonstrated a notable pride in being Cuencan, if perhaps not Ecuadorian.

These last two comments that hint at arrogance and pride are clues to how one can reconcile Cuenca's identity as center of refinement, art, and culture with the more colloquial regional identity that posits that Cuenca's residents are *morlacos*. The word *morlaco* has been used to describe *cuencanos* since the French Geodesic Mission in the eighteenth century; it is thought to be a word of Italian origin to reference mountain inhabitants known to be rebellious, violent, vulgar, and ignorant. It is likely that *cuencanos* earned that reputation because of an incident that occurred in the 1730s when members of the expedition were visiting the city. During their time in Cuenca, one member of the party, the renowned surgeon Jean Senièrgues, who had gone ahead of the expedition and had spent months in Cuenca, became involved in a local personal matter. Manuela Quesada, the daughter of a wealthy businessman, was jilted by a young man who then took up with the mayor's daughter. Senièrgues was asked by Manuela's family to intervene and try to collect the compensation due her and her family for the broken engagement. Senièrgues then moved in with the Quesada family, raising the eyebrows of the community and leading many to presume he was having an affair with the beautiful Manuela. With tensions high, Senièrgues scuffled with the ex-fiancé on a Cuenca street corner, exacerbating the ill will directed at the French, who *cuencanos* believed were "wooing their women and threatening people with their swords" (Whitaker 2004, 136). A few days later, at a bullfight in the Plaza San Sebastión, Senièrgues arrived with Manuela on his arm, making a public spectacle of their affair. Robert Whitaker writes that Senièrgues was far from contrite about breaking local custom and "played the moment for all it was worth, slowly strolling to his box, where he took out a handkerchief and made an exaggerated show of dusting off Manuela's seat" (2004, 143). A fight ensued, resulting in the cancellation of the bullfight. Angered, the crowd rioted and turned on the Frenchman. Senièrgues was attacked and mortally wounded, dying a few days later (Whitaker 2004; Ferreiro 2013). The French took this report of *cuencanos'* lawless and violent behavior back to Quito, cementing the notion that *cuencanos* were *morlacos*, that is, violent, rustic rubes.

The *morlaco* and *morlaca* designation is now ubiquitous throughout Cuenca. A local church in one of the older neighborhoods where members of the French expedition stayed has a Virgen de los Morlacos statue in the vestibule. The city's professional soccer team has adopted Morlacos as a nickname, a moniker that is meant, I think, to evoke toughness. And during the annual celebration of the city's founding in November, they crown a young "Morlaquita" beauty queen. As is often the case with multivocal signifiers, the term has been thoroughly appropriated by *cuencanos* who reworked it over the centuries to index far more desirable characteristics that blended fierceness with more romantic and attractive traits. An undated *Guía Turística* (tourist guidebook) from the 1970s describes Cuencan *morlacos* as deeply religious if not spiritual people with a passion for romantic poetry but also a profound practicality. Similarly, but decades later, a Facebook post describes the *morlaco* as "sharp witted, feisty and unable to continence injustice."[5] The requirements for the 2017 Morlaquita beauty queen were a willingness to do social work and a "strong entrepreneurial spirit" (*El Tiempo* 2017). In 2015 the city of Cuenca published a dictionary of local terms, called the *Diccionario de la real lengua morlaca* (Real Morlaco Dictionary), as part of the public service campaign Cuencanizáte! (Cuencanize yourself!) meant to help the growing expat community understand local customs and language. In it, *morlaco* is defined only as one who is "original" to Cuenca and speaks in an identifiable manner (Cuenca 2018). This definition obscures the rustic rube past of the term and only refers to *cuencanos* being known in Ecuador for a distinctive singsong cadence to their speech.

The embrace of the *morlaco* identity in Cuenca today is curious, to be sure, but the numerous contradictions it encompasses point to the ways elite *cuencanos* consistently romanticize themselves and their cultural identity. Over the centuries the *morlaco* has been transformed from a crude, ignorant, and rustic fellow to one with deep passions who is inspired by nature and finds outlets in poetry, literature, social responsibility, and in a twenty-first-century twist, even entrepreneurship. The *morlaco* stands in for the values that *cuencanos* hold dear and consider admirable in one another. It is almost impossible to pick up any books written by *cuencanos* about their city that do not start with an homage to the landscape, its mountains and rivers, making a clear connection between the natural world and the social values of the city. Nature and culture blend harmoniously, the green mountains sloping down to timeworn furrows, garden plots, and fragrant fruit trees that give way to church spires and orderly city streets. The *morlaco*, notably European in origin, stands as a naturalized human symbol of this tamed yet passionate nature, as it is directed to the noblest of human pursuits including art, literature, architecture, and public service.

But here is where it gets curious. That dictionary would imply that all native-born *cuencanos* are *morlacos*, yet I have never heard anyone personally identify as one. Other than to designate a beauty queen, it does not appear to be used as a marker of personal identity, nor does it delineate a particular category of persons. The idea that *cuencanos* are *morlacos* makes sense, so the phrase "We are *morlacos*" has meaning, but it is not a term of personal identity. "I am a *morlaco*" says nothing about the person but rather indicates only the speaker's abstract identification with Cuenca and perhaps a set of vague social values. It is similar, I would say, to calling oneself a Midwesterner in the United States in that it links one to an inchoate set of homogenized, regional ideals but reveals no socially meaningful individual characteristics.

In contrast, the other potent human symbol of Cuencan identity is the lowlier and hybrid figure of the *chola cuencana*, a designation of paternalistic othering of certain persons rather than one of group inclusion. Much has been written about the *chola cuencana*, who stands as a living but increasingly fading symbol of Cuenca's mixture of Spanish and Indigenous cultures. The term references the ways that class and ethnic hierarchies are both imagined and enacted (Abbots 2014; Mancero Acosta 2012; Miles 2004; Weismantel 2002). The *chola cuencana* is a mestiza woman of rural Azuay Province who wears a *pollera*, a Panama hat over two long braids, and often a distinctive blouse and shawl. It is the *pollera*, however, that most defines the *chola*, and by wearing the *pollera* one signifies a *chola* identity even if the other characteristics are not present. The *chola cuencana* is by far the most significant marker of local identity. The unofficial song of Cuenca is "Chola cuencana"; a statue of her graces the eastern entryway into the city, and just about every tourist brochure and web page pictures a *chola* in her colorful finery. *Cholas* are usually associated with the countryside, where they are noted for their industriousness, and in urban markets, where their commercial shrewdness is often feared but respected. The *chola* carries the weight of Cuencan tradition on her shoulders, and her very bodily presence signifies the ideals of a romanticized past in which tradition was respected, class distinctions were clear and uncontested, and rural peasants knew their place. As *cholas* moved into the city center in the 1970s, they became less folkloric and therefore less likeable, and their presence in the dirty tenement houses was viewed as problematic. Though *morlaco* does not single out a person but rather hints at a set of regional values and civic pride, a *chola*, regardless of how iconic her image, is a particular woman in a *pollera*.

Curiously, the *chola*'s male counterpart, the *cholo*, holds no folkloric value and conjures up no sense of local pride, however wrested from patronizing stigma it might be. Indeed, the word *cholo* is usually used in an insulting manner to reference someone who is trying to be something he is not. The *cholo* is the real rube, not the *morlaco*. *Cholo* is a pointed class reference and one that signals a superiority of the speaker who uses it to denigrate someone else. In the early 1990s the word took a slightly different turn when it was attached to the English word "boy," as in *cholo boy*.[6] The *cholo boy* is a young, usually rural man who goes to the United States in search of wealth and cosmopolitan status, someone who believes the myth of streets paved with gold and who, as the story goes, along the way loses his own cultural heritage. *Cholo boys* wear hip-sagging blue jeans and "I love New York" baseball caps; from the perspective of elites who decry their transnational migration, *cholo boys* have enough money to spend unwisely. The elites of Cuenca say the *cholo boy* has abandoned his cultural patrimony for fast money and the moral decay that accompanies it. Many of those same *cholo boys* have come home from New York, though, and are buying condominiums downtown and renting them to expats.

When I started working in Cuenca in the late 1980s, the *chola cuencana* was as real as she was iconic. In the 1980s it was still common to see a woman of any age in the *pollera* in the city and the countryside. But there were already hints then that times were changing, as younger rural women were abandoning the *pollera*. Like Rosa, who changed out of the *pollera* to please her teenage son, those who moved to the city soon found it easier to wear western-style clothing to avoid social stigma. Women complained that the cost of the *pollera* was too high compared to western clothing, about $80 in 1989 for a top-quality woolen one, and while many tried to tell me this was the reason they stopped wearing the *pollera*, I never really believed them. It seemed much more apparent that the *pollera* signified something that was neither modern nor forward-looking and increasingly was not desirable (Weismantel 2002). Who really wants to be "folkloric" when that designation marks a denigrated racial category, constrains economic potential, and indexes a fundamental unfitness for modern life?

By 2016 the few *pollera* shops in town were in desperate straits. One merchant told me she was lucky to sell one *pollera* every two weeks, excepting the Christmas holidays when it was traditional for sons to buy their mothers *polleras* to present on Christmas Eve. Slowly the nature of the *pollera* shops changed over time, and they sell more novelty costumes made of cheap polyester for parades and saint's day celebrations than they do real *polleras* that women wear every day. A rather embittered storekeeper told me she had to put a stop to giggling tourists who came to her shop to snap photos of themselves trying on *polleras*. This, she told me disdainfully, was what her business had become, and she resented that most tourists walked away with photographs but purchased nothing. A middle-class woman of some means, this shopkeeper had traveled to Rome with a delegation of Ecuadorian craft and folklore purveyors, yet she nevertheless saw me only as a recalcitrant customer. I was introduced to her by a friend from the university who told her of my anthropological interests, but whenever I came to speak with her she pointedly asked me, "What are you going to buy from me today?" And then she would turn away disdainfully when I smiled weakly and shrugged. It seems I was just another *gringa* looking to capture a piece of folklore without laying out money. When I returned in 2018, that shop, which had been there for more than forty years, had closed. Although many market women still wear the *pollera* and many older women in the countryside do, I can quite easily imagine the *pollera* as an item of everyday dress disappearing in another generation.

It is difficult to know what to think of such shifts. On the one hand, it does feel like something is lost when the tangible signs of difference disappear.[7] But who can blame those who once wore the *pollera* and want to distance themselves or their daughters from the patronizing gaze that the *pollera* elicits? So while the public rhetoric might extol the nostalgic virtues of the *chola cuencana* as a symbol of cultural blending and a proud rural past, it is also obvious that the *pollera* is a symbol of a kind of non-modernity. When does the folkloric become the backward? Rosa's mother has worn *polleras* all her life, and Rosa grew up wearing *polleras* and wore them through much of her young adult life. That changed when Rosa was about forty. Her daughters have put on only costume *polleras* for school pageants and parades and have never worn one as an item of ordinary clothing. The *pollera* is not just an article of clothing but a marker of identity. Once a woman is out of a *pollera* she does not go back. It is not a skirt that a woman wears one day and not the next, depending on her mood or the event, but a far more resonant statement about who she is. The elites regularly bemoan the loss of the hardworking and respectful *chola*, and while her extinction surely looks like culture loss, I would not wish to see Rosa's daughters, now respected professionals, return to a life of milking cows as their mother or grandmother had done.

In contrast to other places in the Andes where the *chola* represents Indigeneity, not mestizoization, there have been no real efforts at cultural revitalization of the *chola* in Cuenca, unless one counts the photographs of middle-class young women dressed as *cholas* who pose glamorously for tourist brochures. Given her origins and lifestyles, it is hard to imagine what past, exactly, revitalization efforts could invoke. *Cholas* are mestizas, not Indigenous; they speak Spanish, not Quichua, and their most potent symbol, the *pollera* skirt, comes from Spain. How do you effectively argue for the value of a figure whose origins and ways of life such as dairy farming exist only because of the colonial encounter? Are hybrid figures like this one, created from the domination of one culture over another, better off abandoned? What is lost when they are? And what are they abandoned for? Indigenous groups in Ecuador have been mobilizing politically since the 1990s, sometimes successfully. During Rafael Correa's administration they were granted rights to practice Indigenous justice for crimes committed in their communities, and the government funded bilingual education, important mechanisms for creating a sense of cultural worth. Correa's *sumak kawsay* or *buen vivir* was an homage to Indigenous communities, albeit a politically motivated, romanticized one. From time to time I see Indigenous students and faculty from other provinces at the universities in Cuenca, suggesting that one can be Indigenous, attend a university, and presumably weave Indigenous identity into varied life trajectories. Not so with the *chola*. I have never seen a costumed *chola* at the university; they do not become teachers or doctors or politicians. What this means is that there is no middle ground for women like Rosa's daughters. They must acknowledge at some point, or more often their parents have for them long ago, that success in the city cannot happen in a *pollera* and that the *chola* identity is antithetical to a truly modern life.

Becoming Patrimonial

In 1989, ten years before it was designated a UNESCO World Heritage Site, the *centro histórico* district was feeling the expansion of rural-to-urban migration of *cholas* and their families that began in the 1970s. Once the residential area for Cuenca's middle and upper classes who lived in colonial-era buildings with multiple rooms surrounding a central courtyard, by the 1970s these buildings were in significant decline. Most of the wealthy had begun to move out of the central historical district to the other side of the Tomebamba River. They left the area to retailers, artisans, and small shopkeepers, and their once-grand houses were turned into *conventillos* with multiple families, each occupying a single room or two with a shared courtyard, a washing sink and a toilet, and a paid shower down the street. These rooms were filled by families from the countryside who came to the city for better schools for their children and perhaps better economic opportunities for themselves.

Conventillos provided relatively inexpensive housing to the poor, but they could be crowded and dirty places to live. I saw *conventillos* that housed four to six families, often with several children each, in a couple of rooms and others that housed dozens of families on three floors. Most often residents did not know one another before they moved there, and sometimes relations could be strained between neighbors as they negotiated the use of shared spaces, sinks, and toilets with one another. Rooms did not have water service, so all the washing, of dishes, clothes, and bodies, was done at the communal sinks in the courtyard. *Conventillo* rooms usually only had windows onto the courtyard, and it was common to see the windows covered with paper to provide a small bit a privacy in a crowded space. The only natural light into many homes came when the doors were opened onto the courtyard, so women often sat in their doorways to catch a little afternoon sun to warm themselves. Because so little sunlight entered *conventillo* rooms, they were always cool and sometimes quite musty, and they were invariably crowded with families' clothes, bedding, school supplies, cooking utensils, and necessities packed into a few small rooms. A stalk of aloe hung on the inside of every front door to ward away possible envy of neighbors, a real risk when living cheek to jowl with veritable strangers.

Although at the time elites were critical of the ways their homes had been sliced up to accommodate a new urban reality, the fact that these buildings stayed in use throughout the 1970s and 1980s has preserved them in ways that might not have happened had they been abandoned and left to rot (Mancero Acosta 2012). Because they retained some value as rental properties during a time of little urban investment, they remained intact and are now part of the urban renovations that were initiated after the World Heritage designation and have blossomed with the increasing expat market where "colonial" and *el centro* have taken on a whole new commercial cachet. Today there are far fewer *conventillos* than there were in the 1980s, as little by little they have been renovated to accommodate new businesses, language schools, luxury hotels, and apartments.

A 1979 USAID study on tourism called Cuenca Ecuador's "hidden gem" with significant tourism potential (Gee and Coe 1986, 6), but until the UNESCO designation in 1999 when Cuenca had a theme to rally around, tourism had been quite slow to develop. Throughout the 1970s and 1980s, national tourism campaigns focused primarily on Quito and the Galapagos. Cuenca was at best a half-hour plane ride away and at worst a ten-hour bus ride from Quito, where tourists were centralized. Most tourists who made it to Cuenca in the 1980s were the backpacking kind, interested in hiking or camping in Cajas National Park, or perhaps those making Cuenca a stop on the long trip to the Inca mecca of Cuzco, Peru. As a testament to the type of tourists and their expectations for what they would find in Cuenca in the 1980s, Rosa's fourteen-year-old son Vicente asked me in 1989 why tourists always dressed in shorts and khaki vests like they were "on a safari."

The "touristification" of Cuenca began in earnest in 1999, and little by little, there has been a gradual transformation of the city center from a primarily commercial and residential place to a tourist and cultural center. The city's historic district is hailed by UNESCO as having a high "degree of authenticity."

> The urban fabric of the Historic Centre of Santa Ana de los Ríos de Cuenca comprises a system of parks, squares, atriums, churches, and other public spaces. Around the Plaza Mayor (Park Abdon Calderón), the three powers of society are always present: political with the town hall and the Governor's Office, religious, with its two cathedrals opposite one another, and the judiciary with the Law Courts. Its paved streets are wide and sunlit. Moreover, the simple colonial houses have often been transformed into more important residences, especially during the period of relative economic expansion due to the production and exportation of quinine and straw hats (19th century). This resulted in a specific architecture that integrated the diverse local and European influences. (UNESCO n.d.)

The central plaza, Parque Calderón, was among the first to be renovated with new sidewalks and benches and the performance cupola rebuilt. The newly installed red tile sidewalk is lovely to look at and adds a colorful dimension to the park but becomes as slippery as ice when it rains, which is often. The Tomebamba riverbank, known as El Barranco, which was in fairly poor condition in the 1990s, has become a tourist and visitor attraction. The scrubby, urine-soaked footpath has been replaced with a manicured sidewalk, and buildings that once either were abandoned or provided shabby, worn, inexpensive rooms to let are now upscale homes and restaurants. The washerwomen who lined the river's edge, their drying laundry making a patchwork quilt on the grassy rise of the riverbank, have been moved upriver, or perhaps, as a friend from the university joked with me, they are all home using the washing machines their sons sent from New York.

Among the more controversial renovations have been those of the municipal markets where mostly food vendors sell their wares. The largest city market, the 10 de Agosto, was renovated in 2003–2004 and the 9 de Octubre market in 2008–2009. The city officials argued that the markets were disorganized, chaotic, and unsanitary and that the renovations were initiated for "health and safety" reasons (Mancero Acosta 2012; Orejuela Aguilar 2009). Both of the projects were strongly resisted by vendors and shopkeepers who feared the temporary loss of business could easily become permanent. When the renovations started, vendors were relocated to an outdoor venue for months. Many stopped working when they found the outdoor conditions untenable, and the rest, years later, claimed they had not gotten all of their clientele back. Once the habit of going to the market is broken, the supermarket might seem like a good and more sensible option. As workdays become longer and more women work outside the home, a weekly trip to the grocery store rather than a daily trip to the market is becoming the norm. Some market women opined that the renovations were not initiated for their benefit or even for that of their clientele but rather to make the markets more palatable to visitors and tourists looking for a semblance of an authentic experience. Stalls were reduced in size, so there was little obvious tangible benefit to vendors. The renovation of the 10 de Agosto market was unveiled in 2004 to much fanfare; the escalator was a source of real amusement as heavily burdened, elderly *cholas* tried to navigate them for the first time (Mancero Acosta 2012).

The building of a *tranvía*, a light-rail train system, is another of the many new projects designed to make Cuenca more enjoyable as a tourist and expat destination. Traffic in the city has increased considerably in recent years, and buses loudly rumble down the streets constantly. The *tranvía* was built to reduce the need for car and bus traffic on some of the major streets in the *centro histórico* as well as sections of main roads on its outer edges. Bus drivers who would lose their routes were among those potentially most affected by the *tranvía*. Like many public works projects, the building of the *tranvía* was filled with delays, broken contracts, and political problems. Construction sometimes was halted for months when contractors stopped working as the city waited for the federal government's promised contribution. Streets remained torn up for years. Tempers were flaring in 2016 among local businesspeople who lost customers who did not care to venture down the dusty construction zones, and they complained of the expected rise in business taxes along the *tranvía* route. They feared less foot traffic once the tram line was in place, as there would be no bus interchanges and fewer shoppers arriving in cars, since automobile traffic would be trimmed to one lane. Initially the proposed fare for the *tranvía* was to be one dollar, four times the cost of a bus ride. This provoked locals to declare that, much like the market renovations, the *tranvía* was built for outsiders and not working people. In the end, *tranvía* fares are heavily subsidized by the city, costing riders thirty-five cents, only five cents more than a bus ride. Most *cuencanos* know the *tranvía* subsidy is unsustainable; in 2018 the city debt from its construction was a whopping $270 million (*El Mercurio* 2018). By 2020, photographs of the completed, shiny, red *tranvía* working its way down colonial-era streets became dominant on tourist websites, competing with the *chola* as the new iconic image of the city.

By 2010 the immigration of North Americans really began altering the city's landscape and accelerated gentrification. Heavily marketed online, Cuenca has seen an influx of thousands of mostly older American and Canadian expats. Along with the expats have come numerous new restaurants and bars and renovated housing. Lattes and pizza slices are now commonplace. While their reasons for coming to Cuenca are many, expats generally share with the elites a nostalgic vision of Cuenca as a place that recaptures a lost time. They often extoll the beauty of the colonial architecture and the virtues of the locals whom they see as steeped in old-fashioned family values. Even though they have been the catalyst for much of the city's alterations, expats also weigh in on what they think is important to preserve about Cuenca's culture and the evils of global homogenization.

In 2013 a spirited set of comments emerged on the now-defunct expat website Gringo Tree after the site published an article about the building of a McDonald's restaurant in Cuenca. This was not the first American chain to open a store in Cuenca—Pizza Hut had been there for years—but it sparked lively commentary on the website. Among the comments was this one from Dave: "no, No, NO!!!! I moved to Cuenca to be a part of a different culture than the one of the United States. This type of business brings some of my old culture. I would think that it will displace local vendors of food and of course the profits to McDonald's will not stay here in Ecuador." Another reader wrote a similar comment: "Yuk! One of the motivations in coming to Cuenca is to find 'real' food and get away from all these junk food franchises. Sad that economic development here equals 'N. Americanization.'" And there was this comment from Rebecca: "This is very tragic. The Ecuadorian people are fit and beautiful. I wish this would not change!"

As the city center is renovated to suit the tastes and pocketbooks of tourists and expats and bureaucrats at UNESCO and faculty at the Universidad de Cuenca, it becomes more and more expensive for other local people to live and work there. There are few *conventillos* left, and everyone I knew in the 1990s has moved outside of the city center. This is the usual gentrification that accompanies promotion as a patrimonial site and tourist destination (Scarpaci 2005). Moreover, the city is facing a host of urban problems that it did not have in 1988. Streets are choked with cars and buses, elevating large-particle air pollution levels beyond World Health Organization guidelines (Palacio Espinoza and Espinoza Molina 2014). In contrast, in 1988, there were so few cars in Cuenca that there were only a handful of stoplights in the *centro histórico*. There were primary streets where cars had the right of way and secondary streets where drivers were required to stop and wait for traffic to pass. Traffic lights were installed in the 1990s when power lines were placed underground. *Cuencanos*, one shopkeeper told me, are "very in love with their cars," and traffic, she predicted, would only get worse. The new *tranvía* could help some with congestion in the city center, she said, but she was skeptical that people would willingly give up their cars, especially if they were driving in from the outskirts of town.

The density of the city increased in the 1950s through the 1970s, but as rural-to-urban migration picked up in the 1990s, there has been a reversal of this trend. The city is expanding outward, incorporating once-rural land, and the density of the city center began falling (Hermida et al. 2015). The dispersal means more cars and buses enter the city, spewing more pollution from their exhaust pipes, and green spaces at the periphery are being swallowed up in concrete. When I first went to Cuenca the airport was surrounded by cornfields, not houses and businesses, and rural land extended between Cuenca and nearby towns such as Baños and San Joaquin. Now the city and the once-rural towns appear as one contiguous cityscape traversed by countless cars and buses as well as trucks that often emit a cloud of black exhaust with every shift of the gears. Some newly suburbanized areas are sprouting from farmland as exclusive, gated communities for expats and rich Ecuadorians.

The realities of the unplanned growth of the city, the urban problems of congestion, the loss of green space, and the slow disappearance of the *chola* have yet to alter the ways that the city projects itself even as its advocates try to create a modern, business-friendly appearance. The website Cuencanos .com features articles meant to promote businesses and professionals in town. The audience for the site is unclear, but I presume it is regional or national consumers and entrepreneurs. It may also be intended for Latin Americans more broadly interested in doing business in Cuenca, but it is only in Spanish, so it is not a direct appeal to expats. The site is filled with business promotions, real estate ads, and lists of working professionals in the city, but it also appears to be selling the city itself. It has extensive content about the city's culture and history. At the end of a brief undated introduction on Cuenca's history is this recap: "In summary, Cuenca is a quiet city, enviably healthy, cheerful, and attractive, with hardworking and progressive people and all the resources and attractions that life can offer to man. And to complement this, its inhabitants are friendly and hospitable, with the simplicity and nobility typical of a temperament that overflows with cordiality." I suspect this description was lifted from another, older source and placed on the website rather than being original content. But, the fact that it was chosen tells us that what it is saying has some resonance, for as dated as it is, someone thought it was still a good description of the city and its inhabitants.

The Virgin of Cajas

When I was in Cuenca in 1988–1989, a Virgin appeared. It was quite the phenomenon. Paintings shed tears of blood, the sun danced in the sky, 80,000 people showed up to her conveniently prearranged Saturday appearances, and miracles happened. The story of the Virgin of Cajas, as she came to be known, puzzled me considerably at the time. This was my first trip to Cuenca, and I wondered how often something like this occurred and how the extraordinary visions of a teenage girl could so enrapture the city and the nation. As the events unfolded over the course of months, I read newspaper articles and talked with everyone I knew to get an understanding about it while not devoting myself to a study of it, wary of spreading myself too thin. As one might imagine, people had a range of impressions, from complete skepticism to utter devotion. In 1989 I could not see how the story of the Virgin fit with the rest of my work on rural-to-urban migrant families, so while I collected information I didn't see my way clear to answering the question of why this girl's vision created such a stir. The easy conclusion was that she was wealthy and therefore well positioned to be taken seriously. This seemed like a pedestrian observation, and I didn't write anything about the Virgin of Cajas.

When I returned in 1993, the Virgin of Cajas was out of the news and most people's thoughts. Indeed, I did not think much about her until 2016 when a friend took me to see the large, modern sanctuary built for the Virgin in Cajas National Park. The Virgin, it seems, had not really gone away, and clearly there was enough interest and money over the years to build and maintain the rather large chapel. After that visit, I went back and looked at my old field notes and the yellowed newspaper clippings I collected; I prowled the Catholic bookshops in Cuenca for books about the Virgin, and I read what other scholars had written. There was not much of the latter. However, with the help of a small book by a Norwegian scholar, Gro Mathilde Molstad, I pieced together a critical understanding of what happened in 1989 and why. I now interpret the Virgin of Cajas phenomenon as a kind *cri de coeur* by Cuencan elites for a way of life they could see had already receded.

The Virgin made her first appearance on August 28, 1988, amid a golden glow in the bedroom of Patricia Talbot, nicknamed Pachi, a sixteen-year-old from an elite family. August 28 was the first anniversary of her parents' divorce. Pachi was a popular and pretty girl who excelled at ballet, and she was part of a group of high school girls who promoted and modeled Ecuadorian fashions nationally and internationally. As described in a manuscript about the events, Pachi was awakened from sleep in the predawn hours of August 28 to see a brilliant light in her bedroom. Adjusting her eyes, she saw above her a beautiful apparition of the Virgin Mary. The Virgin spoke to Patricia, telling her, "Do not be afraid. I am your mother of the sky."[1] She asked Pachi to place her hands on her chest in a prayerful position and to appeal for peace in the world. The Virgin also requested that Patricia make an altar to her in her bedroom where the girl was to pray daily. After the Virgin disappeared, evidence of her presence, in the form of the fragrance of flowers, lingered for days in Pachi's room. Only Patricia, her mother, and a few family members knew of this first apparition.

Patricia next saw the Virgin several weeks later during a modeling trip to Mexico City with a group of her friends. While visiting the Catedral Metropolitana de la Asunción de la Santísima Virgen María de los Cielos, Patricia began crying. "The Virgin has appeared, right here!" she is reported to have told her friends, and one of them was burned by the touch of Pachi's hand, which was feverishly hot (Jijón 1989). The Virgin Pachi saw was standing barefoot on a cloud, and she had large, honey-colored eyes, a small, even nose, thin lips, and fine features (11). Her skin was touched with gold, and she carried a rosary in her right hand (11). She repeated to Patricia that she was not to be afraid and encouraged her to continue praying, but slowly and with care, because prayers said on the fly do not reach heaven. She appeared to Patricia three times in Mexico, where Patricia spent more time praying in the church than she did modeling clothing. Her friends noted on the trip that Pachi had changed; she was no longer interested in the superficialities of fashion but spoke to her friends about a life of meaning and prayer. From this point on, the secret of the Virgin's apparitions became common knowledge, first among the elites of Cuenca but soon far beyond that group.

Over the last months of 1988, the Virgin appeared to Patricia numerous times, and a small but dedicated group of followers, mostly composed of friends and family, local elites, formed around her. They prayed together, protected her from too much exposure, and discussed whether and how the news of the Virgin's appearances and her messages would be shared more broadly. Befitting her physical appearance, the Virgin spoke to Patricia using Iberian Spanish grammar, not that of Ecuador, and Patricia understood her easily because she attended an elite private Catholic school whose teachers included nuns from Spain. The Virgin called herself the Guardiana de la Fe (Guardian of the Faith), and she encouraged Patricia to pray and to bring other youths to prayer. She called for the rejection of vanity and trifles, of superficial matters of this world, and for the abandonment of selfishness. She warned of coming disaster, perhaps a world war (Bettwy 1991). The Virgin watched Pachi's prayers carefully, commenting affirmatively when they appeared especially sincere, and she reminded Patricia that the rosary is a shield against the bad things of the world (16). She also began preparing Patricia for a more public role, explaining that they had embarked on a "gran misión" to convert the world (17). The Virgin warned Patricia and other followers to stay true and devoted because Satan was penetrating the churches. "You are my chosen," the Virgin told them. "You must not be afraid to complete the mission" (17).

Soon Pachi was doing more than reporting and writing down what the Virgin told her; in an ecstatic state, she began to speak, using peninsular accent and grammar, as the Virgin. As word spread, people from all over the country began appearing at Pachi's house to pray with her. The Catholic Church, which officially assumed a skeptical stance, began an investigation, as is usual, of the circumstances and credibility of the sightings. In January 1989, popular interest in the Virgin exploded after it was reported in local and then national newspapers that paintings in Pachi's house, one of the Virgin Mary and the other of Christ, had miraculously cried tears of blood and in one case an oily substance. The Archdiocese of Cuenca intensified the investigation, including examining the family's paintings (Calvacho 1989). Cassette tapes of Patricia speaking as the Virgin, recorded without Pachi's consent, were being hawked on Cuencan street corners (Jijón 1989).

People who spoke with me about the Virgin stories did not openly doubt that Patricia believed she had seen the Virgin or that the Virgin was speaking through her, but there was plenty of gossip and commentary about why she might be seeing the apparitions. Among some elites in the university, there was much embarrassed concern about Pachi's mental health and the stress of her parents' divorce on her mother and therefore on Patricia. It escaped no one's notice that the Virgin made her first appearance on the anniversary of the divorce. It was hinted by some that those surrounding Patricia, her mother and friends and family, were encouraging Patricia to see and report on her encounters with the Virgin for reasons that varied from self-importance to creating social leverage. A member of her inner circle ran for mayor on a very conservative platform soon after the apparitions became public knowledge.

Many of my elite acquaintances cringed whenever a new message from the Virgin was reported or when inexplicable events occurred such as the crying paintings. A friend suggested to me that the Virgin sightings were a cry for help from Patricia, who was distraught over her parents' divorce; the friend pointed out that Pachi's mother was an overbearing presence in the girl's life. In an Ecuadorian magazine, *Vistazo*, Diego Jijón (1989) covered the story, writing that Patricia's friends thought her mother was too strict and controlling and put too much pressure on her daughter. In contrast, my poorer friends, while expressing some skepticism about the apparitions, were far less troubled by why the Virgin appeared to Patricia, a girl from an elite family. In fact, this made perfect sense to them. She appeared to be a devoted young girl to them; she was frequently described as shy, and in pictures she was always simply dressed without jewelry or makeup and with her head covered. And she was rich. What did she have to gain by making up untruths? As far as they could see, she was a sincere girl who wanted for nothing but to spread the word of God. If someone was making money from this, it was not Patricia's fault.

As momentum increased, the inner circle of elite friends took the name Movimiento Guardiana de la Fe and saw their role as assisting Pachi in spreading the Virgin's message of faith, devotion, and prayer. They prayed with her daily and were often at her side when the Virgin spoke. Soon it became clear that the Virgin needed more space than what was afforded by Patricia's bedroom, and in June 1989 the Virgin asked Pachi to begin a search for a place to build a sanctuary. Jijón reported in *Vistazo* this remembrance from a follower: "We went to various places with Pachi until she said she heard bells coming from Cajas. . . . There we saw the sky clear and a ray of sun shine down" (1989, 74). Cajas is a large, high-altitude, national park west of Cuenca. Cajas has long held an important place in Cuencan consciousness; it is seen as a kind of pure wilderness with soaring mountain ranges, crystal-clear lakes and rivers, and a safe haven for endangered wildlife. It appeals to many *cuencanos'* ideas of the beauty and value of the intersection of the human and the natural world, and they fiercely defend its boundaries. Cajas is also the source of water for the city.

It is not surprising that Pachi would see in Cajas, a place of natural beauty and wonder, the chosen spot for her Virgin. The manuscript *Guardiana de la Fe* notes that the Virgin appeared to be rather particular about the site of the sanctuary and the way it was to be arranged, asking, among other requirements, that a picture about 1.2 meters tall be placed in a certain location (65). The original locale that Pachi thought the Virgin had chosen was on private property, but she quickly accommodated to a nearby place on public land.

Soon there were regular pilgrimages to the garden in Cajas, and the Virgin became known as the Virgin of Cajas. It was reported that inexplicable events occurred during pilgrimages; the sky was said to open, the light shifted dramatically, and miracles transpired. The Virgin spoke through Pachi in Cajas, and her messages became increasingly clear and directed. She urged people to move away from sin, couples not to live together outside of marriage, and parents to keep vigilant eyes on their children and not give them too much liberty or let them watch too much television (69). The Virgin acknowledged that Patricia suffered but said she needs to continue the struggle in peace and love. Suffering and penitence are part of God's love. At one point the Virgin declared that she has not authorized the sale of cassette tapes of her teachings and that she would speak to people when and where she decided.

By August 1989, the Virgin's fame had spread throughout Ecuador and on the twenty-eighth of that month, on the one-year anniversary of her first appearance in Pachi's bedroom (and the second anniversary of her parent's divorce), a large pilgrimage to Cajas was planned. The Virgin was set to speak on Saturday morning, and by Friday night the streets of Cuenca were packed with cars from out of town, and the hotels were jammed with pilgrims. I did not go on the pilgrimage, but two boys I knew were determined to hear the Virgin speak, and they set out late Friday night. Their plan was to take a bus as far as possible and then hike in overnight. They never made it close. The two-lane road into Cajas was filled with nearly 6,000 vehicles and 80,000 people (Jijón 1989, 74), or in another estimate 150,000 (Molstad 1996), crowded into Cajas to see and hear the miracle of the Virgin's presence. Most people had to abandon their cars or buses as the traffic reached a standstill.

With heads covered and rosaries in hand, the young and the old, the sick and the healthy climbed the mountain passes to reach the Virgin's garden. The civil defense workers of Cuenca made sure there were plenty of oxygen tanks, especially for the coastal *guayaquileños* who made the trip, unaccustomed as they were to high altitude. Some people reported hearing the Virgin speak through the microphones that were set up; some people said they heard a recorded message; others said they heard very little but saw the sun and sky open in an otherworldly sort of way; some pilgrims said they saw the Virgin come out of the clouds; and others wondered if anything at all sacred had happened. A few claimed to have experienced miraculous healing that morning, and others walked away disillusioned. For *Vistazo* reporter Jijón (1989), the real miracle of the day was that no one was killed or seriously injured, given the traffic, the hiking, the cold climate, and the altitude.

Patricia, members of the Movimiento Guardiana de le Fe, and other groups of devoted followers continued to make official pilgrimages to Cajas on the first Saturday of every month and unofficial visits to the Jardin del Virgin (Garden of the Virgin) throughout the next year. The Virgin let it be known that she would come on the appointed Saturdays for six months, until March 1990, and then she would appear no more. Catholic Church leaders continued to hem and haw about the official status of the pilgrimages and the veracity of the Virgin's appearance, and they did not endorse or reject the movement. Several priests presided over the masses held during the pilgrimages. Years later, the local bishop gave approval for the construction of the sanctuary in Cajas. It is now a bit of a tourist stop; you eat trout from a local lake at a rustic restaurant and visit the Virgin's sanctuary, complete with vendors selling rosaries, necklaces, and *llapingachos*, Ecuadorian potato pancakes.

The question that long troubled me about the Virgin of Cajas was why a teenager's visions were given so much attention and managed to capture national and international interest and even provoke belief. To be sure, it struck me that only an elite teenager could have been propelled into the spotlight in this way, but again, the question was why so many people supported her visions. Mass hysteria is certainly one explanation, but it does not solve the question of why this girl with this message at this time. Soon after Pachi's revelations, a girl from a rural community also claimed to see the Virgin, but she was roundly dismissed by all.

In her 1996 book, Molstad offers a convincing theory for why Patricia Talbot's midnight visions were turned into a powerful cultural phenomena that led to tens of thousands of people descending on a remote park to worship a sight-unseen Virgin. Molstad begins by focusing on the message and the messengers. The teachings of the Virgin, she points out, were imminently conservative. The Virgin was no revolutionary, and she spoke of traditional values of family, devotion, selflessness, modesty, individual prayer, suffering, abstention, and penitence. These harked back, Molstad argues, to Catholic practices that had only recently been called into question after the Second Vatican Council, often called Vatican II, which ushered in a series of sweeping reforms that were meant to modernize the Catholic Church. Among the changes brought by Vatican II was the adoption of local languages rather than Latin for Mass and in teachings and a concern for understanding the lives and problems of the poor. This was followed in the mid-1970s by the document *Evangelii nuntiandi*, which encouraged the Church to become involved in social justice concerns and in alleviating social inequality (Molstad 1996, 41). In Ecuador this meant, Molstad contends, that the Church made efforts to democratize its practices, bringing in lay practitioners from the working classes rather than relying solely on the elites for community leadership and publicly advocating for the poor. These changes frustrated the elites of Cuenca, who were dismayed by the changes to their once-exclusive status; they could no longer count on the Church to uphold their conservative political and religious values and their God-given roles as church and civic leaders (Molstad 1996).

What Molstad does not talk about but that surely also figured into the elite perspectives during this time are the multiple changes that were beginning to happen to the city because of transnational migration. Emigration to New York brought new means for making money that was wholly out of elites' control. It was a work-around to the entrenched elitism that kept social mobility out of reach for so many. For the first time in Cuenca's history, substantial wealth was coming into the community that elites did not control. This was frightening business for those who had long seen themselves as the arbiters and gatekeepers of Cuencan society. And they were right to worry. Transnational migration and globalization were shifting social life, providing opportunities to those once excluded, and forcing elites to interact with non-elites in new ways. Molstad writes about their dismay at finding working-class people running church marriage classes, and I heard their disgust at what they saw as the conspicuous consumption of migrant families and loose morals of women and children when husbands and fathers were in the United States. Conditions were changing rapidly for elites, inside and outside of the church, and they found it increasingly difficult to exploit local workers and segregate the poor from educational and employment opportunities. The European Virgin came to reinvigorate an old-fashioned order and denounce material wealth just at the moment when remittances from the United States made the ability to buy goods more democratic.

The Virgin of Cajas was a relief, a welcome throwback to the good old days of conservative Catholic values of sacrifice and modesty and antimaterialism. Even better, the Virgin sanctified elite control over the moral and religious high ground, as she chose them as her confidantes and disciples. She argued against hedonism and consumerism—those *cholo boy* stereotypes come to mind—and urged penitence and respect for authority, just like society used to be before so many changes threatened elite sovereignty. This was a comforting message for those who saw their relevance in the Church and in local economic and political life diminishing.

Patricia turned away from public life after the March 1990 pilgrimage and a few years later married her childhood sweetheart. Some took the news of her marriage as a sign that the whole thing was a hoax. Women who see true apparitions of the Virgin, it seems, never marry. Rather, they enter a life of quiet contemplation, usually in a convent. Patricia's life has been relatively quiet since 1990. Family friends told me that she did not speak publicly until 2012, when she attended a conference of the International Congress in Honor of the Two Hearts.[2] The two hearts are those of Jesus and Mary. Patricia spoke to that conference and a few other Catholic events about her experiences in 1988–1990 and about the need for a life full of meaning and Catholic commitment. Her voice sweet and calm, Patricia described her teenage life as a model as empty and of the importance of prayer and contrition for a good life. Her picture appears from time to time in the Cuenca social pages of the newspapers, always beautifully dressed and looking like any other Cuencan *dama*.

In 2000 the Archdiocese of Cuenca approved the formation of an official Association of the Guardiana of the Faith and the building of the rather large and elegant sanctuary in Cajas. The association today is both real and virtual, with international satellite groups in the United States and Mexico as well as Ecuador. The purpose of the association is to promote a life of faith and service to others. It relies primarily on donations from the faithful. Today there is a website and a Facebook page for the Guardiana de la Fe group. The Virgin also has a Twitter account. History has been remade on the official association website, where no mention is made of Patricia Talbot or her role in bringing the Virgin of Cajas to life.

CHAPTER 3

Single Women in the City

The families I worked with in the *conventillos* in 1988 were, for the most part, young ones, and they had small children in elementary school when I met them and began tracking generational changes. Migrants are future-oriented for the most part, and the families I worked with told me they had come to the city primarily because they wanted to further their children's educations. Schools in the countryside were thought to be of much poorer quality than those in the city, and families made real sacrifices to buy uniforms and school supplies and pay the transportation fees and tuition for private Catholic schools. No one I knew thought the public schools were any good; nothing the government did was good,[1] and most parents did not cotton to the co-ed nature of the public schools. Parochial schools, which are usually single-sex, were generally seen as a better choice. Schooling in Cuenca starts when a child is around five years old with kindergarten, which was optional in 1989, followed by six years of primary schooling and six years of secondary education called *colegio*. Most of the parents I knew in 1988–1989 had not completed primary school, let alone high school, but all of them saw graduation from *colegio* as a worthy goal for their children. There was not much talk of going to the university in those days, and most parents did not see that as an option for their children; that was just too big a leap of faith and imagination for poor families in 1989.

Evidence of school attendance was everywhere in Cuenca then, as it still is today. In contrast to American cities where the central downtown districts are generally devoid of schools and schoolchildren, Cuenca's *centro histórico* is home to numerous elementary and high schools. Some of the largest buildings in town are schools, with footprints occupying, in many cases, complete city blocks. Most schools in the *centro histórico* are associated with parishes; they are tired-looking places that show the decades of wear and tear of countless children who passed through them. They have high walls that shelter inner, concrete, noisy, open-air courtyards surrounded by two stories of classrooms. The worn, wooden floors of the creaky stairs dip slightly in the middle, a testament to the hundreds if not thousands of little feet that have climbed them. The usual classroom is fairly bare and austere, with small wooden desks for students, a chalkboard at the front, and an often rickety desk for the teacher. There are usually maps of Ecuador on the wall and perhaps a picture of the Virgin of Cisne, a local favorite, or the pope, but none of the colorful and messy handicrafts that adorn elementary school walls in the United States. Creativity is not openly admired in Ecuadorian schools. The sun does not reach most lower-level classrooms, and they are often cold, with a scent of musty wood overlaid with the petroleum smell of the floor wax used to keep the wood from drying out too badly. Newer schools are mostly on what twenty years ago would have been the fringes of the city, and these schools have more expansive grounds and far better facilities. The better private schools have large campuses with soccer fields, basketball courts, and inviting green spaces. Mirroring the practices of social exclusion in other domains, school uniforms are distinctive, and as students move through public spaces in their uniforms they declare their social status; everyone knows what color and style of uniform belongs to which school and how exclusive and costly it is.

The high walls might make schools in the city center difficult to identify at first glance, but a casual observer cannot miss the uniformed schoolchildren coming and going to and from classes several times a day in two shifts. The midday rush is particularly hectic as students coming from the morning sessions collide with those going to the afternoon classes. Finding a seat on a noon-hour city bus is a perennial challenge; seats are filled with schoolchildren of all ages carrying satchels and backpacks, pushing their way onto the buses, laughing and shouting. Older siblings watch over the younger ones, holding their hands and tugging to help them make that big first step up into the bus, where they crowd three or four to a seat, uniforms now askew, and their fists wrapped around some sticky treat they bought for a few cents at the kiosks outside the school gates.

Back in 1989 the daily trip to and from school was one of the few times when parents allowed their young daughters to travel through the city on their own. Patriarchal standards of female virtue still mattered, and girls were discouraged from being in the street, a place of strangers and therefore unknowable dangers.[2] Girls were often accompanied to school by their siblings or neighbors if their parents could not take them, but sometimes they went on their own. Even as girls grew into teenagers or maybe especially as they matured, parents kept a close eye on their daughters' comings and goings. Except for short forays to a corner store, girls were rarely sent on errands that took them more than a block or two from home. Girls played at home or in the courtyards of their *conventillos*, where parents could monitor who they were with, what they were doing, and where they could easily be fetched to help when needed.

Members of several families told me they thought girls were more responsible and work harder than boys and, therefore, that their educations were a better long-term investment. Most poor families had no social security or retirement funds, so they counted on their children to help them financially in their old age. The thinking was that girls were more dependable than boys. Moreover, men can always get jobs with their backs in Cuenca or New York, but women need education so they can fend for and support themselves (*defenderse*) if necessary. Without saying so directly, parents made it clear that they did not want their girls to be dependent on bad or abusive men. The term *defenderse* is used in this sense to describe a woman's ability to support herself, in contrast to another commonly used phrase, *salir adelante*, to come out ahead, which is used more generally to refer to an individual's or a family's progress. Jessaca Leinaweaver (2008) describes an analogous term, *superar*, used in urban Peru in similar circumstances; she points out that *superar* connotes economic betterment, a relative term for those in poverty, and that it has a moral component as well. *Superar* in Peru and *salir adelante* in Ecuador mean not just self-improvement but progress that is born from and reflects on a person's connections to family and community. *Defenderse* carries a similar relational morality. Good city parents make sure their daughters are protected and educated so they can take care of themselves throughout their lives. It is also a poignant acknowledgment, if not a critique, of a daughter's potential vulnerabilities. A third term I heard is *hacer algo en la vida*, used to describe getting ahead, to doing something in life. This utterance implies not just achieving economic advancement or progress but having a meaningful, usually professional career.

In 1989 young girls from poor families received conflicting messages about how to achieve success in life, *salir adelante*. On the one hand, they were told they needed to be educated so they could be *bien preparada* (well prepared) to be a *bonita profesional* (pretty professional); on the other hand, they were told that the world outside of the home was a potentially dangerous space for them. Girls were going to school to prepare themselves to move away from a completely domestic future, yet they were encouraged to stay close to home, expected to perform domestic duties, and subjected to practices of routine surveillance by parents who feared talk of lost virtue. Reconciling these conflicting perspectives was not always easy, especially as girls moved into adolescence and sought more autonomy and independence. By the time they entered high school, most girls were far better educated than their parents, who likely did not complete elementary school. Their experiences in the city and their education gave them perspectives and confidence that their parents did not share.

The concern for the virtue of girls and the efforts families made to ensure that their reputations were not compromised were oddly contradicted by a fairly open admiration for sexually provocative media. It was not unusual in the late 1980s for a small business, something as unassuming as a bakery perhaps, to display an often-outdated girlie calendar with bare or nearly bare-breasted white women offering over-the-shoulder, come-hither smiles. I got into the habit of asking people why they had these pictures, and I was routinely told that they are simply "bonita," pretty. Music videos on television became more common in Ecuador throughout the 1990s, and the Spanish-language ones were pretty racy, with scantily clad young women prancing around seductively. People watched these videos uncritically, as far as I could tell, and I recall several times when little girls were encouraged to mimic the provocative moves on the videos. Families would laugh delightedly at these antics. Yet when the television was off, the girl herself, particularly as she entered her teen years, was required to behave demurely, come home directly after school, and learn domestic skills. When Rosa's daughters were in their teens they begged me to talk to their mother about allowing them to go to parties at their classmates' homes, something she refused to permit after their older brother and father left for the United States. Rosa supposed that others saw her girls as undefended and vulnerable without any obvious male supervision. It appeared to me that Rosa was as concerned about her own reputation as a good mother as she was for her girls' standing in the neighborhood. All of their reputations were on the line.

As they matured, the daughters of rural-to-urban migrants I knew struggled with the conflicting role models they saw around them, and tensions between parental values forged in rural areas and modern, urban lifeways became more difficult to manage. It seemed as though having the future ability to be independent was considered a value, but exercising that independence while still an adolescent was not. A girl with a reputation for lingering in the street demonstrated a worrying degree of moral laxity in herself and her parents. While their parents sought to instill a conservative set of patriarchal values about modesty and female virtue, the girls themselves could easily see that the female compliance, reticence, and humility their parents encouraged would not get them very far in the world. In 2000 I wrote an article about what I thought of as the longing of poor adolescent girls to make something of themselves in a world that was stacked against them in multiple ways. Because of the authoritarian nature of their families and the social exclusion of the broader society, there was little chance that poor girls would be able to fulfill their dreams of being professional women who wore crisp uniforms and high heels. Most of those uniformed women were, in fact, in dead-end clerical positions, but their presence on Cuenca's downtown streets with their form-fitting suits, panty-hosed legs, and long, polished fingernails was a source of much admiration among school-age girls.

Little girls were compliant, but by the time they were adolescents there were signs that girls from poor families understood that they were unfairly burdened not just as girls but as poor girls. Despite political rhetoric of inclusion, Cuenca remained a place where social privilege is linked to family name and ancestry, and the children of rural-to-urban migrants had little in the way of *palanca*, leverage that greases the wheels. Given their shallow and unimportant social networks, these young women held out little hope that they could succeed within the system, so many of them openly resisted it by various means. They rejected being demure and silent, pushed back against the authority of their parents and teachers, and made it clear that they were uninterested in marriage if it looked like their mothers'. I found that in the late 1990s, mothers who engaged in rural-to-urban migration generally tried hard to teach ideals of modesty in comportment, believing that compliance with the dominant ideologies for how poor girls ought to behave was the best way for them to get ahead in the city. The girls thought otherwise.

Their daughters, on the other hand, are not so acquiescent. They openly reject the Hispanic model of gender by refusing to be submissive, and they shock both their parents and the upper classes by wearing revealing clothing and makeup. They are much less willing to quietly accept male privilege and aspire to hold men to different standards than did their mothers. Because these girls have gone to school where they were told they could be part of the modernizing economy, they can no longer accept being relegated to the margins of the economic system. They are angry that palanca still is the dominant mechanism for economic advancement, and that few alternatives are open to them as poor females (of peasant origins). They value North American standards for female comportment over local elite ones, and they long for more material goods and for the independence and autonomy they see represented on television. In the end, what these girls have, and often bring into adulthood, is a longing for real social transformation. How successful they will be at creating change however, remains to be seen. (Miles 2000, 70)

Structural Changes and Women's Roles

I have lost track of some of the young women I knew throughout the 1990s, so I cannot say for certain how their lives unfolded. I do know, though, that they came of age at a time when women's roles and rights were changing rapidly and that their lives reflected those changes to one degree or another. The concern for sequestering girls at home now looks a bit quaint. Either from choice or necessity, this generation of women, now in their thirties and forties, is generally better educated than their mothers were, and they have been navigating the world outside the home, whether in school or work, in ways their mothers never could.[3] I have witnessed attitudinal changes such as pushing back against patriarchal constraints that I saw happening in 2000 and meaningful differences in the circumstances of young women's lives; they are less likely to be married, they have fewer children, and they are more likely to be working. Moreover, the steady flow of mostly men to the United States has left many women as de facto heads of household who have to make crucial financial and personal decisions for their families in the absence of their husbands. When men return, if they do, the patterns established during their absences are hard to break, and a noticeable shift takes place in household gender roles after migration. Returned migrants now pitch in around the house, something they learned to do in New York when they lived without their mothers or wives.

Public discourses about women's social roles and more formal, structural changes in women's rights and protections were unfolding as these women were coming of age. Although more symbolic than real, especially in its early days, in 1995 a federal law was passed making violence against women and families a crime, and in 1997 new labor laws required that women represent 20 percent of public workers, raised to 30 percent in 2000 (Valle 2018, 24). But it was only after the ouster of President Abdala Bucaram (El Loco) in 1997 that women's social movements found an opening and started to have significant social and political influence (Lind 2003). At the urging of feminist groups, the 1998 constitutional assembly adopted language that legitimized single-parent households, created greater protections for women and children, and established quotas for female political candidates (Lind 2003). At more or less the same time and mostly separately, LGBTQ rights activists were able to decriminalize homosexuality by galvanizing the outrage that occurred when police raided a bar in Cuenca and arrested dozens of men, some of whom were raped and beaten in police custody (Lind 2003). While the decriminalization of homosexuality has certainly improved the lives of gay and lesbian people in Ecuador, many *cuencanos* are still deeply uncomfortable about homosexuality, and homophobic comments are plentiful.

In 2007, President Correa brought women's concerns to the forefront of his campaign, calling his "citizens' revolution," which was focused on anti-neoliberal economic policies, a "revolution with a woman's face" (Lind 2012). Human rights for all were guaranteed in the 2008 Constitution, and Correa's program of *buen vivir* (good life) promoted equitable and plurinational transformations. Although national development plans during this period emphasized equality, they never directly referenced women's equality or the elimination of gender inequalities (Valle 2018). Amy Lind argues that Correa's political rhetoric and legislative agenda were important for expanding definitions of "the family" but that in practice, his policies reinforced "a maternalist, heteronormative understanding of the family and women's rights" (2012, 538). The rhetoric of equality in *buen vivir* remained mostly that: rhetoric.

Over the years I have been working in Ecuador, the standard statistical indicators of women's status have been steadily improving. Educational levels are increasing for men and women, and people are marrying later and having fewer children. Women's fertility is often linked to education; the more education women have, the more they delay childbearing and the fewer children they have. While still not as low as they are in many European countries, birthrates in Ecuador have fallen considerably in recent decades. According to government statistics, crude birthrates in the country fell 13 percent between 1990 and 2017 (INEC 2018). Nationally, the overall fertility rate declined from an average of 3.28 children for women of childbearing age in 1989 to 2.4 in 2018 (World Bank n.d.). Cuenca's fertility rate mirrors the national average (INEC 2017b).

Marriage rates dropped 8.9 percent from 2005 to 2018; in 2018 it was reported that in Azuay Province, 37 percent of women were single,[4] and that number rises to 45 percent when widows and divorced women are added (Valle 2018, 149). Divorce, once rare in Catholic Ecuador, is increasing in frequency, with rates rising 83 percent between 2006 and 2016 (INEC 2017a). It is difficult to say with certainty what the increase in the divorce rate signifies. Women generally do worse economically after divorce, leading to a decline in their economic standing, but rising rates of divorce might indicate changing mores on women's rights and attitudes about independence. Divorce is at least a partial reflection of women's autonomy to choose whether to remain married. Cheng-Tong Lir Wang and Evan Schofer (2018) posit that increases in divorce rates globally are associated with an increase in the circulation of the "cultural principles" of gender equity (690). They argue that norms about divorce are often shaped by global processes and discourses on human rights and development, including increased female education and employment.

Because women are often disadvantaged in the workplace and frequently have childcare responsibilities, female-headed households in the United States are associated with economic precarity and more poverty, creating what has been called the "feminization of poverty." However, the same dynamic may not be happening in Latin America. Sylvia Chant (2006) contends that because of how patriarchy operates within the home in Latin America, female-headed households are not necessarily poorer than their male-headed counterparts. Women in patriarchal households often have little control over their own fertility, so family size may tend to be larger, and they often have little access to their husband's wages, which are frequently spent in ways that do not benefit the household. Chant finds that in female-headed households, women may earn less but have greater control over the household income. Moreover, even if households are materially poorer without male wage earners, Chant argues that women "may feel they are better off, and what is important, less vulnerable" (147). They may experience an intangible psychological benefit in being able to successfully provide for their families.

Following trends throughout Latin America, labor force participation by women in Ecuador more than doubled between 1980 and 2010, going from 23 percent of women working to 56 percent (Chioda 2016, 110). The rate of increase was about the same for married and unmarried women, but more unmarried women worked, and worked more, than married women (Chioda 2016, 111). Laura Chioda calls the increase in Latin American women's labor force participation and the cultural shifts in education that promote it a "quiet revolution" whose effects reverberate favorably on several cultural and social levels (2016, 107). More realistically, labor statistics in Ecuador are difficult to draw conclusions from, for they report a range of occupations including informal work and agricultural labor, and despite rising rates of labor force participation, Ecuadorian women are less likely than men to have salaried work that requires they be paid a minimum monthly wage and social security benefits, and their average take-home pay is a good deal less than men's. As of December 2017, men's average take-home pay was $369 a month and women's only $295 (Valle 2018, 49). Women were far more likely to be unemployed and underemployed than men, and they reported far more working hours when housework was taken into account (*El Universo* 2018).

Perhaps the most disturbing manifestation of enduring sexism in Ecuador is the seemingly intractable incidence of domestic violence, both physical and psychological. In 2011, six out of ten women reported experiencing violence in their lives, 87 percent of it within marriages (Boira et al. 2017). Rates of intimate-partner violence diminish with educational levels, yet the rate of reported violence among college-educated women is surprisingly high (Comacho 2014). Gloria Comacho has found that 57 percent of women without education reported intimate-partner violence, compared to 44 percent of high school graduates and 34 percent of women with college graduate education (2014, 52). Reported rates of violence have risen significantly in recent years, as have public campaigns and public demonstrations denouncing violence against women. It is possible that better public education and training of police have encouraged women to feel more comfortable reporting domestic violence, but this does not mitigate the very high rates of physical, psychological, and "patrimonial" (property) abuse that takes place. In a troubling study conducted at the University of Cuenca using a variety of quantitative instruments, Santiago Boira and colleagues report high levels of "hostile sexism" among university students and an abundance of stereotypical representations of women's roles and abilities (2017, 10). Even in a university setting, where one would expect to find more progressive attitudes, patriarchy and male privilege are still dominant modes of thought.

On Their Own: Single Women in Cuenca

There are plenty of single women in Cuenca.[5] There are women who have never married, older widows, divorced women, and those who remain married but have not laid eyes on their husbands for decades. These women are single mothers in all but name. In general, when men go to the United States from Ecuador without legal documents, they do not come home for visits; it is far too expensive and dangerous to cross the border more than once. Some men have been gone for more than twenty years and have grown children they have not seen since those children were babies. Most send some money, but rarely is it enough, or consistent enough, to support their families in Cuenca. The "single" women I know living without the presence of a husband, whether they are divorcees or have never been married or their husbands are in the United States, work outside of the home to help support themselves and sometimes their children or their parents. Most unmarried women without children and many with children live with their parents and often help support them.

Much has been written over the past few decades documenting women and work in urban settings in Latin America, and a good deal of it focuses on poor women's mostly unregulated or semiregulated labor in the informal sector. Market women are the specific subjects of many of these studies (Babb 1989, 2018; Mancero Acosta 2012; Seligman 1989; Weismantel 2002). Research on market women in the informal economy in Latin America initially offered a crucial corrective to previous descriptions of Latin American women's acquiescence to male dominance, showing that women did have some agency to make decisions and create economic opportunities. Studies also documented the very real constraints on them as poor, often ethnically marginal women (Buechler and Buechler 1996; Seligman 1993). Informal-sector work is often all that is open to poor women because of a lack of education or connections and pressing needs for childcare or other family responsibilities. Class, race, patriarchy, and *palanca* also play roles in defining some spaces as fit for poor women and others not (Weismantel 2002). The unregulated and untaxed informal sector provides little in the way of job security and in Ecuador, at least until recently, little social security. Women's informal work in urban settings often mirrors the prominent gender stereotypes of women as caretakers, and opportunities are often associated with traditional women's domestic work such as selling food in the marketplace, cooking meals, and working as domestic maids.[6] Other options have arisen, such as direct sales of cosmetics and other products (Casanova 2011). Despite the known pitfalls for participants in these kinds of pyramid marketing schemes, direct sales offer women the flexibility to work when they are able around other family obligations. Erynn Masi de Casanova notes that for poor women in Guayaquil, the affiliation with a global company can "confer a sense and image of professionalism that is valued by the women in the sales force and often respected by others" (2011, 202). This desire for a sense of professionalism is a crucial element in the quest to go forward, *salir adelante*.

While work in the informal sector remains a vital means for many women to support their families, my focus here is on the lives of now single women who transitioned out of the informal sector and are the first in their families to be professionals or otherwise employed in the formal sector. To be sure, the distinction between the formal and the informal sectors is not always as clear as it might have seemed in earlier descriptions. Women often move between jobs that are more or less regulated and that provide them with greater or fewer labor rights and provisions. Definitions of what constitutes the informal and formal sectors have shifted over time, and now a more widely accepted understanding is that variations in work arrangements can produce degrees of formality and informality (Biles 2009). Working for oneself and paying taxes is a step toward formality compared to working for oneself and not paying taxes. Moreover, as with the direct sales beauty product business in Guayaquil, a professional appearance may disguise what is really an informal work arrangement (Casanova 2011). Even women with professional credentials may occupy an in-between status in the formal and the informal sectors. Pilar, a lawyer, rents an office, pays some taxes, and maintains her own social security account, but much of her income is made under the table. While we can quibble about where she might sit on the informal-formal continuum, she sees herself as a professional who takes great satisfaction from her self-made accomplishments and career.

Pilar and other first-generation workers in the formal sectors and formal sector–like workers have gotten where they are by embracing a cosmopolitan, urban vision of competent womanhood. That includes learning how to interact confidently in the workplace and developing skills, usually through education, outside of the traditional domestic sphere. They have also had to defy constraints that others, parents, and ex-husbands in particular might have placed on them. Those same parents who were determined to provide their daughters with a high school education frequently discouraged a college education as too costly and too long a deferment of income earning. Husbands, too, even those far away in New York, make claims about being good providers by supporting stay-at-home wives. Sometimes out of necessity, sometimes out of ambition, and sometimes out of a desire to become something in life (*hacer algo en la vida*), women from poor families have been redefining the roles they will play at home and in the workplace.

The single women I know have defied traditional gender expectations by not privileging marriage over their work or careers. Some have never married, often moving up in their workplaces fairly rapidly, and others have left unhappy marriages and chosen to support themselves. The latter choice often is not something their mothers would have done or felt they could have done, as divorce was highly stigmatized just a generation ago. Several of the young women I met in the late 1980s married relatively early, often in their late teen years, and had a child or two, and then their husbands left for the United States. Blanca's daughter-in-law, Carolina, is one such woman, as is her niece, Pilar. Both women were married in their late teens, and both had children right away. Carolina had one son, and Pilar had two children before her husband migrated. Both women had some financial support from their husbands and regular telephone calls when the men first migrated, but essentially they have been single mothers to their children as they managed their day-to-day lives. Perhaps not surprisingly given the distance, Carolina and Pilar are now divorced from their husbands in the United States. Their ex-husbands still send money or gifts to their grown children from time to time, but they have not sent money to their former wives in many years. While life has not always been easy for either woman, over time and perhaps compelled or encouraged by the absence of their husbands, they have developed a profound sense of their own competencies.

Carolina

Carolina is a pretty woman with an expertly made-up face, gleaming, long, black hair, and an outgoing and enthusiastic personality. She fills up a room with the scent of perfume and her nonstop banter. She rarely sits still, and when she does, her long, painted fingernails are click-clacking away on her cell phone. She is opinionated and will freely share her views on everything from the quality of rice in the market to the moral threat she perceives in homosexuality. She has had a number of sales jobs in her career and by 2015 was working six days a week for a European hair-care company selling high-end beauty products to salons. "I have to look like this," she told me as she jokingly tossed her hair, "or no one will buy my products." She is an impatient person and drives her beat-up Honda aggressively through town, her left hand out the window most of the time as she waves, smiles at, and flirts with other drivers, most of whom are men, to encourage them to let her into their lane. She is expected to drive her own car all over the city and region for her job and receives no gas or maintenance allowance from the company. Carolina has been divorced from her ex, Blanca's son, for many years. She married a second time, but that marriage did not last beyond a few months. Her second husband drank and was abusive and a bad influence on her son. Although she initiated the divorce from her first husband, who lives in New York, she confesses that she still gets jealous when she sees pictures on Facebook of him with other women. Carolina admits her choices in men have not been good. She describes both her husbands as temperamental, argumentative, and abusive, but she also found the wherewithal to leave them.

Carolina had a tempestuous adolescence. She was uninterested in going to the university, and when she was seventeen she started working, selling clothing in a shop and hanging out with a fast crowd. She got pregnant at eighteen and married the father, Blanca's eldest son, Fernando. Carolina's mother was disappointed in her and disapproved of her choices, and for several years they were estranged. That is all water under the bridge now. Since the divorce from Fernando, Carolina's mother has helped her through lean times by sharing meals, providing her grandson with pocket money, and allowing Carolina and her son, Raul, to live in a small apartment attached to her house. Carolina had a hard time making ends meet for several years, especially after her relationship with Fernando soured. He continued to send money, but only to support Raul, and even that was inconsistent. Carolina, therefore, has had to work. For years she had been employed by a personal-care product company, selling affordable shampoos and lotions wholesale to grocery and discount stores. It was a good job. However, when the government raised the import tax on many products, including those she sold, which were made in Colombia, the new taxes put these once common and affordable products out of reach of the average consumer. She worked mostly on commission, so her take-home pay suffered, even though she expanded her territory during this time, driving all over the province and putting countless miles on her already worn car. Frustrated by the poor sales, she left that job to work for the Italian hair-care company.

Carolina's son, Raul, has caused his mother a great deal of anxiety. He completed high school in his mid-twenties, after years of intermittently attending night school. He did not attempt college. He has not been able to find or hold a steady job, in part because he has had serious alcohol and drug problems since his teen years. She has tried more than one approach to his problems, vacillating between being understanding and supportive and giving him tough love by refusing to support him and kicking him out of her house. Carolina has lived for years wondering and worrying about Raul, lying awake at night pondering when or whether he would come home. Sometimes she did not know for days if he was alive or dead. His habits were expensive; he stole money from Carolina and borrowed money from some unsavory characters. He was beaten more than once for failing to pay his debts. It is often worry over Raul that drives Carolina to the church overlooking the city, where she tries to put her problems into perspective.

For a change, in 2018 Raul was doing well, and his mother happily reported that he had a steady girlfriend who seemed to be a good influence on him. He has given up both drugs and alcohol. His mother still supported him, and he worked only from time to time when someone he knew offered him day work, but he was cooking up an idea for a new business venture. He and his girlfriend have a thoroughly modern dream to open a dog hotel to care for dogs when their owners leave town. Such an idea would have been completely absurd in 1989, a time when poor people did not travel, few had pets, and middle-class and rich people had domestic help who stayed home and cared for the house and animals. Raul needed capital to start this venture, most of all to rent or buy property to house the hotel, but at this writing he had not been able to convince anyone to invest. When Carolina talks about her son, she is alternately optimistic that he'll figure something out and worried that he'll fall back into drugs and alcohol and not amount to very much. She wonders about the effects of not having a father's presence in the home throughout his childhood and if Raul would have done better with a father to discipline him. His father had not sent enough money, Carolina said, to compensate for his absence from his son's life.

Carolina's work life is inherently unstable; companies come and go in Ecuador's beauty supply market, but she has not been without a job for very long. Her outgoing personality and boundless energy make her a natural salesperson, and with her years of experience she has made contacts and connections across the region. While Carolina may not like a particular job, she loves working; it gets her out of the house, and she enjoys seeing her clients. Staying home is not an option. Carolina would like to have a responsible man in her life, but there just are not many of those around. Most men her age are married or in New York. By her mid-forties she became accustomed, for better or worse, to her independence; she does not think she'll find a good man, although there are plenty of bad ones to be had, she is quick to point out. She goes to parties with friends and family, but the pickings are slim, and men her age all want younger women, she tells me. She knows she is a handful, she is opinionated and temperamental, and she gets jealous easily, but she has been looking out for herself for too long to change for someone else. She has a funny habit of holding out her hands, cocking her head, and quipping, "Asi soy yo!" (That's the way I am!) when she knows she has said something provocative, as though to clarify that she has no intention of moderating herself. "Perhaps," she says, only half-jokingly, "one day I'll find a rich old widower!"

Pilar

Pilar is very different from Carolina. Pilar wears conservative business suits that tug uncomfortably on her stocky frame; she is circumspect in conversation and slow to give her opinion, doing so only after asking a range of questions. When she has a quiet moment, she is likely to bring out her knitting needles, not her cell phone. Her one real concession to the local beauty standards is wearing high heels, albeit awkwardly. Carolina walks confidently in three-inch heels, commenting that they make her blue-jeaned bottom more attractive. Pilar takes baby steps in high heels and looks for an arm to lean on whenever possible.

When she was nineteen years old, Pilar married a man she did not really love because she was pressured by her family to do so. Her husband was a decent man, she says. He cared for the children and was never abusive, but he was king of the house and controlled everything. She regrets her marriage, although most certainly not her children, and says she tells people, "Don't marry young!" She says women should not marry until their late twenties or early thirties, and men should marry in their forties. She contends that young people do not know what they are doing when they marry and that marriage makes it difficult to complete other goals in life. Pilar speaks from experience. She married right out of high school, and her husband did not want her to continue her education after their marriage, so she did not enroll in the university and stayed home to raise their two sons. When her boys entered primary school, her husband migrated to the United States, where he remains today.

Pilar lived with her in-laws for several years after her husband left, and they shared remittances, childcare, and living expenses. It was an unhappy arrangement for Pilar; she felt scrutinized by her in-laws and was reluctant to share her remittances with them. Like her Aunt Blanca, she parlayed cooking into a business and opened a small restaurant. As the boys grew, she rented an apartment and left the home of her in-laws. Her life was her children, she says, and she worked to supplement her husband's remittances and provide a better life for them. About twelve years after her husband left, Pilar made some financial decisions that led to the dissolution of her marriage. Using some savings and the collateral from the restaurant, she borrowed heavily from local banks and began to build an expensive new home. She did not consult with her husband. This act of independence, if not defiance, set off the unraveling of her marriage. Her husband was infuriated that she had borrowed so much money without his knowledge or consent, and he wanted to distance himself from what he considered her bad debts. They fought over the phone for over a year and then decided on a divorce.

After the divorce, her ex-husband suspended all financial support to her, but when I asked Pilar how she managed, money did not much figure into her calculus. In describing her divorce she said, "For me, it was really good. I was finally free." Freedom for Pilar meant that she could do what she had always dreamed of doing, go to college and earn a law degree. Pilar sold the land and the building materials she bought for the new home, and she now talks about the house as though it was someone else, someone with very different priorities; who ever wanted such a thing?

She continued to work days in the restaurant, and then every evening, from five to eight p.m., she attended law classes at the Universidad Católica de Cuenca. This university has historically been the least expensive option for higher education in Cuenca, and it offers night school programs. Pilar was thirty-six years old when she enrolled and the only older student in her classes. She says she felt awkward from time to time, but she was more motivated and focused than the teenagers in her classes. She graduated in five years and opened a small office downtown in what is known as "lawyer's row." She doesn't make much money, but she loves her job, stays in the office regularly until 7 or 8 p.m., and does what she can, she says, to help people. She mostly practices family and small property law, often representing destitute campesinos who have lost their land, and she defends abused women.

Given her work, Pilar tends to see the unhappy consequences of bad or violent marriages, reinforcing her belief that marriage should not be undertaken lightly. Despite this aspect of her work, her face lights up when she talks about her job, and she still seems to marvel at how she pulled it off: she went back to school and made a career for herself. She has done something in life. Her sons are grown now; one is a Spanish teacher in a high school in North Carolina, and the other is a dentist in Cuenca. She has not talked to her ex-husband in years, but her sons stay in touch with him. She does not interfere in their relationships and knows very little about her ex-husband's life in Philadelphia. Despite her quiet demeanor and studied politeness, Pilar is by far the most outspoken feminist I know in Ecuador. She advocates for abused women, fills her Facebook page with videos about female empowerment, and lectures young women on the value of avoiding the sorrows and constraints that come from an early marriage.

Jessica

Most women in Cuenca do marry and have families, yet I have met many who, for a variety of reasons, did not get married. These women usually stay at home with their parents, since living on one's own is usually not a readily available option. In addition, a childless, single woman living with friends would necessarily have her virtue called into question, and housing is too expensive and salaries too low to support independent living. Beyond those considerations, there also is little desire among the young women I know to separate from their natal families despite the frustrations they may feel occasionally about family obligations that increasingly fall on them as their parents age. Living on one's own is just not commonly done; it displays a worrisome level of independence and freethinking. When I asked young women if they ever thought of moving away from their families, they were rather stunned at the idea; it was not something they had considered. Living at home not only helps to stretch inadequate salaries, but the idea of cooking and shopping and taking care of oneself while holding a full-time job did not seem tenable. They might have had moments when living at home felt constraining or their parents or siblings irritated them, but they had not given any serious consideration to seeking a different living arrangement.

In 2006 I began a multiyear project studying women with the chronic illness systematic lupus erythematosus. I had come to this topic of research because Rosa, whom I had known for so many years, was diagnosed with the illness, and I had a hard time imagining how she would cope with the complicated medical regime it entailed. Lupus is an autoimmune disorder in which the immune system no longer recognizes friend from foe and begins to attack normal, healthy body tissues. It usually starts with inexplicable, severe joint pain and if left untreated can progress to organ damage and death. There is no cure for lupus, but a complicated medical regime can help to keep lupus flares at bay. I wondered how Rosa, with a third-grade education, could manage the medications and home care required to prevent a lupus flare. Over several years I talked with women across the city about their experiences with the illness and how it affected their families, careers, and sense of self. In Rosa's case, her daughters saw to her care; she would not be alive today if not for their vigilance and sacrifice. As I talked with women from various walks of life about their illness experiences, I found myself most intrigued by the single women I met. Their experiences with lupus reinforced the importance of their connections to their natal families and highlighted their reconfigured aspirations for their lives. Chronic illness brought to the visible surface the tensions that underlie many young women's lives as they strive to find their places when marriage and childbearing appear unlikely.

In 2013 I wrote about Jessica, then in her thirties, and how her struggles with lupus had affected her life course; I argued that chronic illness left her permanently in a liminal state between childhood and adulthood and under the overly watchful eyes of her family. Lupus is an erratic illness characterized by periodic flares and remissions, and even when a person is feeling well, she must be careful not to tax or overtire herself, lest any exertions provoke a reactivation. Physical and emotional stress need to be managed. Jessica's lupus was not very severe, and she went through years of remission when she was free of all medications. Despite her mild case of lupus, Jessica complained to me then that her parents and sister constantly surveilled her every mood, worrying that the slightest cough or sniffle portended a lupus flare or some other health crisis. Her life centered almost exclusively on work and family, but she did go out with friends from time to time, something her mother did not like very much. As a teenager, Jessica was raped by a schoolmate, and her mother became exceedingly cautious. She used Jessica's health problems as further evidence that Jessica needed to be closely monitored and that her social life should be constrained.

When I met Jessica in 2005 she was twenty-nine years old and living with her working-class family in their home in an older neighborhood just outside the *centro histórico*. Jessica shared a bedroom with her twelve-year-old sister. Their mother, Carmela, kept a small *tienda* in the front of the house where she sold groceries, cigarettes, and treats. Their father had a small tailor shop. Jessica started to have symptoms of lupus in her late teens and was diagnosed with the illness at age twenty. Although her lupus symptoms were mild, she described her health in general as "delicate," and she has had a series of health problems including endometriosis, ovarian cysts, and anemia. Jessica's periods were so heavy that sometimes she had to leave work because she could not contain the flow of blood.

Jessica graduated from high school and went to work immediately as a bookkeeper for a large, local company with several retail stores in town. She has worked for the same employer now for more than twenty years. She has not had a boyfriend since high school, saying that men run when they hear about her health troubles. In describing the effect of lupus on her life, Jessica told me that her illness had kept her from having a "complete life," that is, one with a husband and children. At one point she entertained the idea of having a child out of wedlock through artificial insemination since she wanted one so badly, an idea that horrified her mother for myriad reasons, least of all the public scandal of it all. Given her ongoing health problems, Jessica did not pursue that idea for long.

Jessica's life since I have known her has been one of continual but relatively minor health problems punctuated by terrible and traumatic personal events. In 2010 Jessica was in good health, and her doctor recommended that she get out more and try to enjoy herself. She was then in her mid-thirties, and her life consisted of going to work and coming home to her family. Out of loving concern and with the best of intentions, Carmela had long made it difficult for Jessica to maintain a social life outside of the family, believing that Jessica's health was too delicate and that going out in the evenings after work would tire her and put her health at risk. In a small act of defiance, Jessica decided to follow the doctor's advice, and she and a friend started going out on Friday nights. Sometimes they went to a friend's house, sometimes out for coffee or ice cream, and a few times they went dancing. When I saw Jessica that year, she was happy; she knew she was making her mother uncomfortable by going out, but it was only one night a week at most, and she enjoyed her time with her friend tremendously. "We mostly just talk," she told me. "It's nice to go out and see people happy." Then, tragedy struck. Her friend and one of the friend's two children died from carbon monoxide poisoning from a faulty space heater. Jessica was devastated by grief. She once again returned to spending all of her free time at home with her family.

Jessica has a close relationship with her mother, who has always kept a keen eye on her daughter. Carmela feels responsible for Jessica's fragile health and her lupus because, as she explains it, she became pregnant with Jessica too soon after her previous baby, Jessica's older sister. She had not yet had a menstrual cycle after the previous birth when she became pregnant with Jessica, and the buildup of "bad blood," as she calls it, "polluted" the fetus, leaving Jessica with lifelong health problems. This explanation also serves to tie Carmela to Jessica through a sense of guilt and responsibility. It is Jessica's mother's fault because of a lack of care in getting pregnant that Jessica has so many health problems. Carmela told me privately that she "feels so much" for Jessica and understands her loneliness as an unmarried and perhaps unmarriageable young woman. Her heart breaks for her daughter. When Carmela complains that Jessica's employers take advantage of her or she is not taking good enough care of herself or her doctors don't pay enough attention to her, Jessica just smiles and nods and rolls her eyes as though to say, "Mothers, what can you do?"

In 2016 Jessica's home life was in complete shambles. Carmela had been in and out of the hospital for months with acute abdominal pain. She claimed that no one in the hospital took her pain seriously until Jessica came and pressured them to do more tests, and they diagnosed pancreatitis. Jessica spent weeks running between the hospital, where she was her mother's health care advocate, her home, and her job, trying to hold everything together. Her younger sister was in college and helped when she could, but it was understood that her priority should be her schoolwork. Adding even more stress, Jessica's father, at seventy years old, was incarcerated. He pleaded guilty to child molestation, a charge Jessica and her family did not believe was true. The fifteen-year-old girl who swept the tailor shop accused Hugo, Jessica's father, of touching her breasts. Jessica said the charge was completely false and was an extortion attempt by the girl's mother. The girl's family first sent a lawyer, who asked for money, and when that was not forthcoming, they went to the police. In a testament to the changing laws about gender violence, the police did not look the other way, and Hugo was arrested. He was convinced to plead guilty to avoid a costly trial and potentially a longer sentence. Jessica said her father was given poor advice from his attorney and should have fought the charges. He was sentenced to two and a half years in prison. The family did not have the money to pay the lawyer and court fees, and Jessica had to ask her employers for an advance of her pay to help cover the legal costs. The stress and anxiety of her mother's illness and her father's legal troubles reactivated Jessica's lupus, and for the first time in several years she was once again taking daily medications.

When I saw Jessica in 2018, the family was in a much happier situation. Her younger sister, Ana, a recent college graduate, was about to be married to a young man the family liked, Carmela's health was stable, and their dad was out of prison and able to give the bride away. In a stroke of serendipity, their neighborhood had been transformed, opening up new economic possibilities. A regional prison had been a dominant presence there for decades; its high wall lined the surrounding blocks, making the streets seem narrow and uninviting, and a watchtower loomed over the neighborhood. The dilapidated prison was not good for the neighborhood property values; it was an eyesore and brought an unsavory element to the neighborhood. Finally the prison was relocated and the old structures torn down; an enticing city park was created on the site with an attractive new viewing tower overlooking the city. The family began considering reopening the closed *tienda* to serve the children and families they hoped would fill the park on Sundays.

Less optimistic was Jessica's career. The company she worked for began slowly failing, and as other employees were being fired, Jessica became even more essential at work. The company had not adjusted to a changed, digital retail environment, and Jessica said the owner's children who took over the business from their father did not know what they were doing.

As a single woman, Jessica's days became filled with work and her nights and weekends with family obligations. Her parents needed her income to help make ends meet, and in times of crisis they depended on the social connections and access to loans that her employers have provided. As they age, they are happy to have Jessica at home with them; it was she who managed the household when Carmela was in the hospital and her father in prison, and she made sure her younger sister kept her grades up. As Jessica's company floundered, her employers were counting on her more and more, and her weekends and evenings were swallowed up by work. When I visited in 2018, Jessica's mother was livid at the endless phone calls coming to Jessica from work during her vacation. "They never leave her in peace!" her mother lamented. I had a different interpretation. I sensed that Jessica liked being needed. She is over forty years old, single, and living at home, and her job provides her with a sense of her worth beyond her household. She is indispensable. Jessica has plenty of real-world work experience but fears that without a college degree she could never get another job. There are too many college-educated accountants out there. Staying at home, she says, is boring and sad.

No one appeared happier at Ana's wedding than her sister Jessica, who wore a beautiful dress with a stunning corsage and a huge smile on her face while greeting friends and family and handing out little satin bags of rice to toss at the happy couple as they left the church. Jessica knew everyone in the church, and she had hugs and a gracious smile for every attendee. She had spent the week before the wedding at home helping her sister prepare for the big day and furnishing a new apartment where the couple would move after the wedding. Yet, because they shared a bedroom, no one would miss Ana more than Jessica. Jessica would be the only one left at home with her aging parents, and her responsibilities to them would no doubt increase. Carmela is a worrier. She regularly asserts that motherhood is fundamentally about suffering, starting with physical suffering and extending to the financial privations endured to provide for children. Then there is the worry over their schooling, who they are hanging out with, what they are doing when they are not home, followed by the fear that they have married badly or won't ever marry and end up lonely, and specifically with Jessica, the fear and concern about her delicate health and her tendency to take on too much. Jessica knows that she eases her mother's burdens at the same time that she contributes to her anxiety and suffering.

Women's Suffering

The kinds of comments that Jessica's mother makes about the difficulties of motherhood and especially the suffering of women echoed comments I had been hearing from women of her generation for decades. Throughout the years, I noticed that women talked about *sufrimiento* (suffering) often and in myriad different ways that defied easy categorization. It took me nearly twenty years of putting together various iterations of the term to understand it. *Sufrimiento* is a concept that cannot be explained by asking people about it. When I did I got pained looks as people attempted to define something they could not. Everyone knows what *sufrimiento* is, but they are hard-pressed to define it. The word means "suffering," but how that suffering manifests in women's lives is hard to put a finger on.

I first heard the term *sufrimiento* in 1989 while working among poor rural-to-urban migrant women who lived in crowded and dilapidated *conventillos* in the city center. They had come to the city mostly to make their children's lives better, but it was not clear that their own lives had improved much if at all. City life offered them few opportunities and far less trusted companionship than their rural homes had. They came from circumstances of rural poverty and had little education and few occupational choices. Many dealt with difficult and abusive husbands and spent their daily lives in a city where their very embodiment of self-identity—the *pollera* skirt, braids, and Panama hat—marked them as targets of social derision. The women frequently spoke of their *sufrimiento* as they described their lives and circumstances. Given the difficulties these migrant women faced, their use of the word made sense to me, and I saw it as a literal description of the objective conditions of their lives.

Yet, I also thought I heard in poor women's descriptions of their *sufrimiento* an underlying critique of the unfairness of their lives. This was a time when resistance theories were prominent in anthropology, positing that the poor analyze and resist their oppression in regular yet often very subtle ways. Resistance theories were inspired by James Scott's 1987 book *Weapons of the Weak*, in which he contends that the poor and marginalized should be seen as more than passive victims of their fate. Rather, he argues, the subaltern make varied critiques about their subjugation and creatively undermine hegemonic discourses and practices. Given what I knew of the social stigma attached to rural-to-urban migrants and the daily indignities their status brought them, I wondered if women's expressions of *sufrimiento* were a kind of resistance, an indirect critique of the systems that oppressed them.[7] The women were not willing to passively accept the objective conditions of their lives, their poverty, and the prejudice against them as the natural lot of the *chola* or as something they deserved. Their *sufrimiento* highlighted their inability to change the difficult conditions of their lives despite their hard work. *Sufrimiento* draws attention to the differences between who they believed themselves to be, humble and hardworking, and the social circumstances of poverty that stigmatized them but that they were helpless to change.

Then, over the years, I heard mature women from various social positions from rich to poor and in a vast array of life circumstances, from very sick to utterly well, speak of their *sufrimiento*. It became clear to me that my first impression of *sufrimiento* as a poor woman's resistance discourse needed to be revised. *Sufrimiento*, I came to understand, was invariably a woman's discourse and not necessarily restricted to the impoverished. Women use *sufrimiento* to describe circumstances, even trivial ones, that are out of their control but that affect their lives or sensibilities in profound ways. For example, an elite friend once exclaimed "Qué sufrimiento!" as we passed a new building that she found artistically ugly. The building was garish and not in keeping with her understanding of local aesthetic and moral values, and it tarnished her beloved landscape. Her critique was about more than taste, however, and expressed a sense of loss of influence over what mattered to her, such as the city's aesthetics and architecture.

What I came to see over time and with many examples is that *sufrimiento* is an expression of women's vulnerability to circumstances and a moral stance in the face of these circumstances. Good women suffer because they are good women in a cruel, sadly indifferent, and unjust world. *Sufrimiento* highlights a woman's vulnerabilities to personal and structural insults stemming from patriarchy, economic insecurity, illness, shifting family or class dynamics, and even her own sentimental or artistic nature. It is an expression of distress and a recognition of a woman's lack of influence over the circumstances in which she finds herself. She has little ability to change what causes her pain, so she must simply endure it. The ability to withstand the suffering that comes from unfairness, be it poverty, illness, or even ugliness, is a declaration of a moral position and character.

Yet, so far, anyway, the younger women I know have not picked up their mothers' idiom of *sufrimiento* to describe themselves or their lives. This is not to say that these younger women do not suffer, because clearly they do. Carolina described awful moments of sadness and fear about her son and her loneliness without a man in her life, and Pilar spent years living with difficult in-laws, unable to do what she wanted. Jessica has had more than her fair share of personal, work, and health problems, yet she smiles while she relates them and leaves the talk of *sufrimiento* to her mother. I have not heard Jessica describe her life or circumstances as ones that provoke *sufrimiento*.

So what, if anything, does this mean? Perhaps their rejection as teenagers of the dominant patriarchal models has meant that they do not see their lives as constrained in the same ways that their mothers saw their own lives. As a generation, they have shown that they can and will divorce their unacceptable husbands and that they will go to school and work outside the home. While these gains have not always left them happy or with the lives they expected or even wanted, the gains also have perhaps mitigated the sense of powerlessness that provokes women to see their lives through a lens of the acceptance of suffering.

Again, I do not want to overstate the case for improvement in women's lives, nor can I pinpoint what mattered most in provoking change—urban values, education, the absence of men, remittances, legal provisions, or larger cultural flows. But I do think something important has been happening. The younger generation of women who came of age in the 1990s and 2000s do have an enhanced sense of their own control in the face of life's circumstances, and the skills and sensibilities they acquired by necessity, hard work, and choice give them the confidence to claim more agency over their own lives. A quiet revolution, in other words.

Alejandra

This is the story of Alejandra, Rosa's eldest daughter. In contrast to the women I met as adults, I have known Alejandra since she was eight years old. The Quitasacas have come a long, long way in the years I have known them, no one more so than Alejandra. Her life trajectory has taken her from a dark, stuffy, windowless two-room *conventillo* with a shared toilet to what by any measure is a comfortable middle-class lifestyle. Her life has been marked by the rural-to-urban migration of her parents and by her brother's transnational migration to the United States. Her parents' newness to the city and fear of its possibilities influenced her early years, and her brother's migration shifted her teen years in unpredictable ways and provided a means for her to move away from the life her mother had envisioned for her. Much has changed in the opportunities available to young women in Cuenca in recent decades, but Alejandra's successes are undoubtedly also an outcome of her intelligence and dogged perseverance. As one of the older children, born when the family was still very poor and the parents unsure of the path to progress, she was not given opportunities, so she fought for them.

In 1989 Alejandra was a shy, quiet eight-year-old whom I noticed but frankly paid scant attention to. When I met the Quitasacas, they were living in a two-room apartment in an old colonial building downtown, one of those places that assails the nose with the smell of rotting wood and poor plumbing. In my early field notes, my impressions of young Alejandra, the next child after Vicente, are vague and almost entirely made of observations rather than conversations, and there were not that many of those, either. Some of that had to do with the children's staggered school schedules and when I was most likely to visit. I found early on in my fieldwork that women were less likely to be home in the mornings, or if they were home, they often did not have the time to talk to me. Mornings are busy for poor women in Cuenca; they often wash their family's clothes in the early morning, a necessity if they have any hopes of the clothes drying before a musty smell sets in; they shop for the day's food and begin preparing lunch, the main meal of the day, by 11 a.m. or so. Vicente, who was in *colegio* (high school) went to school early in the morning and returned home for the day by 1:30 p.m., and Alejandra left for school in the afternoon. Because she was absent when I was mostly likely to visit, in the first four months of field notes I recorded just one conversation with Alejandra. Most of the time I simply acknowledged that when Alejandra was home she was most likely in the bedroom, invariably keeping her baby sister, then a year and a half old, entertained, clean, and quiet and watching cartoons on the small black-and-white television, before it was stolen.

While I often did not notice Alexandra or what she was doing, my notebooks are filled with commentary and snippets of conversations I had with her older brother, fourteen-year-old Vicente. I do not think I was alone in noticing one child and not the other. Vicente was a favorite with his mother; she commented numerous times how intelligent she thought him and how well she thought he was doing in school. Vicente was an engaging young man and filled with the confidence and curiosity that comes to eldest sons whose mothers dote on them. Vicente was six years older than Alexandra, so his oldest-sibling status was firmly rooted in the family dynamics, and he took on an authoritative role with his siblings and his mother with apparent ease.[1] He was much better educated than either of his parents, and his mother in particular relied on him for help of all kinds as well as companionship. Lucho, Rosa's husband, was a long-distance bus driver in 1989 and was gone for days at a time, and when he was home, their relationship could be tense and strained.

Lucho was authoritarian in his home, and I saw Rosa become quiet and acquiescent is his presence. It was different with Vicente, with whom she had an easy companionship and whose competencies she nurtured and admired. She would often turn to Vicente for affirmation of something she said or to ask him to explain something she was having trouble articulating. Vicente helped his family navigate paperwork and bureaucratic hassles, and he was something of an emissary to modern urban lifeways. Rosa listened to him in ways that she did not to Lucho and deferred to his judgment frequently.

Alejandra, however, spoke only when she was spoken to, was slow to respond to my questions, and never laughed at my jokes. Indeed, she never really laughed at all. During school breaks or weekends, Alexandra was usually in the bedroom caring for Cecilia when I came over, while Vicente sat with me in the kitchen, often peppering me with questions like "Don't Americans get sick from drinking milk cold, straight out of the refrigerator?" "Is it true Americans just throw clothes, furniture, and TVs into the street?" and "Doesn't snow hurt the leaves on the trees?" I also noted in Vicente's demeanor a kind of male privilege, and I wrote the following: "Vicente reminded me today of Hector [another teenage boy I knew]. They, in contrast to girls who are quiet and demure, take a real know-it-all authoritative tone. They often say things I know are incorrect but in such an authoritative way, I believe them. I have not met a single young girl like that." Despite this observation, I was thoroughly charmed by Vicente's curiosity and, like his mother, I paid far more attention to him than I did to the rest of the children. In a household with five children, including a precocious fourteen-year-old boy and an adorable eighteenth-month-old baby, a quiet, obedient, eight-year-old was easy to overlook.

My first real conversation with Alejandra took place about two months after I met the family when we were visiting her grandparents in the rural town of Cumbe, a short distance from Cuenca. I was sitting in the one-room, straw-roofed adobe kitchen called a *choza*, watching the grandmother tend the *cuys* (guinea pigs) that she was roasting over the fire. Alejandra sat down next to me on the soot-embedded wooden bench in the smoky room, and we talked about the food being cooked. Alejandra said she did not like watching the *cuys* being killed, and she had learned in school that animals are "like us," that is, they have souls. She then told me she liked to eat only the paws of the guinea pig, which get crispy after roasting. But when her grandmother snapped off the charred feet and handed them to us as a snack, Alejandra tossed hers on the floor for the dogs. She said the nails frightened her. While these comments seemed trivial, I noted them at the time because they clearly established a break between Alejandra and her mother and grandmother, who enthusiastically enjoyed *cuy* and were skilled in killing and roasting a much-favored food. I interpreted Alejandra's reticence to urban affectations learned in school.

I rarely saw Alejandra play, and I noted conspicuously in my field journals when she did. Once or twice when we sat outside in the back courtyard, if the baby was asleep Alejandra would play with another girl about her age who lived in the building. They had few toys; there was one dirty, naked doll that was passed among the girls, and they mostly played an imaginative game of devils chasing angels. Those moments of play seemed like stolen ones for Alejandra because as soon as Cecilia woke and fussed, she was told to go inside and attend to the baby. Even when Lucho or Vicente was home, relaxing on the bed and playing with the baby, Alejandra was charged with the more difficult bodily care of her sister. Alejandra changed the rags that functioned as diapers, soothed Cecilia by walking her around, or gave her a snack or a bottle. Others might play with Cecilia, but Alejandra was her caretaker. There was no time she could play or do her homework that was uninterruptable. Alejandra was never thanked for her help; it was expected, but she was blamed if something went wrong. One afternoon I arrived to find that Cecilia had a swollen lip, and rather than saying simply that she fell, Rosa made a point of telling me that Alejandra "let Cecilia fall" from a kitchen chair, a clear indication that Rosa blamed Alejandra for carelessness and expected better.

The gendered roles of Rosa and Lucho were fairly clear and straightforward in those days, but their children were already learning to be more flexible. Lucho did not cook, clean, or do childcare, and when he was home he expected to be waited on. He might play with his children, but he did not clean or feed them. Vicente was much more helpful around the house. Rosa proudly told me that he could cook simple dishes, although I never saw this, and he would help his mother if she was late by starting the rice or helping her peel potatoes. He was expected to help clean up the previous evening's dishes if there was time before he left for school, but finishing his homework and doing well in school were priorities. Vicente was also allowed to visit friends after school on occasion or go to Cumbe by himself for a weekend and hang out with his cousins. Alejandra was not allowed such liberties. Moreover, her educational achievements were deemed worthless by Rosa, and her contributions at home were expected and therefore unremarkable. While Rosa knew that graduating from high school was important for her children's future success, she also blamed their schooling when Vicente or Alejandra were reluctant to help at home. Toward the end of my first stay in 1989, Rosa complained to me that school was influencing her children's behavior and they were not as respectful as she thought they ought to be.

Despite her expected contributions to household chores and childcare, a pattern more closely associated with rural areas, Alejandra was a city girl, and Rosa, never mind her occasional complaints, wanted it that way. When we took trips to the countryside, Alejandra was always much more stylishly dressed than her raggedy cousins. Rosa made sure of that, with Alejandra's hair carefully combed and held back not in *chola* braids but with brightly colored barrettes and ponytail holders.[2] Alejandra had city manners and expressed fear of the many animals around the farm, even horses and cows, and she insisted that spoons be found for eating potatoes and *mote* (hominy). When Alejandra was six, Lucho's parents asked if Alejandra could live with them in the country and help them around the house, but Rosa refused to let her daughter go. She wanted her home, and she wanted her to go to school. Rosa's sister-in-law, who lived in the country, commented one afternoon when we were chatting about children that her girls were small compared to Rosa's because they worked too hard. "Girls need to be left in peace, not ordered around all the time" if they were to grow well, she commented. Compared to her country cousins' upbringing, Alejandra's life was considered easy.

Toward the end of my first fieldwork stay in 1989, Rosa and Lucho made plans to baptize all four of their younger children at the same time. Even though she was eight years old, Alejandra had not been baptized, nor had her younger siblings. Rosa commented that the family had not had the money to do the baptisms right and that doing four at once saved them a good deal of money. Baptisms are big events in Cuenca and even bigger events in Cumbe. In addition to the costs of the church service, the family is required to host an impressive party, perhaps with a DJ and a rented sound system, and provide endless bottles of beer and sugarcane alcohol (*aguardiente*) and an enormous dinner for all the guests. The godparents are presented with plates overloaded with *cuy*, chicken, rabbit, potatoes, and *mote* in a sign of the new relationship of generosity and reciprocity on which they are embarking. The Quitasaca children were baptized in a church in Cuenca, and then the guests, in private cars or taxis driven by friends or family members, were transported to Cumbe, forty minutes away, for a party that lasted from mid-afternoon to the wee hours of the next morning. Alejandra, as the oldest to be baptized, was allowed to choose her godmother, and she chose me. The other children's godparents came from a working-class family in town that Rosa had met years earlier when she was selling Cumbe milk to her neighbors.

I did not see Alejandra between the ages of eight and twelve, and when I returned in 1993, her world had not changed very much. I had arrived just after the birth of Rosa's last child, a boy, and although it was weeks later, she was still in bed. It had been a difficult pregnancy, and she had no breast milk for the infant, who was being bottle-fed. Vicente was still in high school, at eighteen, but he seemed like a grown man. I saw little of him that summer, as he spent his time after school tending their small, ill-stocked store in Cumbe that Rosa only occasionally opened when she made the trip there. Lucho was driving a taxi locally, so he was home more often than he was in 1989, but his work was frustrating and tensions in the household were growing. Gas prices were rising, and when people were short of money, they did not take taxis. Moreover, Lucho complained, his taxi was old, and some people simply rejected it. This made sense to me, as more than once I saw a friend of mine turn away a taxi she thought was not nice enough. Her thinking was that if she was going to spend the money for a taxi, she wanted a nice ride.

Alejandra was the only one home when her brother was born; she had just sent her sisters to fetch the doctor when Rosa collapsed on the floor. Alejandra found the birth process to be "horrible," and years later when she was studying to be a doctor, she said that experience taught her that she never wanted to be an obstetrician. When I showed up two weeks later, it was clear the household was stressed but, I assumed, only in the way every family was after the birth of a child. Years later, after Alejandra became a physician, she recalled this period as one of the most difficult of her life. She said she thought her mother must have been suffering from postpartum depression or an undiagnosed lupus flare. Alejandra described her mother as emotionally overwrought. Nothing Alejandra or anyone else did was right during that time, and Alejandra had to care for her new brother, as her mother seemed unable to muster the energy to bathe him, prepare his bottle, or soothe him. "It was an ugly, ugly time," Alejandra told me.

While her brothers were free to go to Cumbe every afternoon where they watched their mother's small *tienda* and goofed around with their cousins and friends, and Alejandra's sisters, close in age, still mostly just played like little girls, Alejandra was expected to keep the household together. She did not have the time or freedom to play as her sisters did or explore as her brothers could. During this visit in 1993, and because I am her godmother, I took her out several times for ice cream and once to buy her eyeglasses. I noted at the time how reticent she was to express an opinion, whether for something important like her glasses or unimport-ant such as making a choice of ice cream. I had to read her face and eyes to figure out what she might really want, as she seemingly felt she had no right to ask for anything or express an opinion of any sort.

In 1995 Alejandra was fourteen and already in *colegio*, and Vicente was almost twenty and *still* in high school. He had been held back at least two times, disappointing his parents considerably. Not only was he unable to contribute to the household by working, but his extra years in high school meant extra years of expenses. Rosa was angry about Vicente's failings in school and blamed herself in part for being too permissive with him. "I let him go into the streets," she admitted to me, and he enjoyed himself and did not do his schoolwork. Rosa had allowed Vicente to go to Cumbe after school for years, where he hung out with friends and probably caught the fever to go to the United States, and she freely let him attend school functions and parties at the homes of school friends. She vowed to me then that she would not let the younger children have such freedoms. In those years tensions grew between Vicente and his mother. He would occasionally come home from school complaining that his friends at school were able to buy whatever they wanted, while he had nothing, and he complained that his father treated his mother and siblings crudely. The Quitasaca marriage was under some duress then, with the economy failing while family expenses were growing.

By 1997 Alejandra was chafing pretty badly under Rosa's new approach to raising teenagers. Vicente had been gone to the United States for nearly two years, and Alejandra was in the position of being the eldest child but with none of the privileges that Vicente was afforded. Rosa was determined not to make the same mistakes, and she kept a very tight rein on Alejandra. She was required to be home when not in school. Parties, which she could attend occasionally when Vicente accompanied her, were now a pleasure of the past. Alejandra was supremely irritated by the constraints put on her, and by all accounts, including her own, she rebelled. She started hanging around some rough characters in the neighborhood, ones Rosa was sure were involved in selling drugs or some other illegal activity. Rosa and Lucho were worried sick about her reputation. They just could not understand the deep anger she seemed to have for just about everything. In conversations with her, Alejandra told me she was frustrated about her home life and her family and more broadly about the world she was growing up in. She saw countless friends and family members leave Cuenca for the United States because they saw no future in Ecuador, and she wondered what chance she would have of making a good life in Cuenca without *palanca*. Closer to home, she resented that she had to suffer for Vicente's lapses and that her social life ended when he left for New York. Her parents did not trust her, she told me, and that was infuriating to her. So she gave them a reason to mistrust her by hanging out with the neighborhood hoodlums. Years later Alejandra reflected on that time and marveled that she survived those years.

Alejandra did not exactly know what brought her out of her adolescent rebellion, but from an early age she was interested in going to college. Her mother saw little value in yet more education and wanted her to go to work right after high school so she could contribute to the household, but Alejandra resisted and asked Vicente and me for help in paying for college. We both quickly learned that we had to send the money directly to Alejandra; if it was sent to their mother, she'd spend it on some other necessity. Almost immediately after she started at the university, Alejandra's focus shifted away from the social life in the neighborhood to her studies. In Ecuador, students begin studying for their careers as undergraduates, and her course of study to be a physician lasted six years: four years of classroom and clinical training, one year of internship usually in a hospital setting, and finally a year of rural service. Alejandra did her internship in Quito, living in one room and working sixteen-hour days.

When she was in Quito, I met Alejandra for dinner and asked her how her education at the least rigorous of Cuencan universities was holding up. She admitted she knew less than some of her peers did but, smiling, added, "I just have to work harder." And indeed she did. Following her year of rural service, Alejandra returned to Cuenca to look for a job. She grumbled some that finding a good position required two advantages she did not have: money to buy into private practice or the *palanca* she thought she needed to secure a job in the public sector. She picked up shifts for a while at several clinics around town while she waited for the scores of the standardized examination she took to earn a coveted position as a resident at the Instituto Ecuatoriano de Seguridad Social José Carrasco Arteaga hospital in Cuenca.[3] Much to her delight and surprise, excellence, not *palanca*, prevailed. Alejandra got the top score on the exam and was hired.

Along the way, Alejandra got married to a very nice, soft-spoken man who was working as a supervisor in a factory. Mutual friends introduced them, but it was understood by his family early on in their courtship and marriage that Javier had married below himself. His family is part of the working class of Cuenca, with long ties in the city and a Spanish surname. Alejandra's "Indian" name and rural heritage signaled her family's inferiority. They lived with his family for a few years, and they fought a good deal until they moved out to a rented house by themselves. The in-laws eventually learned to accept Alejandra more, but after the way they treated her she was openly uninterested in them and accompanied Javier only occasionally when he visited them. They did not mix with the Quitasacas at family events, and on holidays Javier spent time with the Quitasacas, who enjoy him tremendously, and then visited his own parents, usually alone. Alejandra and Javier's marriage clearly had difficulties; sometimes when I saw them they seemed quietly companionable, and other times that quietness resembled remoteness.

Alejandra continued her education, obtaining advanced specialization in radiology. She took a teaching position at the best medical school in the city, at the Universidad de Cuenca. In 2016 her days were a blur of activity, with classes in the morning, hospital rounds until early afternoon, and then a shift at a local hospital. She didn't complain about the pace she was keeping because she loves her work. I recall seeing her after a sleepless night on call, and her eyes would be bright as she told of the cases she tended and what she learned. She does not talk about having children. In more recent years, Alejandra took to traveling, and she and Javier visited several countries in Latin America. They liked taking long bus trips and watching the landscape change.

In 2017 Alejandra won a prestigious training fellowship in Mexico, and she spent two years at a hospital in Mexico City. Javier hoped to get a job in Mexico, but he did not, so while Alejandra's days were filled with new friends and colleagues and professional challenges, Javier mostly stayed at their home in Mexico City. He ended up returning to Cuenca early and without Alejandra. After her time in Mexico, Alejandra spent six months in the United States visiting her brother on Long Island and me in Kalamazoo, Michigan. In New York she took English classes, went to art museums, and caught up with transnational family members. As she prepared to return to Cuenca in late summer of 2019, she was fielding offers from hospitals to head up their radiology departments. Soon after returning to Cuenca, she divorced Javier. Their life trajectories seemed impossibly different.

In writing about Alejandra, I came to learn that my old field notes preserve and hint at what I might not have wanted to realize. I found in them a mother who was not just blind to her daughter's quickness but downright dismissive of it. How could she see it as anything but a threat as she counted on her to watch the baby, boil the rice, or run to the store? But what's my excuse? I cannot pinpoint when Alejandra went from being a shy reticent child to a quick-minded student. I did not see it coming; I probably was not paying enough attention. She watched everything in ways I did not comprehend. When and how did that switch turn on that got her away from hanging out with the bad characters in the neighborhood, in part to assert her independence and drive her parents crazy, to staying up at all hours studying microbiology? No one in her home saw the value of what she was doing; she got little encouragement there. So she turned to Vicente in New York for tuition money. I suspect her mother complained about that too. Rosa sees a world of limited good, but even more so, I do not think she could possibly imagine the world that Alejandra saw for herself. It was simply beyond her comprehension that her daughter, one generation away from milking cows for a living, could graduate from the university and embark on a professional career.

The first time I went to Alejandra's home that she shared with Javier, I realized that she truly was middle-class. I saw clearly that she had developed ways of talking and a taste in art and food that were distinctive to the middle class. Her home was comfortably furnished in bright colors; there was inexpensive but carefully chosen modern art on the walls and a golden retriever in the yard. If someone had just met her they most likely would not know that her family came from rural Cumbe and that she grew up in a two-room *conventillo*. Some of her colleagues at the hospital pause when they hear her last name, an Indigenous one, silently reckoning with what they thought they understood that name to mean. In recent years, Alejandra dipped back into her rural roots, delicately, circumspectly, now far enough away from it all to be reflective. She started going more often to Cumbe to visit her grandmother, a woman whose life was miserable from start to finish. She was orphaned as a child and married off to a man who thought he was better than she was, a husband who insulted and beat her for more than fifty years. On her deathbed she told Alejandra her life had been one of relentless sadness and suffering. Alejandra talks from time to time about growing up in the old days, when her parents were strict and full of country ways, but she has no fondness for the past and prefers not to think about her own childhood and youth. Sometimes her family members tell me, when Alejandra is not around, that she can be *brava* (temperamental). Damn straight, I think to myself. Of course she is. There would have been no other way out.

CHAPTER 4

Ni de Aqui, Ni de Allá

In 1989 just about everyone in Cuenca knew someone who had migrated to the United States. There was plenty of talk about who was getting remittances from whom, who should be present for the well-planned phone calls from New York, and what was being delivered in those packages from Delgado Travel, a courier service with offices in Queens and in Cuenca.[1] Even with growing migration to the United States, especially from rural towns and the general buzz surrounding it that circulated, people were often hesitant to discuss openly their own relatives in New York and how they got there. More than once I was only half-jokingly asked if I was from the CIA, and frequently if I tried to ask direct questions about a loved one in the United States, people would give me vague responses. A few women showed me pictures of their husbands in New York, always in front of a well-known landmark so there were no doubts about the location, but I had difficulty engaging people about specific details. The clandestine nature of the emigration no doubt left many people unwilling to talk too freely about themselves or their loved ones, although they had few qualms in speculating about their neighbors. I did learn that much of the migration was made possible by costly loans, falsified documents, and connections to unsavory characters.

Despite the hesitancy to talk about it in 1989, I did make an attempt to systematically study transnational migration, and I spent a few weeks in Corpanche, a rural community about a half hour from Cuenca that was known for its high rates of migration to New York. I lived with an elderly widow and her adult daughter, both well known in the community, and made the rounds in town talking to women whose husbands were in the United States. The town had a reputation for being feisty and gossipy albeit closed-lipped to outsiders. After two weeks I left the town for a long-planned trip to Guayaquil with the intention of returning to the community when I got back from the coast. While I was in Guayaquil, however, a national magazine, *Vistazo*, a cross between *Newsweek* and *Playboy*, with hard-hitting investigative journalism interspersed with pictures of women in skimpy bikinis, published an article about migration to the United States featuring Corpanche and the nearby town of Checa (Abad 1989). The article was scandalous and pandered to the worst stereotypes elites held about the uncouth behavior of rural people with too much money and too little culture. The article pointed out, for example, that consumer goods were covered in guinea pig droppings, and it described the loose morals of local women who engaged in extramarital affairs while their husbands toiled in the United States. My own experience in Corpanche told me that gossip, true or not, has an enthusiastic life there, and those stereo systems and other electronics were treated like shrines, encased in plastic, and put in a place of honor. The *Vistazo* article was written by a journalist who had been in the community well before I arrived and who, I later learned, never made his journalistic intentions known in the community.

By the time I returned from Guayaquil, the article, provocatively subtitled "Tierra de las mujeres solas" (Land of women alone) and with photos of several local women, had been picked up by local media and had spread throughout the Cuenca region. The reaction from the community was not good. When I arrived back in Cuenca, I found a note slipped under my door from a friend at the university warning me not to return to Corpanche; the community was extremely angry, and they were blaming me for the article. I was, after all, the last one seen walking around with a notebook and tape recorder. The local newspaper *El Mercurio* reported that Corpanche had put up roadblocks to bar outsiders from coming into the town and that community members were boarding arriving buses and monitoring who was allowed into the community. I had not been in Corpanche long enough to build the relationships necessary to weather this kind of storm, and I never did return. Today that sort of vigilance is completely passé, and Corpanche seems far less interested in isolation. The town has a Facebook page where community members post pictures of parties, sporting events, and dances, a good way to keep those in the United States apprised of local events. One reposted entry shows a ripped and damaged passport and airline ticket with the caption, "Here's what happens when your dog learns that you are going on a trip without him."

Asking about migration to the United States was delicate in 1989, but by the mid-1990s, much had changed. In a few short years, transnational migration had gone from being furtive and clandestine to an open secret.

A song I heard frequently one summer immortalized migration to New York. The song, "Soy cholo boy," is part rap, part jazz, and part traditional Andean San Juanito style and tells of the odyssey of a young man who migrates to New York City. The musical group that released the song, Utopía, had as one of its members an American jazz pianist and sociologist who was studying transnational migration in the country. The song parodies the popular perceptions of migration in lyrics about men crossing the US border from Mexico, working double shifts in New York, buying plenty of nice things, and taking up with Puerto Rican or Cuban women. The last verse of the song touches on the shared fantasy of most migrants to return to Ecuador, start a business, and only go back to the United States as a tourist to Disneyland. In his 2000 book *Transnational Peasants*, Kyle quotes and translates the lyrics:

> Me vine a la YANY,[2] me vine a trabajar, no importa en que, pero voy a ganar. Los dólares vienen, los dólares van, con toda esa plata, yo voy a comprar: ropita, casita, y el auto popular. Soy Cholo Boy y me voy a trabajar! Tú sabes . . . chulla vida!

> [I come to New York City, I come to work, it doesn't matter in what, but I'm going to make money. Dollars come, dollars go, with all this money I am going to buy: clothes, house, and the hottest car. I am a Cholo Boy and I'm going to work! You know . . . only one life to live!] (17)

> Soy Cholo Boy, y me voy a regresar. Total después de todo, no me ha ido tan mal. Cuando llegue a mi llacta, yo voy a comprar, la casa, la ropa, y el Trooper manejar. A la Cunshi, y a la Rosa, negocio voy a dar. Lo propio, lo nuestro, vamos a exportar. Ya lo tengo bien pensado, y no me va a fallar. Pues, el cuye McDonald's yo voy a instalar. Soy Cholo Boy y me voy a descansar! Tú sabes . . . chulla vida!

> [I am a Cholo Boy, and I'm going to go home. After everything, I didn't do too badly. When I arrive at my farm, I'm going to buy a house, clothes, and a Trooper to drive. To Cunshi and Rosa, a business I will give them. Our own thing we will export. I've thought about it well, and I'm not going to fail. A guinea pig McDonald's I will build. I am a Cholo Boy and I'm going to rest! You know . . . only one life to live!] (158)

The song's lyrics provide humorous commentary about the cultural clashes and yearnings of young Ecuadorian migrants in New York, tapping into local popular culture ideas and tropes about fast living in the big city as well as painful adjustments to American work-time discipline. The ability to publicly address transnational migration in this humorous way reflects the newfound recognition of migration as a popular social advancement strategy. As the economy faltered and collapsed in the 1990s and economic mobility for the average person seemed to be out of the question, transnational migration took on a feverish pitch as people began to see going to the States as the only viable option for them (Kyle 2000, 91). Poor boys with "dark skin and Indian names," as Vicente's brother described himself, understood that given the system of *palanca*, they had little chance to better themselves if they stayed in Cuenca. Young people seeing their friends, neighbors, and relatives go created the sense that migration was the only thing to do, and a "panic to leave" ensued.[3] For young men in particular, migration demonstrated a willingness to take risks to better oneself and hopefully help one's family.[4]

Despite the growing commonness of transnational migration, for an individual family it is an emotionally wrenching and very costly endeavor. Most of the emigration from Cuenca to New York and the surrounding areas that occurred since the 1980s has been undocumented, as very few arrive in the United States with legitimate visas or any other legal paperwork. The distance, cost, and difficulty of entering as an undocumented person means that once someone makes it to New York, they will stay there for many years before contemplating a return to Ecuador. Most returns are permanent, as going back and forth without papers is far too difficult to undertake more than once. In the 1990s it was almost unimaginable that someone from an immigrant's family would get a tourist visa to visit their relatives in New York. In short, migration meant many years of separation from family and homeland. Partings were therefore sad and even maudlin affairs, especially if the emigrant went *andando*, walking across the border. No one knew when they might hear from that person again or, especially in more recent years, what shape he or she would be in when they did contact the family back home. Everyone knew a story or two or three about bandits, aggressive US Border Patrol agents, untrustworthy *coyotes* (traffickers), migrants getting sick and having to turn back, and of people simply disappearing.

Borrowing money from a relative, a friend, or more likely a moneylender was an essential part of the migration process. There were two primary ways to get to the United States without a legitimate visa. The first, *andando*, usually started in Guayaquil by plane or boat to Central America, Panama in most cases. The rest of the trip was overland often by way of countless nighttime bus rides. The trip ended by crossing the border on foot somewhere along the US-Mexico border. Most people I talked with who made the arduous trip north had little idea of where they were at any given time on their journeys, which took months and exposed them to numerous dangers and unexpected costs as well as illness, violence, and robbery. In the early 1990s this kind of trip cost around $6,000, not including shakedowns that might occur along the way. For double that price or more, the migrant could enter the United States documented by purchasing a falsified passport and tourist visa that brought them to New York by airplane. These arrivals were often put through rounds of questioning at the airport by what was then INS (Immigration and Naturalization Services) and is now ICE (Immigration and Customs Enforcement). Everyone I knew who went this way made it through their interrogation. I know people who have taken both routes, and in all cases, substantial amounts of money were borrowed and had to be paid back. Loans came with interest of 18 percent a month or more, and depending on how long it took to pay the loan back, financing costs could climb to well over $15,000. There is a substantial underground economy and network in the region of moneylenders, document falsifiers, and human traffickers (Carpio 1992; Kyle and Goldstein 2011).[5]

The first order of business for most migrants, then, is to repay the loans as quickly as possible so that the interest does not add up. For many migrants, this can take years, and sending money to family members is therefore delayed. But eventually most do send some money back to Cuenca, infusing the local economy in important ways (Kyle 2000, 64). Estimates of the value of remittances vary from year to year; in 2018, $642 million was sent home to Azuay Province and $472 million to the city of Cuenca (Banco Central del Ecuador 2018). These are official figures compiled from courier agencies, banks, and postal services and thus do not include informal transfers of money or goods that tend to go unreported. In a 2006 survey, Ana Melo concludes that on average an Ecuadorian migrant in New York sent $1,400 a year in remittances home, with men who were husbands and fathers sending the most back to their families (40). Remittances were the second biggest source of revenue in Ecuador in 2011, after petroleum (Boccagni 2011).

While documented remittance rates to Ecuador are high and have grown more or less consistently over the years, on an individual level, as my friends in Ecuador explain, they are often experienced as far too sporadic.[6] Even after debts are paid, life in the United States is expensive and insecure. Immigrants often live in make-do housing and move frequently, they are chronically underpaid so they change jobs often, and they are vulnerable to unexpected disruptions such as the tragedy of 9/11 in 2001 and the global economic downturn of 2008 as well as accidents, illness, and other personal problems. An extended illness or an on-the-job injury can mean weeks or months of lost wages, and since most immigrants have no medical insurance, they can find themselves saddled with costly medical bills. There are a surprising number of lawyers' offices in the heart of the Ecuadorian expat community in Jackson Heights, Queens, offering legal services for work-related injuries. Many times these setbacks are not shared with loved ones back home, and families complain that the remittances they receive are not enough and not terribly regular.

Countless times women told me their sons or husbands were having too much fun and had forgotten their families back home. These comments were voiced even from those who were able to build houses with the money sent home but perhaps could not finish or furnish it as they had dreamed. Some of the complaints might also reflect a desire to minimize the amount of remittances received so as to discourage family members who might otherwise make claims over them.

The effects of remittances in Cuenca as a whole are substantial and quite visible on the urban landscape. The first goal of many migrants is to buy land and build a house; there are blossoming neighborhoods on the fringes of Cuenca that are, locals say, "hecho de dolares," made of dollars. Everyone I know with a husband or son in the United States has improved their housing because of the remittances sent home. Housing is about more than a place to live; it is also a symbolic statement about social mobility (Klaufus 2012; Pribilsky 2007). New two-story houses represent upward mobility, and the design choices are meant to convey a cosmopolitan image. But taste is not always shared, especially across class lines, and a design that might be interpreted as cosmopolitan by one group may be read quite differently by others. The new houses built by emigrants' remittances are heavily critiqued by Cuenca's architectural elites, who see them as a rejection of the traditions, values, and old-world aesthetics of the city and call them "monstrosities in cement" (Klaufus 2006, 7). I heard many conversations among elites who readily found fault with the new houses, commenting on what they think of as garish excess or inappropriate styles, as though the houses confirmed something they knew all along. Much like the subtext of that 1989 *Vistazo* article casting aspersions on how migrants spend money, these critiques by elites paint a picture of migrants as devoid of taste and ignorant of and uncaring about Cuenca's European architectural heritage. Their owners ostensibly have been blinded by crass American consumerism and have abandoned their preferred roles as humble, rural peasants.

Because so much emigration from Ecuador is clandestine, it is difficult to evaluate overall trends in migration and determine whether rates are rising or falling. It does seem that the fever or panic to leave, as Astudillo and Cordero (1990) and Jokisch and Pribilsky (2002) have called it, subsided in the 2010s. An analysis of the Ecuadorian census from 2007 shows that emigration from Ecuador peaked in 2000. However, these official sources capture only those who leave with legal visas and not those who board rickety boats in Guayaquil and hope to make it to Panama. But there is just not the same level of talk about migration in Cuenca as there once was. One reason migration may have cooled a bit could be that the timeless myth of America as the place with streets paved in gold has lost some of its luster as stories of the reality of life as an undocumented worker filter home. While there certainly have been some success stories of migrants who made good in New York City, many live in squalid conditions, work at dangerous jobs, and struggle for years with little to show for their efforts. The increased numbers of deportations of Ecuadorians from the United States and from Mexico in recent decades may also have influenced how future migrants view their own prospects.

In addition to increased deportations, since the mid-2000s immigration enforcement on the US-Mexico border has intensified, making border crossings much more perilous. Migrants in the 1980s and early 1990s often crossed the border through fairly accessible points, but by the late 1990s the US Border Patrol stepped up enforcement and adopted a policy known as "prevention through deterrence" (De León 2015, 30). The policy brought beefed-up patrols and infrastructure at the more porous and safer border crossing areas in Texas, California, and New Mexico, a strategy that has resulted in funneling migrants through the treacherous Sonoran desert in Arizona. The trek through the desert takes several days, and Jason De León (2015) points out that it is impossible for someone to carry the amount of water needed to make it across the border. Migrants often have to turn back, drink foul, contaminated water from cattle pools, and intentionally allow themselves to be apprehended, or they die. De León, whose 2015 book chronicles the death in the desert of a young Ecuadorian mother from the Cuenca region, argues that the Border Patrol strategy is designed to cause enough deaths so migrants will begin to self-regulate. As more people learn about the difficulties of crossing through the desert, fewer people will choose to undertake the journey. Since the policy was adopted, thousands of people have died in the desert attempting to cross (De León 2015, 29).

Finally, and more optimistically, as the Ecuadorian economy improved in the mid-2000s, and the cost of a college education was lowered, there appeared to be more opportunities in Ecuador. Young people today are often the children of transnational migrants, educated in better high schools and encouraged to attend college, rather than aspiring to emigrate. Elites occasionally complain that they can no longer find young country girls willing to work as live-in maids because they are all in school.

In the 1990s and early 2000s, those of us studying transnational migration from the region were primarily concerned with documenting mobility, that is, understanding the reasons people felt compelled to take such perilous and expensive journeys, how they did it, and the impacts of remittances and absences on families (Carpio 1992; Kyle 2000; Miles 2004; Pribilsky 2007). The effects on families have been profound, and I have hinted at them already. They include more consumer spending and homebuilding (Boccagni and Peréz Murcia 2021; Klaufus 2006, 2012), greater support for children's educations (Miles 2004; Pribilsky 2007), and shifting domestic arrangements, decision making, and family dynamics (Mata-Codesal 2013; Pribilsky 2007). The divorce rates have no doubt been influenced by migration. Transnational migration from the region was seen as a strategy generally employed by younger men to get ahead in a declining economy that selectively privileged people other than themselves. At the time, migration was mostly talked about by scholars and especially migrants as, at least conceptually, a temporary condition perhaps lasting several years, followed by a return home to Ecuador after earning enough to build a new home and save some investment capital (Boccagni 2011; Pribilsky 2007).

Most of the migrants I know in New York immigrated years ago, some when they were barely out of their teens. Like so many others, they left Ecuador in the 1990s, when things were terrible there, hoping to make a go of it in New York, start a new life, and help their families. Most said they thought they would return home to Ecuador after a few years of dedicated labor in the United States. That rarely happened. Saving money was much more difficult than many imagined, and then as the years went by, going home seemed less and less desirable. Many have now spent two decades or more in New York and have lived longer in the United States than they did in Ecuador. Some have started new families, further distancing themselves from those back home. My friends' lives in New York have not always been easy, and they have an aching feeling that they have let down their families in Ecuador, but their loans are paid, and for better or worse, they now see New York as their home.

When they were young people in Ecuador, they talked often of the future and what it might be like especially in New York. As future migrants they envisioned themselves as cosmopolitans, liberated from the most onerous family surveillance, but also thrust into the role of the person who could change their families' situations in life through remittances and help them *salir adelante*. It was a heroic sort of quest for a kind of modernity that circumvented local elite obstacles, valued family responsibility, and celebrated consumption. The aspiring migrants knew well enough that they would have to work hard and make sacrifices, and they were prepared to do that. Today, as middle-age workers in New York, they are remarkably uneasy talking about the future. When I have directly asked about the future or what they might do in their old age, it was obvious to me that they had no clear plans in place. As undocumented immigrants, they live every day knowing that something could happen tomorrow that would send their lives back to Ecuador. US immigration policies have become far more stringent in the years they have been in the country. But because no one can live every day thinking about that kind of uncertainty, they actively try not to contemplate the future.

Vicente

As a young man coming of age in the 1990s, Vicente, Rosa's eldest son, spent much of his teenage years thinking about how to get out of Ecuador. He didn't excel at high school, so college did not seem like a good place for him, and there were few other opportunities for a high school graduate with an Indian name. In part because his home life was often stressful as his family navigated the economic strains of the 1990s, he spent a good deal of time in the rural town of Cumbe, a place that was becoming defined by the exodus, primarily of young men, to New York. It seemed inevitable that he too would join so many others his age and migrate.

When Vicente left for the United States in 1995, he went, as his father once put it, "the easy way." A year or two before he migrated, Vicente met an Ecuadorian man, Bolívar, who was able to get a green card in the 1986 amnesty program that allowed him to live and work legally in the United States. He had come to Cuenca to spend time with his family, whom he had not seen in many years, and he and Vicente became fast friends. Vicente later told me that Bolívar was reliving his youth on that visit home, hanging out and cutting loose with a much younger crowd. In a stroke of unexpected good fortune, Bolívar offered to lend Vicente the money to go to the United States. Vicente purchased a forged passport and visa for $8,000, and Bolívar offered him space in his home when he arrived.

Before he left, Vicente was coached for days by his smugglers about how to navigate an airport, find his flight, respond to questions he might get from immigration authorities, and repeat the details of the travel history of the person whose name and passport he was using. He had to convince the authorities, if asked, that he had been in New York before and knew exactly what he was doing. He somehow managed to pull that off.[7] Vicente was then twenty years old and had not been farther from home than an overnight trip to Guayaquil with a school group, so his ability to imitate the demeanor of an experienced international traveler was no mean feat. Bolívar met him at the airport in New York, as did a representative of his smuggler to whom he handed over the expensive borrowed watch and rings he wore to solidify his identity as a cosmopolitan and moneyed international traveler. In his first days in New York, his host showed him around town like a proper tour guide and took him shopping for the clothes he would need to make it through the winter. In one photograph that made its way back to Ecuador, Vicente is standing in a clothing store mugging at the camera in his first winter coat. Bolívar introduced Vicente to his contacts on Staten Island and helped him get his first job, busing tables in an Italian restaurant. Vicente paid Bolívar $50 a month for room and board, and he slowly began making payments on his debt.

Vicente lived for several years in Bolívar's house, sometimes with no real space to call his own, depending on how many family members were staying there at any given time. For a while he slept on a couch in the living room, his suitcase with his clothes tucked under the seldom-used dining room table. Even though the arrangement was not always ideal and Vicente missed his own sisters and brothers, he enjoyed being around Bolívar's children and liked the neighborhood feel of Staten Island. Besides, he told me, he spent precious little time at home. Vicente's first jobs were in restaurants, and his hours were late ones; he left for work in the early afternoon and did not get home until one or two in the morning. He started out as a busboy and later became a serving assistant delivering food and drinks to tables but not taking the customers' orders. Despite taking classes, Vicente's ability to speak English did not improve much, and he could not interact extensively with customers. He joked with me once that he went to English classes in Manhattan but somehow lost everything he learned on the ferry back to Staten Island.

Vicente's late work hours meant that he was often in the streets in the wee hours coming home after a shift. One cold winter night he was assaulted and robbed as he came out of the subway; his money and watch were taken, and he was beaten. He was out of work for a week while his face healed. Soon afterward, he decided to buy a car, something he had longed for, so he could drive home from work in safety. Vicente has always had a soft spot for cars; he was saving to buy one, and the assault gave him a reason to do so sooner rather than later. Vicente borrowed money from Bolívar to purchase the car, but because Vicente was undocumented, Bolívar registered and insured the car in his name. The car expenses put Vicente further behind in repaying Bolívar and meant that he sent little money home to his family after the first glorious package filled with gifts of school knapsacks and clothing.

Unfortunately, within a year, Vicente was in a traffic accident that totaled his car and prompted Bolívar's insurance company to cancel his coverage. By now, Bolívar's patience with Vicente was wearing thin, and they often argued. Bolívar was angry about the accident and the trouble it caused him and annoyed at the debts that were accruing. Moreover, the differences in lifestyles between a young, unmarried man and an older married one with children started to weigh on their relationship. Finally, the situation at Bolívar's became untenable, and after four years, Vicente left the house for good and embarked on a far more itinerant life. He lived in several apartments in Queens and one in Manhattan, then moved to Ossining, New York, where he worked in landscaping and learned some carpentry skills. Word from his family during this time was that he was having too good a time and rarely sent money home. He told me he was broke paying off the car loan and earning enough to buy another. Although he did not send remittances regularly, Vicente was prone to big gestures, and on Mother's Day one year he bought his mother a dining room table and paid a mariachi band to serenade her.

I saw Vicente for Thanksgiving in 2002 when he and his father, a recent arrival to New York, drove to Michigan to spend the holiday with my family. Vicente seemed to be doing well, and he and his father had just moved in together with some friends on Long Island. They lived in a small rented house in a poor section of a generally upscale area where work in landscaping, construction, and domestic labor is plentiful. Back in 1989, his father, Lucho, had told me that he would not go to the United States because he believed children need a father in their lives; they need someone to guide them and offer counsel and discipline. He was a hard worker, often working from 8 a.m. to 8 p.m. as a taxi driver to support his family. But like many others in the late 1990s, he found it impossible to make a living. Gas prices were rising and customers weren't taking taxis, and if they did, they often did not choose his battered, twenty-year-old Datsun. With his children growing up, he figured it was time to do something to provide for his old age.

Lucho's plan was to go to the States for a couple of years, set aside a small nest egg to build a house, and maybe start a business. In other words, almost every migrant's dream. Lucho joked about going to the United States for so many years that when he actually did go, no one saw it coming. One night he came home and asked his second son if he could borrow his backpack. When asked why he needed it, Lucho said, in his usual offhand way, that he was going to New York the next day. It was typical of Lucho to make this sort of joking comment, so no one believed him. The next day he got up, packed a few things, enough to fill a schoolboy's backpack, and left the house. He told everyone he was off to New York that morning, but no one took him seriously, and that is how he wanted it. Lucho said he could not bear the stressful emotional buildup that a planned departure would provoke, so he carried on as though nothing was in the works. He wanted a clean getaway.

Unlike his son, Lucho came to the United States the hard way. He took a fishing boat off the coast of Guayaquil where he and a dozen or so other men were forced to spend days below deck tossing and turning and retching. He arrived in Central America, he does not know where, and was taken at night in buses to Mexico. There, things got dicey. Every smuggling story includes a shakedown, and every bandit knows the hiding places of the migrants, so the money stashed in toothpaste tubes, sewn into the hem of blue jeans, or in a hidden pocket in underwear was all taken. That was not enough for the thieves, though, so Lucho and a few other migrants were detained in a small house near the border where they waited until their relatives sent money from Ecuador. No stranger to adobe houses, Lucho made a nighttime escape by digging under the wall of the house, found his way to a shelter, and waited for Vicente to send him money. He joined another group heading for the border and made it across on his first try. He says now that he thought for sure that he was going to die in the desert. He eventually found his way to New York, living first with his brother-in-law, then with his niece, and then sharing an apartment with Vicente and a few of his friends.

Lucho tells plenty of stories about his time in New York, and they are peppered with the handful of English words he picked up while there. His stories are never of the fun he had while in New York or the things he saw; they are singularly about work, looking for work, what happened at work, and the relationships he formed with several "rich people" on Long Island who employed him. Lucho went to New York to make money, and that, he said, was all that he did. Lucho's stories are usually wildly amusing as he takes on the role of a naïve but scrappy entrepreneur, a stranger in a strange land who does not take long to figure things out. Learning only the English words he needed for work, Lucho became good at selling himself. He understood that he was old and small and not always an employer's first choice, so he grinned, joked, tossed out his assorted English vocabulary, and made it clear he intended to work hard. Lucho spent much of his time doing day labor, and after a few years, he developed relationships with several homeowners who regularly employed him as a gardener or to do small jobs.

Being accustomed to the patriarchal work relations in Cuenca, Lucho found the easygoing attitudes of Americans confounding. In one house, he was brought inside by the owner, shown the refrigerator stocked with beer and sandwich fixings, and told to help himself as he liked throughout the day. Lucho found this inexplicable, and he wanted nothing to do with it. He would happily eat whatever someone served him, but there was no way he was going to open someone else's refrigerator and root around for something to eat. Best left alone, he figured. Landscaping jobs were spare in the winter, so Lucho parlayed snowstorms into moneymaking opportunities. Equipped with a shovel over his shoulder, he went door to door in the nicer neighborhoods offering to clear sidewalks and driveways of snow. He found the work easy, he made good money doing it, and he was often treated to hot chocolate afterward. He found Americans curiously quick to part with their money, and he was always willing to help them do that. He learned that Americans are uncomfortable bargaining, and they generally paid whatever he asked, within reason. He went home after ten years to a new house built from his hard work.

I did not see Vicente from Thanksgiving 2002 until 2019, when I went to Long Island to visit him. In those intervening years, he had turned from an energetic young man into a paunchy middle-aged one, and I almost did not recognize him. As a boy and a young man he was a cheerful and enthusiastic conversationalist; now he was slow to smile and reticent to talk. His life, I came to learn, was not going well. Several years earlier, Vicente was arrested for driving under the influence of alcohol and spent two months in a New Jersey correctional facility. This was during the Obama administration, when those with criminal records were subject to deportation. Vicente was given a voluntary deportation order, which means that he was ordered to leave the country within a designated period. A voluntary order allows the person time to put their affairs in order, sell any property, and leave the country on their own without the shame of an immigration escort or loss of all one's accrued wealth. Vicente ignored the deportation order; he moved to another residence, changed his phone, and got a different job.

When I saw him in 2019, Vicente was living in the basement of his cousin's house on Long Island, and his life had narrowed. He no longer posts on Facebook, and he worries about getting in a traffic accident or simply being in the wrong place at the wrong time. He goes to work every day, including most Saturdays and Sundays, but he usually just comes home and watches TV afterward. Alejandra, who was visiting when I was there, said Vicente has no life in the United States and would have no life if he were to return to Ecuador either. The construction skills he learned in the United States are a dime a dozen in Ecuador, and he would not easily find work. He told me his life was on Long Island and after twenty-four years in the United States, he could not imagine living anyplace else. Vicente expressed a kind of resignation about the deportation order, saying, "If they send me back, they send me back," and until then, he would continue to live his life, albeit more cautiously. Vicente has an impressively big, gently used, BMW SUV to show for his labor, the one indulgence in his life. The car is registered in his cousin's name. He drives it judiciously and carefully, as one traffic violation could mean his immediate deportation.

Vicente is moody, and weeks can go by when all he does is go to work and come home and watch TV. He has a separate entrance to his cousin's home, and his basement quarters has a small kitchenette. He does not call Ecuador very often anymore, in part because his parents are always asking him for money and he has none to spare. He still has car loans to pay. Vicente said he sometimes feels that his parents only talk to him to ask for money. Vicente's love life, or the lack of it, also leaves him feeling lonely. He has dated quite a few immigrant women over the years, but his former girlfriends all drained him financially. Perhaps the BMW has something to do with that, but so far, he has only attracted young women who want him to pay for everything from a dinner out, to a manicure, and in one case, a car. He is tired of feeling used by the women he dates, and he wonders when, and how, he will meet a woman who loves him for who he is, and not for what he can buy her. Living in his cousin's basement is not getting him closer to finding the right woman.

Vicente's cousin Marta is from Cumbe. She left Ecuador several years after Vicente, when she was eighteen. She left, she says, to get away from her father, who she thought was too strict. Now that she is a mother herself, she says she understands better why her father was so vigilant with his children. Like Vicente, Marta also came the easy way, with forged documents, paying a borrowed $13,000 up front for the visa and passport and ultimately, with interest payments, nearly $20,000 total. It took Marta almost ten years to fully repay her debt. Before she moved with her husband to Long Island, she lived on the Lower East Side of Manhattan and in Queens with various friends and family members, including her uncle Lucho. Marta met and married another Ecuadorian from Cumbe while in New York; they knew each other only in passing as children in Ecuador.

Marta's husband, Eduardo, came to the United States when he was fourteen years old to join his parents, who already lived here. Eduardo came the hard way, walking across the desert. He recalls stopping to help a pregnant woman who was having trouble keeping up, and they both lost track of the rest of the group. With no chance of continuing on their own, he and the woman waited and hoped for immigration authorities to find them. They did, and he was detained for almost a week until his parents paid a fee and sent him an airline ticket to New York.[8] He picked up English quickly and was a good student, graduating from Queens Technical High School in New York. He has DACA (Deferred Action for Childhood Arrivals) status that allows him to legally work and live in the United States. Eduardo owns a construction and renovation company on Long Island, and he has more work than he knows what to do with. In the summer he does mostly outdoor construction, and in the winter, when most of the summer people are gone, he does indoor renovations. Like Vicente, he works seven days a week. Unlike Vicente, he is loquacious and confident, almost to the point of arrogance. He insisted on speaking English with me, even though I continued in Spanish, thus setting himself and our conversation apart from his wife and her cousins, who are uncomfortable in English.

They live in a primarily well-to-do summer community that swells from Memorial Day to Labor Day and has a more modest year-round population. Marta works as a housecleaner, part-time during the winter months when many houses are closed for the season, and more than sixty hours a week throughout the summer. She spends her summer days in the large homes of the very wealthy, some of whom she considers friends. Marta's marriage is rocky, and at least twice Eduardo has moved out of the house for extended periods. He has an expensive girlfriend. Marta and Eduardo have three children, the oldest and youngest fourteen years apart in age, who were born in the United States and are American citizens.

Their three-bedroom house on Long Island was a fixer-upper that Eduardo renovated and is now bright and modern with a marble island in the kitchen and large, high-end, stainless steel appliances. They live what appears to be a typical suburban American life, with three kids, two cars, two jobs, and mounting debts. Living near the shore of Long Island is expensive, real estate taxes are high, and keeping up with the Joneses takes on a completely new meaning there. Their eldest son planned to go to college, about which his father said, "He's going to cost us a whole lot of money soon." Marta tries to save money where she can, and many of their home furnishings and children's toys come from the constant garage sales held during the summer by the rich. "These people are always buying new things," she explains.

After years of living undocumented in the United States, Marta seems remarkably unconcerned about her status and the risks that housing Vicente might hold for her. It is fairly common knowledge that when ICE raids a home looking for someone with a deportation order, they sweep up everyone who is undocumented, regardless of whether they have criminal records or not. This has been going on since the Obama administration. Marta has a lot to lose if ICE came looking for Vicente in her home. Her response to my questions about her perception of the risks was based on what she has seen; she knows that ICE does not have the resources to track down everyone, and she figures that Vicente is a pretty low priority. "There are drug dealers they don't come for," she pointed out. When I was there visiting in 2019 we took a ride to the beach, a five-minute drive, and they piled two of the kids into the back cargo space of Vicente's SUV for the ride. This is common practice in Ecuador but wholly illegal in the United States. When I pointed this out, Marta simply replied, "It's just five minutes." I did insist, however, that she drive and not Vicente, just in case we were stopped for a traffic violation. I did not want something happening to Vicente because of me.

Vicente has spent more of his life in New York than he has in Ecuador, and he has no regrets about his time in the United States. He said America "is the place where you find yourself," explaining that in the United States you can set goals for yourself, like buying a nice car or a house, and with hard work you can achieve that goal. "You learn to depend on yourself," he added. Vicente also likes being part of a multicultural community and has friends from all over the world. "It helps you grow and see other perspectives," he said. While Vicente has curtailed his social life since the deportation order and does not drive if he has been drinking, he also does not live in constant fear of deportation. "The fear has always been there," Marta noted, speaking for Vicente. "You just get used to it." Marta's worries were much closer to home; the mounting bills and her husband's infidelity were far more pressing concerns for her than her undocumented status. She knows there is little local will to remove immigrants. "All these people here depend on us," she explained. "We take care of everything."

Back in the early 2000s, when I talked to Vicente about his early life in the United States, he told me that his life was "like a river running by." What he meant was that as an undocumented immigrant he felt very little control over where his life was headed. He felt akin to a bystander to his own life because his choices seemed limited. While Vicente expressed more agency in 2019, saying that he has achieved certain goals such as buying a nice car, he remained without much to anchor his life, similar to the way he was in 1999. He remarked to me dejectedly that he had no wife and no children and that he was stuck in a numbing routine. He did not use that hard-earned car to go anywhere except work and the occasional visit to his uncle's house in Queens. His free time was spent with his cousin's children watching TV in his basement apartment. But when I asked him if he thought about going back to Ecuador he responded, "What would I do there, Anita? I'd have to ask you for a dollar to buy a Coke."

William

For William, migration to New York was simultaneously an exile and a liberation. As happened in many families of modest means in the 1990s, William and his two brothers were struggling to find work while dreaming about going to the United States. Of the three young men, only William was in college, studying journalism; the other two were working odd jobs and helping their mother sell food from time to time. Yet, when the family finally got a loan to send someone to New York, it was William who was selected. He entertained the idea that he was chosen by his parents because he was the most likely to send money home. He was by far the most family-oriented of the boys and did what he could to help out at the restaurant, but he suspected that there was probably another reason. William said he thought his parents, especially his father, wanted him gone from Cuenca because they were ashamed of him. It was becoming noticeable that William was different from his brothers. He was uninterested in girls and too interested in fashion. He was not openly gay; in the 1990s, no one was, really, but people were making comments. Having a gay son was considered shameful and a stain on the family, and William's father was disdainful of him, crudely calling him a *maricón*, a derogatory slur for a homosexual akin to "faggot" in American English. When I asked William if he thought his parents might have been protecting him by sending him away, he replied, "Mami, maybe yes, but my father, he just wanted me away from there. He was ashamed of me." William has no love for his father, now divorced from his mother, Blanca, and recalled only beatings and abuse as a child. He has made a point of sending money only to his mother despite his father's occasional pleas and requests.

Will's parents borrowed only enough money to send him *andando*, and his migration story is one of the more harrowing ones I heard. He traveled by plane only as far as Panama and then through Central America on a series of buses, always in the care of a smuggler who extorted more money along the way. He didn't know where he was or why they spent long stretches of time in one place or another. The journey took months. He fell ill at one point and was unable to hold down food, but he could not stay back from his group. Thin to begin with, he became skin and bones while on the road. Days blended together as he was shuttled from place to place; he cannot recall much about the trip except feeling sick and sleeping through endless nighttime bus rides. When he reached the US border, he recalls having to run through a tunnel that appeared to grow narrower and narrower as he went along. He was ill prepared for the walk through the desert, having brought only one bottle of water, but he found a six-pack of beer in the tunnel and grabbed that on his way. He laughs now about what a bad idea it is to drink beer in a desert, but at the time it seemed like a godsend.

The desert was a dangerous place in so many ways, and his group was robbed by men brandishing machetes. All he had left after the robbery were the clothes on his back. His small group was then abandoned by their guide, and shortly thereafter they were picked up by US immigration. By then, he said, he was so exhausted he was actually relieved to have been found. INS processed him quickly, and because he claimed Mexican citizenship, as so many undocumented Ecuadorians in transit do, he joined a busload of detained migrants and was escorted back to Mexico. He stayed at a shelter there for several weeks, regained his strength, had more money wired to him, then tried again to cross the border. This time he made it to a safe haven in Phoenix, and a cousin in New York sent him money and an airline ticket. This was just prior to the 1996 rule requiring airline passengers to present identification to board a plane. Throughout his journey, William's biggest fear was that he would be apprehended and sent home, where he would have to face the wrath of his father. Without the money William would earn in the United States, there was no way they could pay back the loan they took out to get him there. He would cross or die, but there was no going home.

Following a well-worn path, William lived for a brief while in Queens and worked in a garment factory, a job he said was terribly boring, hot, and poorly paid. Before long, he moved to Manhattan, where he has lived for most of the time he has been in New York. William has mostly worked in restaurants, first as a busboy, then as a waiter. He said he knows "just about everything there is to know" about restaurants, including cooking and managing the "front of the house."

For years, what I knew about William's life in New York I saw in photos his mother, Blanca, showed me. Some of the photographs led me to speculate that William is gay, but Blanca never said a word to me in that regard, and I did not share my thoughts with her. William told me in 2019 that he never hid his sexuality once he was in the United States, but he also did not tell his family for many years. The distance and the difficulties in communication early on worked in his favor, and he kept his phone calls few and far between. The family practiced a kind of "don't ask, don't tell" policy, facilitated by a lack of easy communication and perhaps some intentional distancing. Sometimes months would go by without a letter or phone call from Will.

When William finally did tell Blanca that he is gay, during a visit she made to New York, she cried. She had little experience with understanding and accepting sexual differences, and she is deeply Catholic. All her life she was taught that homosexuality was immoral, a sin, and deeply shameful. William was the first openly gay man she has known in her life. In Ecuador, especially until very recently, such matters were rarely publicly revealed. Supported by her youngest daughter, who has urged understanding and tolerance, Blanca has come around to accepting William's life. Now they talk every day. Even though she and I have talked about Will countless times, Blanca has not breathed a word to me about his sexuality, nor did she speak up at dinner in 2018 when her former daughter-in-law, Carolina, made some awful remarks about homosexuals having predilections for pedophilia. I hadn't asked Blanca any direct questions, mostly because I did not want to out William if he had not done so already. I too was practicing a kind of "Don't ask, don't tell" strategy.

William loves New York, where he feels free to be himself. There, no one cares that he is gay; it has not affected his job prospects or his ability to make friends. He spent some pretty wild years there when he first arrived, enjoying the nightlife and moving in and out of relationships and living arrangements. He kept in touch only sporadically with his family during this time. Today, much has changed; he is older and more settled, and he is close with his family. He works at an upscale Latin restaurant downtown and has friends all over the city from the various restaurants where he's worked. His English is excellent, he knows every inch of the subway, and his phone is filled with pictures of friends and family in various New York settings and restaurants. When we met at a chic midtown restaurant in the summer of 2019, he was greeted by friends coming and going from the restaurant, and he introduced me to the bartender, a good friend from Argentina.

In his mid-forties but looking years younger, William was confident and debonair. The day we spent together he wore a colorful, untucked, tailored shirt over white jeans, and he looked every bit the urbane, modern man. He told his mother I was coming to see him, and he was touchingly concerned about my visit, texting me several times about a good location to meet, what kind of food I preferred, and whether there was something special in the city I wanted to see that he could show me. While we had lunch, he WhatsApped his mother, and we all talked. Will clearly also adores his nieces and nephews in Boston and Cuenca, and he shared pictures of them together and recounted their antics. One of his brothers in New York continues to shun and insult him, but he does not put much importance on those kinds of comments. "Life is too short," he told me, "for that kind of hate." He is also fiercely protective of his mother and sisters, even from so far away. He has no tolerance for his father or his mother's on-again, off-again relationship with him, and he dislikes both of his sisters' husbands, whom he sees as crude and domineering.

William has built a rich life in New York and cannot imagine going back to Ecuador. He does not see himself as particularly at risk of deportation, he does not have a criminal record, he has a legal driver's license but does not own a car, his English is good, and he works in small restaurants where an immigration raid is very unlikely. He has thought about forced deportation and maintains an attitude similar to Vicente's: that if it happens, it happens. But he cannot live in fear, so he simply accepts that deportation is a possibility and moves on. He said he does not think he could ever return to Cuenca, where there is too much gossip and no open gay community, so he imagines that should he be deported, he would move to Quito, where he knows no one and has no family reputation to worry about. He could easily get a job in a restaurant catering to tourists. In the meantime, he is doing his best to enjoy life. He is a frequent poster on social media and fills his Facebook page with photos of himself in restaurants dining with friends and in photogenic tourist spots. He often reposts humorous memes and accompanies many of his photographs with tags in Spanish such as "Keep your dreams, you never know when you will need them," "Being happy is a matter of attitude," "Be who you want to be, not who others want you to be!" and "You can't escape what you carry inside you." Life, for William, is a work in progress.

Contemplating the Future

Neither Vicente nor William has long-term plans for the future. Now in their mid-forties, neither one knows what he will do when he gets too old or sick to work. Neither one has much in savings; money they sent home went to help their parents build houses or send siblings to school. In a strange sort of irony, Vicente's remittances helped Alejandra achieve a cosmopolitan life and a professional career that entails international travel, while his own dreams of sophistication faded and his life slowly became smaller and more restricted. When pushed to consider their long-term futures, both men say they assume that one day they might be forced to return to Ecuador by deportation or necessity such as a debilitating illness. Neither is young anymore. By 2019 New York City had begun a program that offers health insurance to undocumented immigrants called NYCares that would pay for hospitalization and reduce the cost of medications and doctor visits at public hospitals. William is considering signing up for it. Vicente cannot, as he tries to avoid all entanglements with institutions. If he were to become unable to work for any reason, he would probably have to return to his family in Ecuador. One of his sisters is preparing for this and opened a voluntary individual social security account for him, but he neglects to fund it. Vicente shudders at the thought of returning home; life there holds nothing for him except the realization by all that he is a failed migrant who returned with nothing to show for the effort.

For those with American children, like William's brothers or Vicente's cousin, the situation is different. At least while their children are still young, they give little thought to their own precarious futures. They want their children to be raised and educated in the United States, and they refuse to imagine separation from them. As the wife of a DACA recipient and the mother of three American citizens, Marta holds out hope that one day she will be documented, and meanwhile, she does not perceive any real risks. She lives in New York State and has a legal driver's license, and her day-to-day life is like many suburban mothers'; she goes to work, attends her children's school functions, and meets with extended family on the occasional weekend. She told me she knows Ecuador has changed, but for her it remains frozen in time just like when she left more than twenty years earlier. Returning there seems like an impossible passage, not just in space, but also in time. Her siblings who stayed inherited a small window-glass shop from their father, and they are barely getting by. She does not see herself returning to that kind of poverty.

When I first met Vicente, William, and Marta, they were young teenagers whose lives were constrained by poverty but also by Vicente's Indian surname, William's homosexuality, and Marta's female gender. Each saw in the United States a way out of the constraints on them and a way to make better lives for themselves and maybe for their families. Speaking

English only very poorly, Vicente and Marta seek employment goals unlike Alejandra's, that is, to have a meaningful career; their aspiration is simply *ganar dinero*, to make money, through any means necessary. Marta has little education, so work for her means cleaning homes for others. Vicente's legal problems have left him with little hope of managing beyond the day to day for the extended future. For William, things are a bit different. His jobs in various restaurants have led to lifelong friends spread across the city and a sense of pride in his value. He talks of opening a catering or event-planning business in New York with some of his friends. Saving enough money to open a business, albeit usually in Cuenca, is the dream of most migrants.

All three have struggled since coming to the United States. They have worked awful jobs to pay back loans and lived in roach-infested apartments with countless roommates. And they have missed and been missed by their families. Especially in the early days when the absence was raw, technology was less developed, and visas were all but impossible to get, their families and Ecuador seemed terribly far away. For years, and for Marta more than a decade, they toiled to get out from under loans while trying to attend to the requests from their family members back home. William helped his mother buy her home and bury his sister, and Vicente and Marta have sent money home to help defray the medical expenses for their parents. Vicente's mother has lupus, and Marta's father, who died several years ago, had chronic kidney disease and was in and out of hospitals for years. Now, they pay for their mothers to come see them in New York every five years or so, and they show them the town. While Marta and William seem to be happy, it is less clear to me what sort of life Vicente has. It is one of drudgery, to be sure, and one that he cannot escape. His life in the United States will remain painfully tenuous, and he will keep looking over his shoulder, but the last thing he wants to do is to go back to Ecuador.

Plenty of migrants, like Lucho, have returned home to Ecuador. Many who go back willingly, that is, those who have not been deported, go back to new homes with an array of consumer products in them. Some have parlayed their savings into new business ventures, perhaps putting a down payment on a taxi or a small restaurant or store. A select few have been able to use their English-language skills and American cultural competence to create opportunities for themselves in the expat community. Returned migrants act as drivers, companions, caretakers, and general facilitators who help expats navigate complicated bureaucracies or arrange home repairs. They are the new culture brokers whose experiences in New York help make the transition to life in Ecuador easier for older Americans.

Others come home because they are exhausted or sick or a family crisis compels their presence, and they return with little to show for the years away. Lucho was convinced to come home by his daughters before he saved as much as he wanted. His earnings were spent on the house and paying medical bills, and he had no savings. Back in Cuenca, he cannot find a job, and time hangs heavy for him with little to do. He gardens, built a wood oven on the patio, and generally putters around. He says he wants to go back to the United States, where he at least could make some money. The family's day-to-day expenses are covered by the rent they collect from the second-story apartment in their house when they have decent tenants, supplemented by earnings of their two daughters, the youngest an accountant who lives at home, and Vicente's occasional contributions.

Postscript

As a measure of how much and how fast things can change, I drafted this chapter before the effects of the Covid-19 pandemic on the Ecuadorian economy became evident. Emigration from Cuenca was on the decline, probably in part because of greater enforcement along the US border but also likely due to increasing opportunities in Cuenca. Certainly, during Correa's administration, construction and government employment grew steadily, as did college attendance. The risk/benefit calculus seemed to be weighted less toward migration than it was in the 1990s during the financial crisis. That changed in 2020 with the pandemic, and it appears there is a new and sizable exodus from Ecuador. Stories in Cuenca's daily newspaper *El Mercurio* have noted the long lines at passport offices (2021a), reported on the increasing local labor shortages (2021b), and documented several cases of Ecuadorian migrants dying, missing, or being kidnapped (2020b). In August 2021, responding to the large number of Ecuadorians arriving in Mexico, that country reinstated a visa requirement for Ecuadorians entering Mexico. It was reported that in the first part of 2021, of the 50,000 Ecuadorians who arrived in Mexico, only 12,000 left that country through an official border (*El Mercurio* 2021d). That leaves 38,000 people unaccounted for. Not being able to travel to Ecuador myself, I can only guess at motivations for the emigration, but it does seem that Ecuador has returned to such bad economic conditions that undertaking this very perilous journey to the United States makes some kind of sense.

DATELINE 1989–2020

Blanca

Over the years I have maintained friendships with several women and their families, but few have taught me as much about life in Cuenca as has Blanca, Will's mother. Blanca's biography reveals the multiple strands of how rural poverty, rural-to-urban migration, gender dynamics, transnational migration, the gentrification of the city, and family life cycle come together in the experiences of one person. Her life is a poignant reminder of the multiple vulnerabilities that poor women face, as women and as willing and occasionally unwilling participants in the modernizing projects of the city and their family members. Her later years have been marked by the absence of her sons, all three of whom have migrated to the United States. Their remittances help ease her financial burdens, yet at the same time she mourns the loss of their presence in her everyday life. Blanca's life story, representative of an older generation of women, makes an interesting contrast to Alejandra's biography. Blanca's life was far more constrained by poverty, as a child and later as an adult, and by patriarchal gender configurations that kept her tied to an abusive man for many years.

Although Blanca is only twelve years older than I am, back in 1989 when I was young and single, I thought of Blanca as a wise, motherly type. Blanca started her family early in life, and I did so late, and so for years the age difference between us seemed much greater than it does now. When we first met, Blanca was raising children ages six to eighteen years old, and caretaking seemed to be a kind of default position for her. In fact, one of the first things I wrote about Blanca was that her social graciousness was not limited to me, a *gringa* and potentially someone of social significance, but was bestowed on the most humble of workers who came to her house. She stood out to me then, as she does now, because she is kind when others are often dismissive, suspicious, or condescending.

Eventually it would become clearer to me how adept Blanca was in moving seamlessly between social worlds. It was Blanca who put an amulet on
my daughter's creased little wrist when she was four months old to ward off
evil eye when we headed out to the countryside. "Anything could happen,"
she told me sagely. Years later it was Blanca's phone number that I tucked
into Izzie's jeans pocket when she was sixteen and worked in a day care
center at a city market in Cuenca. If something happened and I could not
be reached, I knew Blanca was competent and assertive enough to handle
anything that might come up. Even though she is the daughter of rural
peasants, Blanca could perform all of the confident courtesies expected of
the modern urban matron while living much of her life firmly rooted in
the daily routines and concerns of her chaotic market neighborhood, the
quintessential transitional zone between rural and urban. This kind of
social balancing act is not all that easy to pull off.

I met Blanca when I was interviewing rural-to-urban migrant women in
the *conventillos*. Because of the entrenched race and class hierarchies, it came
as no surprise that when I knocked on doors to conduct interviews I was
frequently greeted with serious skepticism. In my field notes from that time
I wrote about how especially affronted I was at the brush-offs I would get
from young children, usually boys. They would ask in brusque voices, "Que
quiere?" (What do you want?) and respond with an off-putting, "Para que?"
(What for?) when I asked to speak with their mothers. I often debated with
myself how little I could tell a ten-year-old to get past him and how much
of what I did tell him made any sense to him. Really, what was the point
of trying to explain my puzzling research goals to a six-year-old? I finally
landed on the common *cuencano* supplication (always in the diminutive and
spoken in a slightly singsong tone, to lessen its impertinence), "No seas
malito. Llama a tu mami" (Don't be naughty. Call your mommy). Once I
got over my pique, though, what became obvious to me was that a stranger
at the door was an unwelcome sight, and children had been trained early
to give nothing away. *Conventillos* were often temporary residences filled
with people who had come to the city from places where people knew their
neighbors, perhaps for generations. Otherness is never to be trusted, and
given local configurations of power, white otherness least of all. Living
close together in the city and sharing the open spaces did not bring people
together. Most had only a passing sort of cordiality with their *conventillo*
neighbors and a healthy suspicion of strangers.

After the first interview, I made an effort to revisit all the women I
spoke with in an unblushing attempt to try to find a way into their family circles. While anthropologists generally do not like to put it in these

terms, this kind of calculated and strategic friend making, at least initially, is largely what ethnography relies on, but I did not have as much agency as one might expect. In the end, only those who had some interest in me in the beginning allowed me "in" both literally and metaphorically. Quite understandably, given local histories, there is no pushing or even cajoling an Andean woman to be more trusting or forthcoming than she is inclined to be, so from the start the relationships I had with women were foreshadowed. Those who answered the door with curiosity or who were kind to me during that very first interview stayed with me, at least for that first year or so, and some for much longer, but I was challenged to try to bring around those who resisted my overtures.

I could not help but ask myself if these women's experiences were fundamentally different from those of the friendlier or more curious ones. So, I dutifully went back two or three times and awkwardly tried to ignite some spark of understanding, humor, or interest. A few women simply did not open the door a second time, but most did. However, they continued to answer my questions with as few words as possible, usually saying only "yes" or "no" or the most dreadful of all, "I don't know." There is no obvious follow-up to that response, no way to coax an elaboration. In the end, my efforts were futile, and I never brought someone around who was not seemingly already predisposed to talk to me. I could not blame them for their reticence, as my presence made so little sense, really, and objectively, their resistance was far more understandable than my attempt at friendliness.

To be sure, there were others whose embrace of me was so enthusiastic that, while initially quite gratifying, quickly became suspect. These women and men were far friendlier than is appropriate in Cuenca, often turning the tables on me and asking a host of personal questions, including why I was unmarried and whether I was interested in marrying an Ecuadorian. Sometimes they revealed their not-so-hidden pecuniary interests by clumsily peppering me with questions about money and finances, including what my father did for a living, how much he was paid, how much I paid in rent, and how much money my grant gave me to live on. Some were about as blunt as could be in getting at the heart of the matter and would simply declare "You're really rich" on finding out my father's occupation (a marine surveyor) or my monthly allowance from the grant. To avoid these uncomfortable exclamations and the requests for loans that often followed, I began to skim the truth in my responses, usually saying as little as possible.

The personal questions and the awkward moments they engendered were not unusual in the late 1980s, and given how often they were asked, I do not think they were considered terribly rude by those who asked them.

The United States seemed a million miles away, and very little in the way of information had yet come back from those migrants who left. While I sometimes bristled at the questions, I also understood that people were trying to get a handle on the scale of things and figure out where to place me in their understandings of social power, influence, and potential. I interpreted the questions to mean that people saw in my white foreignness the potential for improving their *palanca*, the social leverage so crucial to social success in Cuenca, or they thought I might possibly be a financial resource or a connection to legal immigration. More than once I was only partially jokingly asked if I wanted to take a child or husband back to the States with me. For others, it was clear to me that by associating with me they gained a small amount of cachet within their own circles of friends and family. When I was introduced to neighbors and family it was often with the line, "This is the *gringa* I was telling you about." Knowing me made them seem more cosmopolitan and worldly and perhaps socially significant. Gringos were a little-known quantity then and full of potential. This might still be the case, but it plays out very differently today.

At Blanca's I never had to work at being welcomed. When I returned after our initial interview I was greeted with "Venga, niña" (Come in, child), as though she was expecting me all along. A chair was always found for me and dusted off, and a child sent out to buy a soda, as though that was the only thing I could possibly want to drink. Blanca's home was right around the corner from where I stayed, so I often found myself salvaging an otherwise fruitless afternoon by visiting her on the way back from some other, less successful outing.

Blanca did not live in a *conventillo* but a place just as bad as the worst of them. The big difference was that this place was hers, and it had a future. Blanca sold a small parcel of land in the countryside she was given by her parents to secure the mortgage on the property, and she was slowly making changes. Her place, I can hardly call it a house, was right in front of the 9 de Octubre municipal market, a hectic commercial zone during the day with itinerant vendors loudly hawking their wares and a dodgy place at night when the alcohol flowed freely from the nearby shops and dispensaries. The area was noisy at all hours as vendors of pirated music tapes (and later CDs) blasted their offerings, cumbia in the 1980s giving way to reggaeton in the mid-1990s. Moreover, the Plaza Cívica, an open space between the market and Blanca's house, was a regular festival and protest site. In early 1997, hundreds of *cuencanos* descended on the plaza for days protesting the corrupt administration of President Abdala Bucaram, who was ousted soon thereafter.

Blanca lived down a funny little sidewalk in the middle of a commercial block across the street from the market and plaza. That walkway led nowhere except to her place. In 1989 the property housed a ramshackle collection of construction detritus, mounds of stones, old furniture, piles of new bricks and sand, and a newly built concrete stairway leading to what were to become second-floor bedrooms. Blanca, her husband, and their five children lived in two large rammed-earth rooms in the back of the small courtyard. Before they bought the property, the rooms had been a charcoal warehouse used by vendors who cooked sausages, pork, and guinea pig on open grills to sell to late-night crowds coming and going to the nearby bus interchange. The walls were still blackened by charcoal soot, and the rooms were crowded with beds and clothes hanging from ropes tied across the ceiling.

Blanca worked cooking and selling simple food such as *guatita*, a tripe stew, in huge pots that she had her sons haul out to the street twice a day at lunchtime and in the evenings. She also earned extra money by renting space to market women to store their goods overnight. There was steady traffic in and out of her place of market women and *cargadores*, the latter the most lowly of manual laborers who haul enormous quantities of goods on their backs. It seemed to me that the job was so often filled by men too old and boys too young for that kind of labor, and they were among the most down-and-out people to be seen. Except for the dead drunks. Many of the *cargadores* slept curled up in the corners of the market at night and the during the midday doldrums when business all over town slowed to a trickle. They were recognizable by the tools of their trade, the frayed ropes wrapped around their ragged shoulders and hunched backs.

Blanca actively performed a kind of urban working-class feminine identity, with a short, stylish haircut, wearing only western-style skirts with stockings and heeled shoes, and displaying confident mannerisms of speech and comportment, such as that "Venga, niña" endearment she gave me. She did not, however, assume the common urban affectation of looking down her nose at those who could not or chose not to engage in the same class identity work. She sympathized and fed the skinniest *cargadores* and found common cause with the hardworking market women who often had little support from the men in their lives. "Women do everything," Blanca told me one day as we watched women haul goods from their storage places, because, she said, "men are lazy." I never did figure out what her husband, Luis, did in these early years. Whatever it was, it involved buying and selling things, and I assumed, by the way he talked about it and the unpredictability of his work, that it was not an entirely legal operation. So many had their hands in something that was illegal or barely legal, and I mostly figured this out by how evasive people were about the details of their work. Luis was a wily sort of guy, street-smart and cocky unless he was drunk, and then he was maudlin and sappy if he wasn't mean.

The only private space in their home was the dark back rooms; the courtyard was a public domain filled with people, market women coming in and out, workmen beginning the construction of the house, a host of friends and Luis's drinking buddies, and a revolving door of visiting relatives. Because their house was located just steps from the market, friends and relatives often stopped in on their way to or from shopping. In that public, private, home, work space, Blanca was a tough mother to an unruly bunch of teenagers, the tolerant wife of a ne'er-do-well man whose jokes and commentaries lurched unexpectedly from stupid to funny to insulting, and a hardworking and savvy businesswoman who had to negotiate prices with wholesalers, keep on top of collecting rent on the warehouse space from vendors who were themselves struggling to make ends meet, and present a polite if not caring front to customers.

I saw Blanca's demeanor of confident competence crack only a few times, usually in the presence of Luis's far more successful brother-in-law. Jorge, a retail salesman, showed up at their house in a suit and tie and seemingly had no qualms about critiquing Luis and Blanca and giving unwanted advice. His commentary ranged from how the house ought to be designed to childrearing tips. He seemed to want to impress me, to show the *gringa* that he was made of better stuff than his relatives, and I found I could hardly tolerate him. I wondered why Blanca and Luis put up with him until I learned that Luis occasionally borrowed money from him. Dealing with his pretensions was part of the deal. Once, after a twenty-minute whirlwind of Jorge boasting about his own children, Blanca, with a stricken look on her face, simply said about her offspring, "We have no high school graduates or marriages among them." Jorge's wife responded that there was still hope for the youngest child, six-year-old Gloria, who might well become a "pretty professional with green eyes." Those eyes marked her as "white" and bode well for her future success.

Little by little, Blanca's house and business improved considerably. By the mid-1990s she had finished constructing and furnishing a two-story home with a restaurant occupying the first floor and the upstairs housing three bedrooms, a sitting room, and a bathroom. The restaurant, which also served as the family kitchen, was an unpretentious one selling mostly *almuerzos*, lunches on a fixed menu of a simple soup, a rice dish, and a juice. At lunchtime the tables were filled with *cholas* and laborers, and in the afternoons, with men having a few beers before going home. Blanca regularly employed one or two young women to help cook and clean, as her own children did not much take to the unglamorous work. Blanca's restaurant did pretty well; it was the closest sit-down lunch spot to the market, and she got good deals on the ingredients from the wholesalers and market vendors. It was her earnings that paid for the new house, and it was enough to keep her solvent when Luis finally left her. Luis was never a good husband; he drank, was more than occasionally violent, and worked only sporadically. He had other women on the side (all told, Luis had twelve children by four women, but he only ever married Blanca), and for almost a decade Blanca helped raise one of his daughters by another woman. Then he left Blanca for good, or so it seemed, in 2000. In a move that still evokes Blanca's derision today, he took up with the fourteen-year-old girl who cleaned the floors of her restaurant.

Luis was not the only source of constant heartbreak in Blanca's life. Blanca had five children. One died in early infancy, and the next girl, Blanquita, was four years old when she suffered a tragic accident that marked her for life. At the time, Blanca and Luis were living in the small, provincial town of Santa Isabel about an hour and a half outside of Cuenca. Luis was raised in Santa Isabel and Blanca nearby on a farm in the warm valley of Yunguilla, where her parents grew sugarcane, tomatoes, naranjillas, and mangos. Blanca's mother, Etelvina, was a well-known healer and midwife who attended births throughout the countryside. Etelvina stopped attending births when she was in her seventies but continued to perform *limpiezas* (ritual cleansings) at her home in her nineties. Although deceased for almost a decade in 2016, her name still had renown in the area among older adults, many of whom she delivered. The farm sits atop a hill and is eyeball distance from the town of Santa Isabel.

In 1975 Blanca was pregnant and had an infant son, so when Blanquita begged her parents to let her stay with her grandparents on the farm, they acquiesced. She liked being held tight in her grandmother's arms while riding on horseback to the homes of birthing women, and even more, she craved the rich chicken soup made with *runa* (indigenous or free-range) chickens that her grandmother shared with her after the births. These were lean times for Blanca and Luis, so the steady offerings of *caldo de gallina* seemed luxurious to the young Blanquita. Chicken soup was an essential part of the postpartum diet in rural Azuay Province, as it was thought to cool the body after the heat of childbirth. The soup is put on the fire when labor begins, and the midwife partakes. Traditionally, when women had kin nearby who could help, new mothers refrained from working and ate special meals for forty days after giving birth. Given the outmigration from the countryside and the thinning of kin support networks, that lengthy lying-in period has been lost for decades. Blanquita enjoyed keeping her grandparents company on the farm; Blanca was a short distance away and came often to visit. No one saw this as a permanent arrangement, as Blanquita would be starting school soon.

There was no electricity in the countryside of Yunguilla then, and the grandparents regularly used kerosene lamps in the evenings. The sun sets year-round at 6:30 on the equator, so nights are long, and lamps were a necessity, especially since Etelvina was often visited by patients asking for cleansings in the evenings, or she was called out into the night to attend a birth. One afternoon Blanquita was unsupervised, and left to her own devices, she poured gasoline instead of kerosene into a small lamp and, imitating her grandparents, tried to light it. It exploded, leaving Blanquita seriously burned. Her grandmother, hearing her screams, rushed in from the fields and bathed her and applied cold compresses. She may have done more harm than good; there was no potable water in Yunguilla at the time. When Blanca and Luis were sent for in town, they were told by a cousin that Blanquita had sustained only minor burns, but when they arrived at the farm they found half of her face and all of one side of her body charred. The child was in agony and had been for hours, and she was slipping in and out of consciousness. They took her to the regional hospital in Santa Isabel where they were scolded for their lack of care. A few weeks later they moved her to a hospital in Cuenca, where she stayed for many months while a heavily pregnant Blanca slept on the floor next to her. Her recovery was long, with some sores festering for years, and her face, including her lips and gums, remained scarred and disfigured the rest of her life.

Blanquita started school in Santa Isabel two years later, and the children teased her mercilessly for her disfigurement. They called her a *longa quemada*, burned Indian. *Longo* or *longa* is an especially cruel insult for an Indian, and it implies stupidity, foolishness, and filth. Eventually the family moved to Cuenca in part so she could go to a better school where they hoped she would be bullied less. That did not happen, and she never liked school and had difficulties making friends. She grew accustomed, no matter the weather, to wearing a scarf around her neck that she pulled up over her mouth to hide the worst of her scars.

When I met her at age eighteen, she was helping her cousin sell clothes at the hectic El Arenal, a *feria libre* (open market), and was embittered about her life. She told me then that she was uninterested in getting married; she saw her father as a model for what might be in store for her if she were to marry, and it was not inspiring. Early on, Blanca was hesitant to talk about Luis and the ways he was or wasn't a good husband, but Blanquita had no such qualms. Blanquita was desperate to live elsewhere, saying that Cuenca was too small and she was tired of it. More than anything she wanted to go to the United States; she was enamored of American pop culture and watched TV incessantly, but she'd settle for living in Quito. Neither of those options came to pass for her.

Blanquita did not have Blanca's warm heart that drew people to her. She was not one of those people who was made better by horrible trials. Quite the opposite: it made her bitter and very unhappy. She was obsessed by her appearance and focused much attention on those parts of herself that were untouched by scars: her hair, which she had cut, permed, dyed, curled, and styled relentlessly, and her small feet, on which she often wore delicate and brightly colored high heels. By her early teens Blanquita was hard to handle and rebellious, and by fifteen she had a baby out of wedlock. There was no question of marrying the older man who fathered the child. I heard different accounts of Blanquita's relationship with the father; Luis called him a rapist, while Blanca claimed he was a seducer. Blanquita herself didn't talk about him.

While not making a secret of her granddaughter's birth, Blanca raised the child, Gloria, as though she was her own daughter, allowing Blanquita to live a teenager's life. I found scattered throughout my notes from 1989 a sort of incredulity and confusion about the openness of the complicated family dynamics. At one point I wrote, clearly shocked, that Luis described six-year-old Gloria's father as a rapist right in front of her and then said, "But I'm your real father, and I'm the one who loves you," drawing her onto his lap. Both Blanca and Luis showered Gloria with affection and called her their daughter, although they made no real effort to hide her origins. For years I wondered how confusing this must be for Gloria, and how they could possibly maintain this complicated and seemingly unclear set of relationships for a lifetime. In the end, I think I was the only one who was troubled or confused by it. They seemed to move in and out of avoiding and revealing the truth, but I didn't gather that it caused them much anxiety one way or another.

Blanquita didn't finish high school; she held a variety of jobs, many of them, like her father's, on the shifty margins of the informal economy. Her mother was often displeased with her and her interest in late-night parties, but eventually Blanquita met and married a simple, decent man who became a good father to their children and who seemed to love her. Blanquita and her husband, Diego, continued to live with Blanca on and off throughout their married life, using Blanca's home as a temporary refuge from economic setbacks. Things were relatively stable in Blanquita's life until tragedy struck. In 1998 the couple's second child, an eighteen-month-old daughter, suddenly died of diarrheal disease. I was in Cuenca when it happened; quite literally, Salma, named after the actor Salma Hayek, was fine one day and dead the next. The funeral was held in the restaurant with the tiny white coffin placed in the center of the dining room. Blanquita's and Diego's grief, intensified by shock, was the rawest I have ever witnessed. In the days following the baby's death, Blanca's Catholicism saw her through, and she grieved not for the baby, who was "happy by God's side," but for her daughter, who would not stop crying. Blanca tried to mitigate her daughter's guilt about not consulting a doctor sooner by pointing out how the baby often looked up to the sky and held her hands toward God. She was never meant to live anywhere else but heaven.

The 2007 renovation of the 9 de Octubre market changed Blanca's life completely. Her property was down an odd, narrow passageway, and her house and one other were all that stood in the way of making a mid-block pedestrian walkway between the 9 de Octubre market and the Plaza Cívica in front of her house and the Plaza Rotary behind it. The Plaza Rotary is Cuenca's best-known artisan market, with handcrafted wooden furniture, iron tools and decorations, tin and clay kitchenware, baskets, and children's toys. An obligatory stop on the tourist route, the Plaza Rotary is one of the few places left in Cuenca to buy locally made handicrafts. Blanca was indemnified, her house razed, and a clear path constructed between the two plazas. Only she and one other family were removed. Today, the site where her house and restaurant once stood is a public toilet. Gloria now talks of the shame she feels that her childhood home has been converted to a public restroom, and she abashedly joked, "Stall number three on the women's side was my bedroom. To think people now urinate where I slept . . ."

With additional help from her sons in the United States, Blanca took the money she was paid by the city for her property and purchased a small home on the outskirts of the *centro histórico*. On the surface, her new house is quite a step up from the old one, which had no windows or green space and was permeated with the noise and smells of the market. Her new house is like most buildings in the center, connected to those on either side with windows facing only the front street and the back courtyard. It has two stories, three bedrooms, two baths, and a patio with garden space and a small, basic apartment in the back. The house is on a quiet residential street that has little traffic. In so many ways, this house represents the fulfillment of Cuencan working-class aspirations; it is a nice house in a quiet neighborhood in town. And that is how Blanca tried to present it to me when I first visited her the summer after her move. "Oh, I'm so comfortable here. It's so peaceful and quiet. I've gotten used to living here so quickly," she told me as I sat awkwardly in her living room on furniture encased in plastic. In the old place, I usually sat in the kitchen by the stove, picking at scraps in the pots, joking with women who worked for her or were visiting, and dodging dogs and cats. Blanca's new place is out of the way just enough that I have to call now before I come over. There are no more drop-in visits.

It was years before Blanca told me what I supposed all along. The move made her miserable. Blanca lived for more than twenty years in front of the market where everyone knew her. Anything she needed for her kitchen was steps away, and she had embedded relationships with market women who had done business with her for decades. She was somebody on that street; her neighbors all knew her, she was a businesswoman of long standing, a mother who raised children in the neighborhood, and a woman respected for her personal charm and professional accomplishments. She was never alone unless she wanted to be, and there was always something for her to do or someone who needed her. Not only was a lifetime's worth of relationships disturbed if not severed by the forced move, but Blanca's livelihood, her restaurant, was taken away as well. She first tried opening a restaurant near another municipal market, but rents were too high and it was a forty-minute bus ride from her home. Then she tried putting a coffee shop in the front of her new house, but there is just not enough foot traffic on her street to support even a small café. She spent most days alone in the house, as her two daughters and their husbands worked and the children were in school. What seemed very clear to me is that despite decades of performing a working-class urban matron identity, Blanca's sense of self-worth, her connection to community, and her personal identity were constructed in that chaotic market space where she had carved out a role as a respected and respectable woman.

For a while after their daughter's death, Blanquita and Diego seemed to do pretty well, finding solace in one another, and they had another child, a son. Then things slowly unraveled and year by year their relationship deteriorated. Blanquita was obviously not happy with Diego, and she never failed to tell me how homely she thought him. I found myself liking Diego for how he remained a good father to their two children and a hard worker in the face of his wife's clear disfavor. Eventually Diego was relegated to the cold back apartment in Blanca's yard, and he and Blanquita lived mostly separated. Blanquita and Blanca continued their tempestuous relationship, and sometimes they would not speak to one another for months at a time.

Gloria grew up to be the kind of pretty woman Blanquita admired, with the much-coveted light skin and green eyes that I was told were her inheritance from her biological father. At first, when Gloria was a little girl, Blanquita acted very much like an older sister to her; she teased Gloria or ignored her. Then, as they grew older and Gloria became an adult, they would slip in and out of a mother-daughter relationship, with Gloria sometimes calling Blanquita by her name and sometimes calling her Mami. Gloria's temperament was sweet and cheerful, where Blanquita was angry and despairing, but they shared a fascination with fashion, music, celebrities, and then social media. Gloria graduated from high school and started college but didn't finish. After she left college she started working as a traveling sales representative for a cosmetic company. She married in her early twenties and had a daughter, and she and her family have lived in Blanca's home. Blanca cared for Gloria's daughter, whom she calls her granddaughter, until the girl started school, giving Blanca something to do during those years. At its fullest, Blanca's house was home to her two daughters, their husbands, and their three children, making for a chaotic household with people in and out on various work and school schedules.

Then, the unthinkable happened. On a September night in 2011, Gloria and Blanquita were on their way home, just the two of them, after midnight, from a family party on a mountainous country road. Gloria was driving her own new car, purchased on credit. They hit a curve at "excessive speed," according to a newspaper article, and the car rolled over at least once. Gloria, who had to be extricated from the car by firefighters, was hurt but eventually recovered. Blanquita, who never wore a seat belt, was killed instantly. Blanca claims that Blanquita foretold her own death in dreams several weeks before the accident, lending a strange and otherworldly dimension to the event in Blanca's mind. The morning after her dreams, Blanquita made her mother promise to look out for her children when she died.

Five years after the accident, when Blanca talked about Blanquita, she was overwhelmed by their mutual suffering, something she avoided discussing while Blanquita was alive. Blanquita suffered the physical and emotional traumas of being burned and scarred, and Blanca endured the daily trial of seeing her daughter disfigured, angry, and unhappy. Blanquita was temperamental and often took out her anger on Blanca. "You have no idea how we would fight," Blanca told me. She feels responsible for what happened to Blanquita as a child, and her early death seems like the final injustice. Blanca's inability to help her daughter did not cease, and Blanca shamefacedly told me that she had only eight dollars at her disposal when Blanquita died and could not even pay the fee to have her body released from the coroner's office. She had to wait for friends and relatives to pitch in. She has turned to her Catholic faith for comfort, even attending a weekend women's retreat at which she said she found some tranquility in the silence, meditation, and prayer.

For years, Blanca's life settled into perhaps too quiet a routine of caring for her granddaughter and preparing lunch for her family, whose members came in only sporadically to eat. Blanca did most of the cooking in the household, and there was often a pot of soup and rice on the back of the stove. Eating meals together was not something the family was accustomed to; Blanca had spent most of the mealtimes in her life feeding strangers. She complained about being alone, mentioning that she had five children and only one continued to live with her or even nearby. Her three grown sons were all in New York. Her grandchildren did still live with her, as did Diego, but they were busy, and she feared that they would all find their own homes soon enough, leaving her truly all alone.

That is, until 2015, when Luis came back. His young lover, with whom he had two children, tired of him and threw him out, leaving him living in a series of single rooms and eating in the street. He had been sick, and Gloria begged Blanca to take pity on him and let him live in one of the back rooms. So now, Luis, after a fifteen-year absence, was back in Blanca's life, but with conditions. Luis lived in the back apartment, and their lives, Blanca said, "are completely independent." He had no right to ask her where she went or when she would be back. She cooks for him most days, and he occasionally does favors for her, but they do not socialize together outside of the house. He has his life and she has hers. When I was there in 2016, Luis would often come home from a morning hanging out with his retired cronies in Parque Calderón and sit and talk with Blanca and me for a while, then head to his room. Blanca seemed a little sheepish that she took him back after years of talking about how shameless he was, but she rationalized it this way: "I'm alone and he's alone. He can't ask anything of me, but it's nice to have someone to talk to." She really enjoys his company; he is a teller of tall tales and crazy schemes, and he is amusing, if nothing else. Blanca laughs when he is around.

I was surprised not only to find Luis back in Blanca's home if not her bed, but it also seemed that he had altered with age. An event in 2016 demonstrated his now far more tranquil nature. On a national holiday, Blanca left early to spend the day with a relative, unaware that the lock on

Luis's apartment door had broken and he was locked in for the day. He spent the day watching TV and lounging around, and rather than being angry, he laughed about it. The story he told about his day was charming and amusing. The old Luis would have been livid about the indignity of it all, not to mention the day of hard drinking with friends that he missed. Blanca seems surprised at her own ability to assert her independence, proudly telling me with a glimmer in her eye that she left the house for a Sunday outing with me without saying a word to Luis about where she was going or when she would be back. This kind of independence is unheard of in marital relationships, and to her was an obvious sign of the new configuration. But it seemed to me her newfound independence had limits, and old habits and perhaps old feelings are hard to change. On our way home that Sunday and after countless stops to try local delicacies like roasted pork, sugarcane juice, and homemade popsicles, we made one last stop, to buy a roasted chicken so Luis would not go hungry that night.

When I arrived in Cuenca in July 2018, I found Blanca beaten down by the guests in her two back rooms. A year earlier, her ninety-five-year-old father came to live with her from the country, and he was bed-bound and, Blanca said, "like a baby." Blanca had to care for his every need, including changing his soiled diapers. Sometimes she did not have enough cash on hand to buy diapers. She also was no longer speaking to Luis, who occupied the other room and who now only slept in the room, leaving early in the morning and not coming back until late. Six months earlier, he had come home one evening to find Blanca in the living room entertaining an old friend of the family, a man. Luis blew up, hurled verbal abuses at everyone, and started swinging his fists at Blanca and her guest. Things got ugly. Blanca tried to have Luis removed from her home after that, even seeing a lawyer about it, but she was told that given his age he had "protections" and could not be removed from his place of residence. So now he slips in and out, not talking to Blanca, who has forbidden him from entering her kitchen. Given a chance, she will still talk endlessly about Luis and his shameless behavior.

In addition to the two "guests," as she ironically calls them, Blanca's house now serves as the site of a new business venture formed by her son-in-law who left what he called the "corrupt" police force, and Blanca's grandson, Blanquita's son. They started an updated version of the same business Blanca was in when I met her, selling food on the street. Early in the morning they prepare chicken sandwiches with a special aioli sauce and take them to various buildings in town to sell to office workers from mid-morning through early afternoon. So far, the business is going well;

they are turning a small daily profit and hired two itinerant vendors to work the streets and offices. One is a dual US-Ecuadorian citizen, the son of an Ecuadorian immigrant to New York who returned to Ecuador, and the other, a woman, is a refugee from Venezuela. For now, Blanca moves between the bustle of the international kitchen crowd, which she sometimes complains is too noisy, and the sad back room where her decrepit father is living out his last days. The highlight of her day comes at the very end, when she curls up in bed with her granddaughter, who always sleeps with her, and talks to Will in New York on the phone.

CHAPTER 5

The Gringo Invasion

Time and Technology

One of the ways I keep track of the changes in Cuenca over time is to think about the various places I have lived. I remember those places because I can picture my growing daughter in each one. The first place she stayed, at three months old, was along the Tomebamba River. It was a scruffy place, so humid that slugs oozed across our kitchen walls at night. It had no phone, television, or internet, and while safe enough for a babe in arms who never touched the ground, it gave way as the years passed to far more comfortable situations with ever-increasing amenities. When my daughter was a preschooler, we found a new short-term apartment rental complex near the Universidad de Cuenca. It was rented primarily to foreigners. In the mid-1990s it seemed to appeal especially to Europeans in Cuenca for weeks-long stays as they finalized the adoption of orphaned children. The apartments came fully furnished with a limited but functional set of kitchen supplies, and there was a phone in the main office that I was allowed to use in the mornings when the office was open. That phone was adequate for a quick conversation, such as setting up a meeting, but not for extended and personal conversations, as there was no privacy. Most of the time I walked a few blocks to a nearby phone-calling center where I could use a phone in a private booth.

In 2006 and 2007, I had a grant that allowed me several months of fieldwork each summer, and we rented an apartment at the southern end of town near the Yanuncay River. The apartments were nicely furnished with a microwave and a television, but they were not move-in ready, as we had to supply most of the necessities, from bedsheets to matches to light the stove. We generally spent the first days of every trip laying in provisions, as not so much as a roll of toilet paper was provided. We stayed in that building four times over six years, storing our accumulated goods such as brooms and sheets with a friend between stays. We liked the place for its location near the river and park where my daughter could play and because it was clean and secure. We were always the only gringos in the building. The rentals operated on a cash-only basis, so a friend had to put down a deposit for me to reserve our place before we arrived.

The apartment had a phone, the first time I had one in Ecuador, and I could make local calls but not to cell phones, as those were considered long distance. Calling out was straightforward, but it was, unfortunately, a cumbersome system to dial into, and most people had difficulty calling me. Calls had to go through a central switchboard, and the young woman who managed the office worked only a few hours a day. Given these encumbrances, it is hard to convey now how thrilling it was then to hear a phone ring in our apartment. Cell phones were available then, but they were costly and clunky, and in the early days, you could only call someone whose cell phone service provider was the same as yours. Because of the hassles, I didn't bother getting one. Instead, when I needed to make a phone call to a cell phone, I did what I had done before: I walked down to the corner store, where there were phone booths. The last time we stayed in that building was for a few weeks in the summer of 2013. I had a cell phone that year, but reception was so poor in the building I had to stick my head out the window to make a call.

By then, Wi-Fi was ubiquitous in Cuenca, yet the building still had not installed it. The manager said guests or their visitors would regularly steal the routers. I wasn't sure if that was true or simply what she supposed would happen. Nevertheless, when I needed to check email I went to an internet café around the corner and paid thirty-five to fifty cents for an hour of computer time. Internet cafés were everywhere in the first decade of the 2000s, from semiprofessional operations with plenty of work stations, varied software programs, and games and lots of customers, to homespun versions located in residential neighborhoods. I regularly went to one that consisted of two computers in a family's converted living room. Only a handful of internet cafés remain today now that smart phones are so common and public Wi-Fi easily available.

In 2016 I spent three months in Cuenca on sabbatical. By this time my daughter was in college, and for the first time in twenty-five years, I was in Cuenca for a goodly amount of time by myself. I called the usual apartment building by the river hoping it had been updated, and I asked if it had Wi-Fi installed yet. The response was no, but they could help me install it myself in my apartment. I declined that offer. And I could now. Renting a furnished apartment, one complete with sheets, towels, Wi-Fi, satellite or cable TV, a security system, and possibly even a washer and dryer in Cuenca is now much easier than renting a hotel room on graduation weekend in Ann Arbor, Michigan. In the past decade or so, apartments have been scooped up by expats and Ecuadorians, renovated, outfitted with technology, and put up for short- or long-term rent. Now, when I arrive I have almost everything I need at my fingertips including, in some cases, far more technology than I have at home. In 2018 I rented a place in the *centro histórico* through Airbnb from a North American (I think) with Roku TV, Amazon Echo speakers, a motion-detecting security system, and two super-fast and completely reliable internet connections.

The technology that makes Airbnb possible is exactly what has fueled the expat migration to Cuenca. Not only do North Americans use the internet to learn about retirement and expat living destinations and conditions, but they would have found the Ecuador of 2000, let's say, with its spotty dial-up cable internet and inconstant telephone service, to be unlivable. The gringo invasion relies on technology and digital communication to sell Ecuador as an idyll and make it less strange. Expats can now sit at home and watch CNN or for some, Fox News, stream hundreds of movies, chat on Skype, and read about events in town in English in a digital newspaper. All of this has made life in Cuenca easier and less strange for expats, allowing them to manage difference in small doses.

"Ugh. Those People Are Insufferable!"

While I enjoy my time in Cuenca, I never thought of it as a place that is easy for older foreigners to navigate, so the arrival of North American migrants took me by surprise. In contrast, say, to San Miguel de Allende in Mexico, a premier expat destination where the sun shines just about every day, Cuenca is frequently cloudy and a good deal brisker. Cuenca is close to the equator and nights come early, and it is situated at 2,400 meters above sea level in the heart of the Andes, which means that the days can be cool and the nights downright chilly, although that is changing and January and February are far warmer than they were in the 1980s. Because of the cool evenings, there is little café culture in Cuenca and little sense of the leisurely pace that typically accompanies a retirement haven. Cuenca is also more congested as new developments sprout out of what was once the countryside, and buses spewing black smoke connect these blossoming new neighborhoods to the city center. Traffic is heavy throughout the city for most of the day now, and pedestrians have to remain highly vigilant while navigating the city streets. Cars invariably have the right of way, and they take it.

Watching my field site turn into an American retirement haven provided me with a new research topic, but it also challenged my ethnographic sensitivities and sensibilities in distinctive ways. Anthropologists, including me, have a strange relationship with studying retirement migration. The reactions I got from colleagues, both senior and junior to me, when they learned I was researching this migration were very telling of the uncomfortable sentiments these retirees bring forth in some anthropologists. The way I saw it, my field site was being invaded by a bunch of old folks, and I was both attracted and repelled by the spectacle. The attraction was propelled by curiosity. How did they get there? What do they do? How do they manage without speaking the language? What sort of community building do they engage in? The repulsion had to do with a sense that *my* place, the place where I built my professional reputation, was now a marketed commodity for older, and obviously culturally incompetent, expats. I found myself impatient with them in ways that did not quite add up. That is, I was every bit as impatient with the idea of them as I was with the actual people.

I was not alone in my anthropological wariness. When professional colleagues heard what I was studying, reactions were cool if not downright hostile. One senior and very well respected anthropologist simply looked at me, scrunched up his nose, and asked, not at all expecting an answer, "Is that anthropology?" No one had asked me that question in my years of studying Ecuadorian migrants in the United States. Clearly, this migration was of a different sort and just did not make the grade. I was so taken aback I did not probe my colleague further, but I could not help but think that his comment reflected the assumption that anthropology still filled the "savage slot" (Trouillot 2003). In other words, our job remained to describe the other, who necessarily stands in contrast to westerners, ourselves, reifying the separation between us and them. That this distinction was still salient, more than twenty years after we began critiquing it by pointing to its colonial origins and neocolonial assumptions, hints at how entrenched it remains in the discipline. Another colleague who encountered elderly American migrants wrote to me when he heard I was doing research among them, saying, "Ugh, those people are insufferable!" Under what other circumstances, I wondered, would a cultural anthropologist feel so free to disparage an entire group, one he had only cursory contact with, in this way? And why did I kind of see his point? There are both simple and complicated answers to these questions.

First, the simpler answers. Some of my resistance (and that of the "ugh"-producing colleague) to being an empathetic ethnographer among retirees seemed rightly placed, albeit, to be sure, a tad self-righteous. Some expats simply are, and among themselves they acknowledge this, to put it bluntly, "ugly Americans." They are brash, unaccepting of Ecuadorian ways, and demanding of public and private services, everything anthropologists try not to be in the field. Retirees often come to Ecuador with deeper pockets than the locals, and they generally expect the world to work the way they want it to. Stories fly freely in the expat community of how, when faced with intransigent bureaucracies, or even people speaking Spanish, tempers have flared. Anthropologists, and rightly so, I think, interpret the whole phenomenon as a neocolonial project in which Americans get to stretch their retirement dollars by (yet again?) taking advantage of others in the developing world. Who else has the kind of privilege it takes to move to another country primarily for leisure and expect that there will be an improvement in one's lifestyle? Retirees frequently have maids for the first time in their lives, and they extract promises from one another not to "overpay" them and ruin it for the rest of them. Less obviously, I noted, retirees also gleefully report that they pay the senior citizen bus fare of twelve cents instead of the regular twenty-five-cent fare without any recognition of the social contract that goes along with reduced fares for students and the elderly, that is, that students will pay into the system and the elderly already have. Ecuadorians, it seems to me, are unfairly subsidizing the retirement of Americans.

The question of how we as ethnographers come to terms with research participants whom we do not like or whose motivations seem unpleasant to us is not a new one, and we have been writing about these kinds of accommodations for years. Peter Metcalf discusses in his wonderfully revealing *They Lie, We Lie* (2001) that people sometimes even actively thwart us by lying or avoiding us or talking against us. But to be clear, that wasn't happening here. These expats willingly came to talk to me. In fact, it had never been easier to recruit participants, as retirees have time, and they were to the last polite, even when self-aggrandizing. I was surprised at how willing if not eager they were to collaborate. I would usually ask one interviewee to give my name to another, and more than once that second person called my cell phone to discuss meeting before I even got home. Hanging out in a bar could land me days of home visits. Over time, though, I came to realize that despite their willingness to engage in research and their cosmopolitan self-image, in many ways they were as naïve as any other anthropological participant might be in terms of understanding the critical lens that we as researchers might bring to bear on them.

As I came to know more retirees, I was able to distinguish among them, and not very admirably, I found myself thinking of some as sympathetic and others as, well, not so sympathetic. Those I find sympathetic are excruciatingly concerned about cultural differences, work hard to form relationships with Ecuadorians, and worry about their intrinsic privilege. They often speak in romantic terms about Ecuadorian values and culture or seek charitable ways to "give back." In many ways, they are not so very different from anthropologists. We too worry about power dynamics, write a good deal about resistance and resilience, and wonder how we can do more. While we might critique charitable enterprises as patronizing manifestations of neoliberal dynamics, I don't imagine we would think any better of the expats if they did not engage in charitable endeavors. Although Ecuadorians voice mixed opinions about the elderly expats in their midst, they invariably point to their charitable work as a good thing.

Those I found the most sympathetic were the self-described health care refugees, those who engage in what Meghann Ormond calls "disability impelled migration" (2014, 7) These are people who struggle with disabilities or chronic illnesses that they cannot properly attend to in the United States, mostly for financial reasons. Moving to Ecuador, where costs of in-home care are far lower, offers a solution to the problem of how to manage needed care, at least until Medicare kicks in. But why, I wondered, did I have to reserve my ethnographic empathy for those I identified as vulnerable in some way? Why did the average migrant who just wanted a change of scene or needed to save money or sought adventure fail to arouse my sympathies, or worse, annoy me? Here is where the answers become more complicated.

For better or worse, anthropologists have long defined our discipline if not our identities as forged through fieldwork and ethnographic engagement. It is what makes our "rough and ready discipline" (Geertz 1988, 137). Although sociologists and others increasingly embrace ethnography as a method, anthropologists still own the practice as a signature feature of our discipline and a kind of rite of passage to a claim of professional identity. It historically has been what gives our descriptions, interpretations, and theories resonance. "Where do you do your work?" is among the first questions an anthropologist asks another, and we easily refer to ourselves as "Latin Americanists" or "Andeanists" or "Ecuadorianists." Perhaps less comfortably, fieldwork is also what captures the popular imagination about the anthropologist. The idea that we leave our homes for extended periods to live among the "natives" has given anthropologists a kind of popular and perhaps even personal cachet. While I am not one to build up my field site or field experiences as particularly exotic or difficult, all the same, the idea that my work takes me to another place where people do things differently and that I have in some ways become adept in navigating this dynamic lends a certain authority to my claims. Given this, the threat to us is obvious: Will we still have that special authority when everyone's granny is doing it too? This thought leads me to wonder whether we dislike the expats because we think they are neocolonialists who exploit Ecuador, exerting their white privilege and living the good life, or because they destabilize our images of ourselves. Are expats insufferable because we see in them our own profession's failed tropes about otherness and our pretensions about understanding it? Does their presence in our field sites force an examination of our own privileged mobility to come in and out of cultural spaces?

Expats in Cuenca

Anthropologists and sociologists who have committed to working with expats in Latin America and elsewhere generally refer to this type of migration as "lifestyle migration," a term that very clearly outlines how this population differs from other types of immigrants (Benson and O'Reilly 2016; Croucher 2012; Hayes 2018). The term "lifestyle migration" stresses the relative affluence of the migrants and that they do not cross borders for political reasons or economic necessity but rather for leisure or to improve their lifestyles by moving to a place where the cost of living is cheaper. Matthew Hayes points out that the term implies a type of "coloniality" between the host country and the usually white, western migrants who, rather than being subject to the exclusionary practices so many migrants the world over face, are generally welcomed and their path to legal immigration is cleared (2018, 20). Although cumbersome paperwork abounds, expats in Cuenca encounter few real legal hurdles to gaining residency or citizenship as long as they have steady monthly incomes. Given the lower cost of living in Cuenca, expats usually have enough disposable income to buy or rent homes in good neighborhoods, purchase health insurance, and dine out with regularity.

Americans in Cuenca generally reject the term "migrant" or (worse yet) "immigrant" for themselves, preferring to be called "expats." I heard

a lively discussion of this at a writers club in Cuenca when a bilingual Ecuadorian writer referred to them as "immigrants," to much consternation
among those present. Immigrants, they argued, are poor and migrate to
work, while they, on the other hand, came to spend money and experience another way of life. One member went so far as to say that expats in
Cuenca are not breaking any laws and that their mobility is fully documented. Therefore, they cannot be "immigrants." Another member of the
group mentioned that she wasn't sure she liked the term "expat" because
she did not see herself as being an "ex" patriate but that it was preferable
to any other term. I was struck by two things while listening to this conversation. First, and perhaps naively on my part, I was taken aback at how
disparaging the word "immigrant" had become in popular parlance. Once
a nation of immigrants, some Americans now see those who migrate as
fully marginal, economically, legally, and socially. Second, this seemingly
select group of expats, that is, writers, presumably people who care about
the significance and power of words, had not considered their privilege
in being able to label themselves or question the imposition of wholly
undesirable qualities to the word "immigrant" that they facilely imposed
on others. They accepted the disapproving connotations as definitive and
positioned themselves in contrast to that status.

For their part, Ecuadorians use at least two words to describe the
Americans in their midst. More colloquially, expats are called "gringos," a
term that most expats do not seem to mind. As used in Cuenca, "gringo" is
usually a matter-of-fact acknowledgment that someone is a white foreigner;
sometimes it is used by Ecuadorians to humorously or indulgently point out
cultural differences in behavior. Depending on the circumstances and tone,
however, it can also be interpreted as a derogatory term signaling annoy-
ance with arrogance or ineptitude. In embracing the term for themselves,
expats call their own gatherings "gringo nights," for example, effectively
neutralizing the term as a potential insult and leaving only the objective or
humorous connotations. More formally, the Cuenca newspaper *Diario el
Mercurio* generally uses the word *extranjero* (foreigner) when referring to
someone in the North American or European expat community, reserving
the word *imigrante* for the often undocumented Venezuelans, Colombians,
and Peruvians in Ecuador or in stories about Ecuadorians in the United
States or Spain. In distinguishing the terms, news media are in lockstep with
those in the writers group in seeing immigrants as somehow fundamentally
problematic or marginal to legal processes and, perhaps not obviously,
in reinforcing the idea that darker-skinned people are immigrants, while
lighter-skinned people are something else.

Despite their claims that expats are not economically motivated, it is fairly obvious that the Great Recession of 2008, which resulted in high unemployment of older workers, accelerated expat migration (Hayes 2018). Suddenly thrust into financial peril, older Americans searched for ways to live less expensively, including participating in lifestyle migration. What is less obvious is how these folks found their way to a midsize city in Ecuador. That was facilitated by technology and the intensive marketing of Cuenca online, especially by *International Living Magazine* (*ILM*). The magazine is a one-stop lifestyle-migration resource with an extensive media presence. It puts out a yearly list of the top ten retirement destinations that is frequently picked up by other news sources, including major television networks, *Huffington Post*, and Yahoo News. Cuenca topped that list several times starting in 2009 and has remained on it for more than a decade.[1]

In the online discourse of *ILM*, international retirement migrants are described as being smarter than those who sit home and wring their hands, and a general atmosphere of entitled privilege is cultivated. Expat living is portrayed as an agentive activity, one in which anyone can participate if they just know a few tricks. Refrains like "You deserve this!" or "You worked hard" are commonplace, making financial freedom seem like an inalienable right. Indeed, *ILM*'s free guide to retiring to Ecuador is titled "Ecuador: Live like Royalty on Your Social Security" (*International Living Magazine* 2020). *ILM* creates an image that domesticates the exotic in appealing and accessible ways, flowering gardens perhaps and friendly locals, so a person in Missouri can see himself there. "We're just normal people living exceptional lives," expats seem to be saying to themselves and to others.

Conversations with expats in Cuenca revealed that a variety of circumstances contributed to their decisions to migrate to Ecuador. Some came because they had long yearned for adventure and this was their last best chance. A retired schoolteacher, Glenn, who spent every winter teaching and every summer working in landscaping, had wanted to travel and live abroad, and retirement finally gave him the chance. He found Cuenca a daily delight of new experiences. He lived right in town, attended plenty of social events, and spent his weekends touring the countryside on a motorcycle with Ecuadorian cycling enthusiasts. He called the years he spent in Cuenca "among the happiest of my life." Much against his own wishes, he returned to the United States after five years because his wife wanted to be closer to family. Others lost their jobs in the recession of 2008–2009 and found their lives and retirement plans completely upended. In a process Hayes (2018) calls "geoarbitrage," migrants look for inexpensive places to live to stretch their retirement savings or Social Security checks. An unemployed fifty-five-year-old has few job prospects or only very poor ones in a global recession and little means to support herself and pay for health care (Hayes 2018; Viteri 2015).

Some left the United States when Obama was president because, as they described it, they did not want to live in a "socialist" country. I had difficulty not laughing aloud at this rationale; it appeared to me that they had moved from an imagined socialist country to a real one, and they seemingly had no idea. By 2009 Correa's twenty-first-century socialist agenda was in full bloom. This expat group seemed to be the least happy with life in Ecuador. They complained to me about the "mañana" attitude of workers or their constant concern that Ecuadorians were cheating them with "gringo pricing." Most spoke little Spanish, and a few seemed unwilling to try.

Many migrants who come to Cuenca as health care refugees are people who lost their health insurance along with their jobs in the recession of 2008 and who have costly health problems they could no longer attend to properly in the United States (Viteri 2015). One couple I met came to Ecuador because the husband needed nearly full-time care for Parkinson's disease, but his wife could not afford to stop working and lose her health insurance. Private insurance in the United States for someone over age fifty-five can be as much $900 a month with very high deductibles of $7,500 to $10,000. If the couple stayed in the United States, the wife would have to continue to work in order to keep her health insurance, but she did not make enough money to afford a full-time home health aide to watch over her husband while she was at work. Every day she went to her already stressful job, worried and frightened about what might happen to her husband, whom she left unattended at home. In Ecuador, given the lower cost of living and the affordability of private health insurance, she did not have to work and could stay home to care for her husband, and she could afford health insurance. She even hired a part-time caregiver, a returned Ecuadorian migrant who spoke excellent English, so she could take some needed time for herself. This couple did not see themselves as permanent expats but planned to return to the United States when she became eligible for full Social Security and Medicare benefits in a few years.

Another couple, Jim and Amy, had been taking care of Jim's disabled brother, Gerry, for years and found financial and personal peace for the first time in decades in Ecuador. They had a problem for twenty-five years, they told me, and Ecuador solved it. Jim's brother had sustained brain damage in an accident decades earlier and needed full-time care. Good care was hard to find in the United States and far too expensive. Gerry lived for a time in a group home but was kicked out; he could be belligerent and hard to handle, and he would slip out of the group home from time to time. Once, Gerry was arrested for purchasing alcohol for minors. In the United States, Jim and Amy had to stagger their work schedules so that someone was home to mind Gerry; it was a difficult and relentless arrangement. They hardly saw one another on a day-to-day basis and had not had so much as a weekend away in years. In addition to being unable to afford good care on Gerry's limited disability benefits, Jim and Amy also could not regularly pay for all of Gerry's needed medications. The couple explained that they found themselves in a Medicare "doughnut," at the top end of expenses at one level of coverage but unable to qualify for the next level of benefits coverage. Their out-of-pocket expenses for medications therefore were sky-high.

In Ecuador, Gerry moved into a newly opened assisted living facility that the family liked very much and could easily afford. It was a homey place, and Gerry had a private room with an en suite bathroom and cable TV. When I met them, the couple was almost giddy about their newfound freedom. For the first time in years they could relax without worrying about what Gerry might be doing or about money. The facility was located in a reno-vated colonial building downtown. It was pricey by Ecuadorian standards but very affordable to an American with disability benefits. An Ecuadorian gerontologist opened the facility, and the accommodations, care, and prices were targeted to appeal to middle-class Ecuadorians and expats. There are a few other homes for the elderly and disabled in Cuenca, but most elder care in Ecuador happens at home, provided by either family members or hired caregivers. The facilities that exist are usually for the abandoned and the indigent, and they are not places expats generally find appealing or even acceptable. Staff do not speak English, and there are no private rooms.

In discussions with expats between 2011 and 2016, many of them, including Jim and Amy, told me they had no health insurance in Ecuador and said they were "self-insured." I found this choice of wording fascinat-ing, as it seems intended to obfuscate what amounts to being uninsured. Indeed, the first time I heard it I paused and had to double back and ask, "So you have *no* health insurance?" There is certainly more agency in the term "self-insured" than "uninsured," as the former sounds like a choice rather than a predicament. One woman told me she preferred that term because she could afford insurance but simply chose not to get it. Most explained that they elected not to get insurance because they had enough savings to pay out of pocket for any medical care they thought they might need. I heard many stories from expats and Ecuadorian physicians alike about expats who were availing themselves of all kinds of medical tests, procedures, and care at the public hospitals and private facilities and in some cases left the hospital and the country before paying. As tolerance and the national budget grew thinner, private facilities started asking for payment up front, and in 2017, Ecuador passed a law requiring all expats who apply for residency to have health insurance.

Affordable health care is not the only reason to migrate to Cuenca. Some expats choose to move overseas, as Glenn phrased it, to "reinvent" themselves. This reinvention usually includes an exciting backstory, often of secret government service or international intrigue. Glenn sarcastically noted a "shocking number of ex-CIA agents" living in Cuenca. I met one of them. Frank was in his seventies, overweight, diabetic, and pasty. Despite claiming that he worked for years for the CIA in Latin America, he spoke no Spanish. He regaled me with tall tales and claims to have witnessed crates full of money being delivered to various Latin American governments and said he was "in the room" when dictatorships toppled. He was especially wary of Cubans, saying they were responsible for unrest throughout Latin America and "a force to be reckoned with." He considered himself a student of the US Constitution and said the United States was "going downhill fast" because of "too many damn regulations!" Before he left the United States, he found himself wanting to reach for his gun and shoot his television whenever he watched the news. Other reinventors are grifters who try to lure expats into making real estate deals or business investments. These unsavory types are fairly itinerant, moving from one retirement destination to another as people tire of them.

Shysters aside, a surprising number of retired expats do try to turn their migration experience into moneymaking ventures. Expats rent apartments to each other (and me), act as facilitators for prospective expats, open cottage industries selling pies, jams, and barbeque sauce, or write promotional columns disguised as "postcards" for *ILM*. One expat told me, "You have to keep your eyes open. Someone is always trying to sell you something," and he was talking about his fellow expats. Early arrivals Edd and Cynthia Staton made a career by selling their experiences in Cuenca, first as paid bloggers for *ILM* and then as independent retirement consultants who help people achieve the retirement of their dreams. They went to Ecuador as economic refugees of the 2008 recession, which they claim on their website sent them from the "penthouse to the poor house."[2] They have written several books on how to retire economically and on their website invite prospective migrants to take a "master course" in how to do it right. Their pitch is that anyone can retire on what they have as long as they go someplace with a lower cost of living, that is, by practicing geoarbitrage.

Edd and Cynthia have not done that themselves, though. They started a business selling that idea to others instead.

In the early days of marketing Cuenca, *International Living Magazine* focused on leisure and retirement, talking up how one could live well abroad and finally enjoy oneself in retirement. Moving somewhere less expensive meant one's quality of life could be improved. Maids and gardeners were not out of the question. More recently, yet still before Covid-19, *ILM* shifted to describing the business opportunities in Cuenca. Moving to Cuenca began being pitched as an entrepreneurial endeavor and the city a place where expats can make money, largely from other expats, as Edd and Cynthia have done. A writer in *ILM* explains, "With fiber-optic internet connectivity and a large but tight-knit expat community, word of any new business spreads fast. Whether your goal is to continue to work full-time, or simply supplement your Social Security income, Cuenca is brimming with opportunity" (Dwyer 2019).

One of the most important considerations for those contemplating international retirement destinations seems to be the quality and openness of the expat community. If making friends starts before an expat even arrives in Cuenca, once in Ecuador the opportunities to build on these friendships are plentiful. Gringos hang out at an English-language bookstore, join reading clubs and writing circles, teach each other how to cook at high altitudes, and do charitable work. A woman who moved to Cuenca on her own gushed, "There's something every night to do. I've never had so many friends and so much to do. Everyone is so helpful and friendly!" There are "gringo nights" a few times a week at local bars and restaurants where new arrivals can meet people. I attended several of these, once with my then eighteen-year-old daughter. She likened the event to lunchtime in her high school cafeteria. She pointed out the popular guy, flitting from one table to another, the "queen bee" presiding over a table of admirers, and a few shy introverts who sat by themselves and looked around the room awkwardly. A few expats told me they tired of the gringo nights quickly because of this kind of gamesmanship, and one likened them to freshman mixers, noting that the new arrival's wide-eyed innocence grows irksome after a while. Others complained that the expat community could be "gossipy." Political discussions are tacitly avoided, as the adventurous hippies and the socialist-avoiding libertarians rarely see eye to eye, so conversations often turn to discussing one another.

While many expats appreciate the larger gringo community and what it has to offer, especially in their first months in Cuenca, over time their social lives tend to move toward smaller groups of people whose behavior and orientations to Ecuador are similar. People sort themselves out. The political orientation that expats bring to Ecuador generally predicts whom they will socialize with once on the country. María Amelia Viteri (2015), who has studied expats in northern Ecuador, notes that there is much consternation among some in the gringo community about the possibility of being marked as an "ugly American" who is insensitive to local customs and imposes his culture on others. Some expats will consciously avoid gringo hangouts and events to prevent these associations, and many will eventually start to limit their networks to special-interest groups such as for hobbies and charities.

Finally, transitioning one's social life away from other gringos and toward Ecuadorians is the real sign of having made a successful, authentic adjustment to expat life. I noticed that expats would frequently try to impress me with their cultural competence by telling me about their Ecuadorian friends, neighbors, or adopted families. Indeed, part of what makes Cuenca a good place to retire to is the romantic imaginaries expats have about Ecuadorians. In this view, Ecuadorians are extraordinarily family-oriented and big-hearted and always willing to bring strangers into their warm family circles. One often-repeated tall tale I heard was that Ecuadorian physicians are so civic minded that they regularly donate half of their time volunteering in public clinics. This is far from the truth. Most physicians have private offices where they see patients on a pay-as-you-go basis, sometimes successfully and sometimes less so, and they supplement that with work in the public sector, where they receive regular, mostly dependable salaries. Expats mistakenly assumed the public-sector work was volunteer labor rather than steady, remunerated employment.

The origins of this myth might lie in the very real experiences expats have with Ecuadorian physicians. As a group, they receive very attentive services from physicians, including long consultations, follow-up phone calls, and house calls. Having worked with poor and middle-class Ecuadorian women with lupus, I can confidently say that expats receive far better treatment from physicians than the average Ecuadorian does. One expat likened Ecuadorian doctors to the vintage television character Dr. Marcus Welby, a family physician who made house calls and knew all of his patients. In a more cynical light, the physicians' attentive treatment to expats has an instrumental purpose. The expat population is older, uses a good deal of medical services, usually pays up front, and provides a lucrative patient pool for physicians struggling to build successful private practices. A good recommendation from an expat posted on an online forum is a boon to business.

In the expat imaginary, however, Ecuadorians are helpful to expats and act as good neighbors and friends because they share old-fashioned family and cultural values of caring and trust. In discussing physicians, an expat said to me, "In terms of technology they are ten years behind, but in terms of doctor-patient relationships they are thirty years behind. That's a good thing!" These popularly circulating discourses reveal nostalgic images of the value of interpersonal and community caring performed by Ecuadorians, something perceived as lost in contemporary America, and they expose American tropes of privilege and paternalism. An expat characterized Cuenca in an interview by saying, "Women don't get raped here, children are not abused. It's like the Alabama of my youth!" The first two claims, about women and children, are patently untrue, and the last statement was no doubt a reference to his life in the Deep South as a white boy before the civil rights era.

Another wrote on his blog, "As I see Cuencanos make their way to the cabinas, the local barber or beautician, the little neighborhood family-owned stores and bakeries, or just watching neighborhood women gathering to chat; I see the kind of community that once existed in the United States" (Mola 2011).

This tendency of lifestyle migrants to see their destination localities as somehow outside of the stream of modern time and global change mirrors similar tendencies among tourists looking for what they believe are "authentic" experiences of difference (Benson 2011; Urry 1990). Lifestyle migrants and tourists often feel alienated from modern life and seek a sense of an authentic community in their destination locations, where they believe people share a set of values that are tinged with a nostalgia for an imagined past. Expats told me glowingly of their helpful Ecuadorian neighbors and adopted families and how important these relationships were to their sense of belonging in Cuenca. The expats were included in family dinners and holiday celebrations, and had someone to call if they needed help. I couldn't help noticing how this attitude contrasted with what rural-to-urban migrants told me all those years ago. They rarely trusted their city neighbors, did not form close bonds with them, and did not expect that the neighbors would look out for them.

Some real ironies emerge when listening to expats extol the virtues of Ecuadorian old-fashioned family values. The very fact that the expat has left the United States is a marker of their own inability or unwillingness to make similar relationships in the United States or at the very least a willingness to readily abandon those ties if they did have them. What then, beyond the cultural competence it displays to other expats, makes the

Ecuadorian family ties so appealing in ways that presumably such ties are not valued back home. The answers to this, I think, vary but rest mostly with the unequal power dynamics of these relations. Relatively speaking, American expats are privileged migrants who carry with them racialized social and economic advantages (Hayes 2015). They come to their relations with Ecuadorians as respected individuals because of their age, race, and economic status. The deficiencies in their Spanish language skills may contribute to these relations being constructed, at least partially, on mutual stereotypes of one another. The role of the rich, patrician American contrasts nicely to that of the attentive, caring, family-oriented Latino. Rather than being "put out to pasture," as one American metaphor has it, the retiree finds himself a respected new member of a social group in which he receives respect and attention almost entirely on his own terms.

Of course, like physicians, everyday Ecuadorians have their own reasons for including expats in their social circles, among them curiosity and caring but also more instrumental reasons. I know this not because I was told it by anyone but because I have been navigating these same dynamics for more than thirty years, reinforcing my conviction that expats and anthropologists share a good deal more than anthropologists would readily like to admit. A cultural cachet can come from befriending a white foreigner, a sure sign of a person's cosmopolitanism. In a place where whiteness and foreignness are admired, it is not surprising to see expats embraced by Ecuadorians. Then there are the economic advantages. Expats usually pay higher rent, willingly pay for help doing simple tasks, and are generous with gifts. And knowing someone with more money is useful. Borrowing money is common among friends and family in Ecuador, and expats who are brought into families are expected to engage in some form of reciprocity. Finally, expats have connections overseas that might be helpful to family members already in the United States or teenagers thinking about college abroad. In an increasingly global world, expats are good connections.

Achedemics and Gringos

In his 2015 article "'It Is Hard Being the Different One All the Time': Gringos and Racialized Identity in Cuenca, Ecuador," Hayes analyzes the white privilege experienced by North American expats in Cuenca. He explores the anxiety expats feel about their race in Cuenca but also how they often unknowingly reap the benefits of a postcolonial order that privileges whiteness. Hayes's article was picked up by the online gringo newsletter *Cuenca Highlife* and was shared broadly with the expat community (Higgins 2015). The article did not appear in its entirety on *Cuenca Highlife* but rather was condensed, and while it was overall a fair portrayal, the reprint lost some of the article's original complexity about the ambivalence and discomfort of some expats. The abridged version of Hayes's article was followed by a critique from an expat described as "an economist and a professor at three Midwestern universities" who commented that he thought the article was mostly accurate, but he accused Hayes of having "tunnel vision" in seeing race where it wasn't and in deploying perplexing academic terms like "racialized" (comment on Higgins 2015; comments have since been deleted).

The first public comments on the article appeared very quickly after it went live and set a reactionary tone that foreshadowed the bulk of the responses to Hayes's article. Relying on shared stereotypes within the conservative right that equate critiques of white privilege with an assault on democratic values, the first online commenter called Hayes a "typical socialist, liberal." He then invoked racial stereotypes meant, I think, to further discredit Hayes by linking him to Black people the writer did not trust to speak fairly about race and racial inequality. The commenter need not say more than drop their names and associate Hayes with them to discredit him: "He could be a press agent for Al Sharpton and Jesse Jackson. Or maybe run for Mayor of Baltimore." Another reader went directly after academics, calling them "achedemics," a term I had not seen before and could not find on Google, but I presume it refers to the "bleeding heart" cliché about academics. This commenter continued the substitution of class for race started by the first one when he called Hayes a "socialist."

> I believe that the article is a traditional achedemic effort that focuses on the traditional socialist mantras of inequality and how horrible it is to the downtrodden lower classes. If you look at the source you will see very likely a fairly well to do Canadian achedemic who bleeds orange and green and who has wasted his parent's money obtaining a more or less worthless degree in social sciences and perhaps liberal arts. (Comment on Higgins 2015)

By erasing Hayes's discussion of race and focusing on the generic but classist "downtrodden," accusations of socialism can be flung and Hayes insulted and maligned with impunity in a way that a defense of racism could not allow. By shifting the conversation from race to class, the commenters feel free to defend themselves and their positions. Class is something that can be debated; race, seemingly, is not. Several expats told me they left the United States because of the socialist president (Obama) but seemed blithely unaware that Ecuador's President Correa was an avowed "twenty-first-century" socialist. Many expats expressed enthusiastic support of Rafael Correa, seeing him as a guy who gets things done. I will not belabor the irony here.

The class argument emerged in a different way by a woman who wrote a response accusing Hayes of only interviewing rich expats who stick to themselves and do not mingle with the locals.

> You talked to the wrong people, with all due respect for your interest in this subject. I live in an apartment with a local family above me who owns the house and who has totally adopted me into their family. I spend more time with them than anybody else and have friends here who are in similar situations. This family is not wealthy by any means but very endearing people who share what they have with me and teach me about their cultural ways which is important to me. So in the future don't talk to "wealthy" Expats who do tend to flock together and cultivate only others of their financial status both with Expats and locals. Seek out more of the "real" people in Expats that live here, please. Then write a different article about what you have learned. I find this a biased article from the start. (Comment on Higgins 2015)

Unwittingly, this writer reflects exactly the dynamic that Hayes analyzes in his article. Ecuadorians, even "endearing" ones, usually do not adopt people into their families and "share what they have" willy-nilly. Generally the city is a place where neighbors are strangers and therefore suspect, and it is not usual practice for urban neighbors to form tight bonds and kin-like relations. Hayes was trying to critique exactly what the author claims as a counterargument: that the extension of quick friendship and family adoptions of expats by Ecuadorians are based in part on mutual racialized stereotypes of the helpful native and the relatively rich white expat.

The comments about Hayes's article reflect more than an attempt to refocus from race to class and replace the indefensible for the defensible; they point to the emotional delicacy of the privileged, "white fragility," as some have called it, that makes conversations about race excessively fraught for white Americans (DiAngelo 2019). Perhaps because of wishful thinking or denial or ignorance, well-meaning expats cannot see themselves as participants in a racially charged hierarchy, so it must be Hayes who is mistaken or prejudiced. He is the one who sees race and racism where it does not exist. He is the problem. One writer went after Hayes's relative youth by implying he is inexperienced in the world and saying that he wasted his parents' money and that "this youngster should get a 'D.'"

There were also responses that sought to turn the tables on exploitation; these commenters accused Hayes of exploiting them, the new "natives," or of ignoring the double standards that white people must endure simply because they are white.

> Hayes is a classic example of gringo imperialism. He goes to a foreign country, observes a few locals, pays them nothing for their time, exports his data back to his motherland, then turns it into highly profitable papers that denigrate the locals, while advancing his academic career and the possibility, perhaps it's too strong to say likelihood, that he will receive tenure. And since it is a far off place and no one will read his articles, no one will call him out on his superficial insights.

> Do the chinese in china-towns across the US bother themselves learning English, and "integrating"? Do the muslims and africans flooding into Europe currently care one iota about "social justice" and improving the living conditions of the countries that have so kindly allowed them asylum? (by the way why are all those so-called war refugees flocking to Europe in boats nearly all men of working age?)

> White people are like the world's punching bag. We just keep giving and giving. Then when we want to associate with our own kind, we're the horrible racists. And its always the leftist self-loathing whites who are first to throw their own people under the bus. Disgusting. (Comment on Higgins 2015)

The overwhelming majority of responses reflected the kind of deflection, anger, and defensiveness highlighted here, but to be fair, there were also reasoned responses that discussed the race-class hierarchy in Cuenca, the role of colonialism, and the uncomfortable privilege that some experience. A few of these commenters were Ecuadorians who had spent time in the United States and had both a distance near and a distance far view of their city. They wrote that they understood how charged conversations about race are in the United States and how assiduously *cuencanos* avoid talking about the subject.

Race is rarely discussed openly in Cuenca; typically it is subsumed into other discourses tinged with romanticism and nostalgia for the folkloric or "patrimonial," and racism is not often discussed as a social problem (Weismantel 2002). Most commonly, race is reframed to look like ethnicity, and that looks like folklore, and that is something to be proud of and commodified. Similarly, the expats who responded to Hayes's article deny race as a determinant of inequality and privilege and redefine it as a purely political or ideological position or argument they are confident they can address and dominate. Little more needs to be said beyond throwing out the term "socialist" to completely discredit the speaker. While this kind of deflection is not new or particularly creative, it does tell us something about the dynamics of conversations about race and racism. For these commenters, it was such a hot potato that the messenger had to be thoroughly delegitimized as a young, bleeding-heart Canadian who speaks gobbledygook and the message almost instantly repackaged as a socialist class project.

Shifting Views

While expats, anthropologists, and sociologists worry about themselves, each other, and sometimes the effects of their presence on the local community, both good and bad, Ecuadorians too have some opinions of the expats. In the early days, many saw them as a source of amusement if not bemusement. Watching gray-haired North Americans struggle to speak Spanish and find their way around town intrigued some Ecuadorians. "What are they doing here?" and "Isn't it great people like Cuenca so much?" were some of the first comments I heard about the expats. It was a source of some pride to think that a foreigner could like Cuenca so much that they would uproot themselves to live there. Other Ecuadorians pitied them. One woman who lived in a crime-riddled neighborhood talked about seeing an older man struggling to make himself understood in a store: "They wander around without knowing anything, poor things." Another thought it tragically sad and disturbing that anyone would choose to spend one's golden years away from one's own family and friends and possibly die among strangers in a foreign land. "There must be something empty in their souls," she told me, to be so unconnected to one's people and home. Others were more instrumental and saw them as sources of money. Doctors, fixers, drivers, translators, and real estate brokers popped up all over the place, creating whole cottage industries around providing services to expats. Ecuadorian elites complained that some expats were uncultured but others were welcome residents. They spoke favorably about the expats who supported the symphony, ate at restaurants, and contributed to charities.

Over time and as the effects of gringos became more pronounced, I started to hear more derogatory comments from Ecuadorians about expats.

Some complaints echoed the classic descriptions of the ugly American, that gringos were loud, demanding, and disdainful of the ways of others. Almost every merchant in town has a story to tell of an expat who became infuriated when he could not understand the merchant and yelled at and insulted them, invariably in English. Equally resented is the cheap expat, the one who looks for bargains everywhere, complains about negotiated prices, or consistently orders the least expensive dish on the menu. A restaurant owner told me, "Some of these gringos are low-class people without manners. They're not cultured people at all."

By 2016 the tourist industry was outraged about the economic impact of Airbnb rentals on hotel occupancy rates. Airbnb owners generally do not pay the taxes and fees that hotels do, and they can therefore offer cheaper accommodations. Hotel industry representatives argued for stricter rules and greater enforcement of tax laws. Ten years into the migration, everyone seemed to understand that the gringo's ability to pay more for housing, food, and goods raised prices for everyone. Real estate prices rose;[3] higher-end restaurants, often owned by gringos, replaced more modest local eateries; and as one man told me, because expats do not know how to bargain in the market, everyone is paying higher prices.

The first wave of expats was composed mostly of older North Americans; gradually the expat community in Cuenca seems to have shifted away from primarily North American retirees toward younger immigrants, many with families, from Europe. However, it is difficult to keep track of who comes and who goes and when. In recent years, several events have stained Ecuador's reputation as a retirement haven. An earthquake in 2016 that especially hit the coast revealed the insecurities of life in Ecuador. Houses were destroyed, sometimes because of shoddy workmanship; insurance claims were left unattended, and repairs to infrastructure were slow and difficult. Economic and political instability has intensified. As the price of oil continued to fall during the 2010s, Ecuador's economy constricted, and Correa's government relied heavily on Chinese loans to keep the economy afloat. When he left office, his successor, Lenin Moreno, pivoted away from China and toward the United States and the World Bank, and the country was encouraged once again to return to implementing neoliberal policies. In 2019 the country erupted in demonstrations and riots over new austerity measures, especially the removal of subsidies for cooking gas and gasoline. The streets of the *centro histórico* were filled with protesters attempting to impede business as usual, and events turned violent. Storefronts were damaged and small fires lit in the middle of the street. The protests dragged on as shortages of food and cooking gas became commonplace. Curfews were in place for more than a week as violence by protesters and the police mounted. Moreno eventually reinstated the subsidies, and calm was restored, but economic crisis was not averted. Unemployment, poverty, and crime increased, leading some expats feeling less secure there.

When Covid-19 reached Ecuador in 2020, Cuenca locked down before there was widespread community transmission, while Guayaquil made international news of dead bodies left in the streets as the health and sanitation departments became overloaded. It appears that some expats left Ecuador as the pandemic approached, and others stayed on through a strict quarantine that lasted months. Whether those who stayed would remain for the economic hardships to come has yet to be seen. A commenter in a Quito expat forum online wrote in June 2020,

> I've been here for 9 years now. The Covid thing does not really bother me, because everyone I know is taking all of the precautions necessary. What worries me is the economic situation. Unemployment and under employment is rampant. The country is broke, salaries of public employees have been reduced, crime is up. The government is corrupt, the politicians are robbing the country blind, the health system is on its last legs since it also is being robbed blind by the officials. Police corruption? Nothing new, still corrupt. Aside from that, Welcome to Ecuador. As for me, I'm starting to look for other places to relocate.[4]

The ability to pick up and move this migrant describes highlights how expat privilege operates. The writer knows that he has options, and it is his choice to stay or go and select his next destination. In contrast, Vicente and William in New York do not have those options. Their international and even local mobility is hampered if not prohibited by their Ecuadorian identities. They are undocumented immigrants from the global South, not documented expats from the North. These distinctions are not solely ones of word preferences but signal the presence of larger hegemonic practices about mobility, power, affluence, race, and class.

Soon the Tourists Will Have the Place to Themselves

In the eyes of Cuenca's city officials, the Plaza San Francisco in the heart of the *centro histórico* had long been a place in need of a major overhaul and, given the fierce objections of the feisty vendors who occupied the plaza, a prickly political problem. The plaza, just steps from the huge 10 de Agosto municipal food market, was a somewhat chaotic jumble of commercial activities that grew organically over time. In the heart of the plaza were makeshift and jerry-rigged market stalls where vendors of inexpensive shoes, rubber boots, blue jeans, and shiny pots and pans sold their wares to the rural and urban working classes. The stalls created a labyrinth of close alleyways where vendors sat on small wooden or plastic stools with their goods spilling around them, talking or looking at their phones as they waited for customers. Except for the presence of cell phones, the plaza in 2016 looked almost exactly as it had in 1989; until then, it was one of the few public sites in the city's central core that had escaped the renovation fever that began after the UNESCO World Heritage designation. That would not last long.

Despite the appearance of business as usual in early 2016, the fate of the plaza was being fiercely debated across multiple sectors of Cuencan society. Plans for renovations were being hatched, and the various interested parties, from architects to vendors, were mounting arguments to support one or another vision of the plaza of the future. The known history of the market and the UNESCO World Heritage discourse were employed by each group to make rhetorical and real claims about how the plaza space was to be reimagined and renovated. Two themes emerged from the long battle over the fate of the plaza, the patrimonial discourse had become ubiquitous by 2020, and governing elites were determined to make the city appealing to outsiders.

For several decades the plaza has been divided into distinct areas. The western half housed the haphazard stalls of the vendors of everyday items, with a small parking lot buffer that separated the vendors from the universally maligned public bathroom on the eastern end. That half is where day laborers congregated, smoked, and often started to drink when work did not come. Along the north side of the plaza, under the archway of a row of colonial-era buildings, was the Otavalan Indian market, where artisans offered weavings, blankets, and sweaters that mostly attracted tourists. The Otavalan vendors often dressed in traditional clothing, for women a long, black or dark-navy wrapped skirt with a woven belt and a flouncy, embroidered white blouse, and for men white pants and a dark fedora. The Otavalan were much more aggressive salespeople than the other vendors, and they constantly surveil the narrow passageway stacked with their goods, calling out to passersby, "What are you looking for? Sweaters? Blankets? Shirts?" Because the plaza is a block away from the picturesque flower market in one direction and a block away in the other direction from the busy municipal food market, it was a kind of transitional space between the ordered, regulated tourist center and the bustle and hustle of the peasant food marketplace.

The plaza has a long history, and the space was demarcated in the earliest mapped configurations of the city before the plaza itself was established (López Monsalve 2003). It is difficult to find historical descriptions of the plaza, yet in 2016 the elite of Cuenca were promoting a singular version of the plaza's history, one that then allowed them to defend a particular vision of its future. This version was written about in the newspaper *El Tiempo* and was then reprinted online by the Centro InterAmericano de Artesanías y Arte Popular (CIDAP), a government institution that promotes popular art and culture in Cuenca, thus giving the newspaper account official legitimacy. The article extensively quotes two local authorities, the director of the Instituto Nacional de Cultural Patrimonial (National Institute of Cultural Patrimony) and a well-respected historian at the Universidad de Cuenca. According to these authorities, the plaza was recognized as open space as early as 1563 but did not become fully public space until later in the colonial period, in the eighteenth century (CIDAP 2016). The colonial-era buildings surrounding the plaza are "quality," indicating that the plaza at one point was home to people with money. During the early republican period, the plaza was formally named the Plaza San Francisco for the church and convent that occupy the southern side, and it was the site of varied public functions, including the executions of those deemed traitors in Ecuador's war of independence from Spain.

By the early nineteenth century, the main plaza in town, two blocks away, was cleared of itinerant vendors who then settled in the Plaza San Francisco, and the plaza became a commercial space known especially for the selling of meat and produce. However, the article points out, and this is important to the city's narrative, the food vendors in the plaza were historically transitory occupants, coming only on market days and special holidays. They did not establish a permanent, daily presence in the square. The plaza was otherwise an open space where occasional public festivals and celebrations could be held. "It was not just a market . . . but a Plaza!" one of the authorities explains (in CIDAP 2016). This is a crucial distinction for city planners who argue that renovations would recoup the true historical uses and purpose of the plaza. This purpose, they argue, had been hijacked by the unregulated commercial vendors who came to the plaza in the 1950s after the transitory meat and vegetable vendors were permanently relocated to the newly opened 10 de Agosto municipal food market just steps away (*Revista Avance* 2016). The article in *El Tiempo* reports that the city "lost control" over the building of kiosks on the plaza in the early 1950s under a weak municipal government (CIDAP 2016).

In addition to historians and administrators, the *El Tiempo* article quotes extensively from interviews with longtime local residents and merchants. An elderly storeowner on the plaza, Flor María Salazar, recalls the plaza of her youth.

> Donde usted ve esas casetas horribles de lata (sobre la Presidente Córdova), había unas cuatro o seis casetas de madera donde se vendía carne. . . . Junto a esos puestos estaba una señora de apellido Maruri, que vendía frutas; era la típica chola cuencana: trabajadora, seria, honesta. . . . Era ejemplar la señora.
>
> Cuando mis cuatro hijos eran pequeños jugaban allí con los niños del barrio. . . . Era una cholería infernal de muchachos jugando en bicicleta, pateando la pelota; era una plaza segura porque era completamente despejada. Luego se fue invadiendo de personas y haciéndose peligrosa. (In CIDAP 2016)

> (Where you see those horrible metal kiosks there were four or six kiosks of wood where they sold meat. Near these was one of a woman named Maruri, who sold fruits; she was a typical *chola cuencana*: hardworking, serious, honest. . . . She was exemplary.
>
> When my four children were little they played here with the children of the neighborhood. . . . It was an infernal ruckus of children playing

on bicycles, kicking a ball; it was secure plaza because it was completely open. Later it was invaded by people and it became dangerous.)

There is plenty of elite discourse to be parsed here, such as the romantic description of the long-lost virtues of the historical, hardworking *chola cuencana* and the far less romantic "invasion" of working-class vendors. Of greater interest, though, is the clear intent to present a consistent narrative that the plaza was and therefore should be an open space. Such spaces are purportedly safer and resonate with the historical memories of particular classes.

One of the first redesigns for the plaza proposed by the city and the university architects in 2013 consigned the vendors of commercial products whose permanent kiosks occupied the open market square to an underground mall out of sight. The Otavalan merchants, more folkloric and therefore a more desirable presence, would be relocated to a nearby renovated building, and they too would be out of the open air. The plaza would then be a clean, wide-open space where, in videos of the architectural plans posted on YouTube, diners could sit at outdoor cafés, take in the sun on benches set out around the periphery, and enjoy the central fountain. That plan was roundly and loudly decried by the vendors, who suspected all along that the city's intentions were to get rid of them. In the end, that plan was also rejected by UNESCO because the underground shopping space, it was feared, would compromise existing historical structures.

In 2016, I attended an open public forum about the latest iteration of the design. That proposal showed portable kiosks that vendors would have to take down every evening and reassemble every morning. The meeting was held in the early evening in an auditorium at the Universidad de Cuenca and convened by faculty members who had worked on the architectural plans and conducted social research among the users of the space. The architects and the sociologist sat on the dais, and perhaps in a move to demonstrate their populist inclinations, they were in surprisingly casual wear, blue jeans and open-collared shirts. The presenters began the meeting by showing a video of the latest plans, and because the video had been online for weeks in advance, it seemed like many people in the crowd of about seventy-five people had seen it before. Several people in the audience groaned when the video started and shook their heads dejectedly. The design had a clear pedestrian-only walkway from the flower market to the large open plaza, with a fountain in the middle, several sidewalk cafés, and portable wooden kiosks for vendors. The computerized design scheme showed figures walking diagonally across the space, something that was not then feasible because of the vendors' stalls. Perhaps as a consequence of the computer software used, the vast majority of human figures that animated the design simulation were clearly white and dressed in stylish Euro-American clothing, confirming local suspicions that the intent of the architects was to attract a different sort of crowd than the ones that occupied the plaza. Later, the designs on YouTube inserted a few nonmoving figures of *cholas*.

At the forum the architects spoke first and discussed the various changes they made over time and how the comments of present users and the architects' own understandings of the "universal historical value" of the plaza guided their work. They argued that the space should be "multifunctional" in ways that it had not been in decades; in particular, they wanted the space to be capable of hosting public festivals as it did before the vendors took over the plaza in the 1950s and built permanent stalls. From their perspective, the new design accommodated the vendors, albeit in portable kiosks, but more importantly, the design would return the plaza to mixed uses in keeping with the values of a World Heritage Site. Borrowing the rhetoric of UNESCO that those sites reflect "universal human values," the speakers stressed the importance of "democratic values" in shaping how the plaza was designed and how it was to be used in the future (Long and Labadi 2010). They emphasized that the community as a whole needs to be accommodated in the design and that space and how it is used reflect a city's values. The architects insisted that their working principle was that open spaces reflect and create democratic "character."

The first public comments at the meeting came from the leader of the Otavalan merchants collective, wearing traditional pants, long braid, and poncho; he made clear from his opening words that their group was distinctive from the commercial vendors. He emphasized that artisan production is part of Ecuador's ancient cultural patrimony and that the Otavalan's work represented more than petty commerce because artisan work "keeps alive Ecuador's Indigenous past." He further stated that to be an artisan means the worker "creates with his hands" and sells in the same space, something the new design did not accommodate, as it had no obvious space for workshops.[1] The new plaza, then, would be a threat to centuries-old Indigenous artisan lifeways and a cultural loss for everyone. He admitted that the plaza was crowded and that everyone would like to see it cleaned up, especially the bathrooms, but the design presented that evening would result in further hardships to the artisan way of life in Ecuador and a clear break from the stated municipal goals of promoting cultural patrimony.[2]

Dressed in a simple jacket and shirt, the leader of the commercial vendors union was next to speak. An articulate and practiced public speaker, he represented the group that was most opposed to mobile kiosks and probably had the least trust in the city's intentions. This is the group frequently portrayed as "illegitimate" users of the central plaza space since their kiosks were built without the city's approval. These are vendors of everyday commercial products and the ones the city planned to "throw away like garbage," a vendor told me, in a space underground. Their leader argued that the mobile structures would mean much more work for vendors, who would have to set them up every morning and take them down every night. He pointed out that there was no clear storage plan but also, much more ominously, the very mobility of portable kiosks signaled a less-than-permanent future for the vendors. And that, he said, would be an erasure of a part of the city's historical patrimony. He continued by arguing that the vendors had more than thirty years' presence in the Plaza San Francisco and that the *casetas* (stands) they had built represented their history as laborers and providers for their families. He argued that the new design would negate their historical contributions to the city's development and make them only temporary actors whose place there can be challenged at a moment's notice. Whatever plan is adopted, he continued, must ensure the livelihoods of the vendors. He said the right to work is guaranteed in the Ecuadorian constitution, and the plaza design must be responsive to the needs of the vendors to feed their families. The renovation of the 9 de Octubre market completed five years earlier resulted in vendors losing space, and he said commercial vendors of Plaza San Francisco had little trust that the architects or the city would do right by them and guarantee them a place to work.

The next speaker was a small, slim, elderly man in an ill-fitting suit who was the leader of the taxi cooperative whose designated stand was located along the southern side of the plaza. Even though there had been several designs by this point and a series of social impact studies, a taxi stand was still missing from the design shown that evening. Speaking in a calm and dignified manner, the speaker noted the absence of a taxi stand in every design and asked the group on the dais why they consistently ignored the presence and work of the *taxistas* for whom the plaza was their dedicated stand. "Why is our cooperative left out of all the plans?" he asked. "We too make our living on that plaza!" Similar to those who came before him, the taxi leader also made his claim for inclusion by pointing out the historical significance of his cooperative. "Our union is one of the oldest taxi cooperatives in the city," he said by way of establishing the legitimacy of his concerns. "Why are we not in the plans? Where are we supposed to go? What will happen to us?" he asked simply and plaintively.

The biggest audience response of the evening came when a fairly prominent local businessman whose office was on the plaza got up to speak. A big man with the speaking cadence of a preacher, he was by far the most skilled public speaker, and his confident voice filled the auditorium. Acknowledging again that everyone wanted the plaza cleaned and restored, he pointed out that the plan for a supposedly democratic open space did not make much sense, and the outdoor cafés the models depicted were an aspirational rather than reasonable prediction of the evolution of that space. Speaking directly to the architects several times, he repeated the phrase "Be realistic," and each time he did, the attendees cheered and nodded. "Lights won't get rid of crime," he argued. "Just look at the 9 de Octubre," where crime is worse than before the renovations. He accused the architects of not understanding "our reality," asking, "Do you really think that changing the space will change how people come to use it?" His point was a good one. The plaza is just one block from the flower market and the cathedral, both clean and bright tourist sites, and it is equally close to one of the busiest bus interchanges in the city and the biggest and smelliest municipal market. Trucks and goods and shoppers and vendors crowd the streets and the surrounding sidewalks leading to the 10 de Agosto market. Where and how was all that activity to be controlled and managed so the more genteel version of the plaza could emerge? Who would lose what when all was said and done? The leader of the market women's union of the 9 de Octubre market, one of the last to speak that evening, had an answer: the vendors would lose. The renovation of that market, she explained, resulted in smaller stalls, no better controls over unregulated itinerant vendors who don't pay for the right to sell there, a loss of parking space, and a sustained downturn in business because the market closed for months on end and customers went elsewhere. "Don't believe the city" was her best and last advice.

I learned at the forum that fifteen years of being declared a UNESCO World Heritage Site left a mark on public discourse; nearly all the speakers at the event framed their positions, and thus the legitimacy of their arguments, by evoking a historical narrative. The discourses about the value of patrimony had filtered down to all citizens, and everyone seemed to understand that any claim to the future of the plaza had to be phrased in historical terms if it was not to be wholly discounted. What was also apparent was the distrust and frustration vendors and those who lived and worked on the Plaza had toward the city and the official vision of its future. Their skepticism was well founded. Small concessions to vendors were made, in the end, and no surprise to anyone, the elite vision of an open-air plaza prevailed.

The struggle over the fate of the Plaza San Francisco had been long and wearying, and by the end of 2016 a plan was agreed upon between vendors and the city that provided permanent stalls ringing the periphery of the plaza. Construction began in early 2017 after vendors were removed from the plaza and given space along several nearby side streets, and it continued until March 2019, when the plaza was reopened. The plaza is now mostly open space. In the center is a fountain that seldom has water flowing. On the east end, in a nod to the touristy aspirations of the architects, the city's name is spelled out in large, lowercase, standing letters. It is hard to say for sure if the plaza is appealing to tourists. In 2021 it had a 3.5 rating on Tripadvisor, with one reviewer writing, "It's big but uninspiring. A bunch of vendors selling chintzy souvenirs just did not appeal to us. The main square one block over is way better and livelier. Have your picture taken in front of the big red letters spelling Cuenca and move on."[3]

Vendors now ring the periphery of the Plaza San Francisco, but there are far fewer than before, and their stalls are much smaller. The city and the vendors had difficulty agreeing on the costs that vendors have to pay for their new stalls and how long they could take to pay in installments; city officials wanted a two-year window, and vendors asked for six years. The total cost to a vendor to purchase a stall is more than $4,000. Many could not afford to purchase a kiosk and therefore did not return. Months after the plaza reopened, numerous stalls remained unoccupied, and vendors complained of more crime and more itinerant workers there than before (*El Mercurio* 2019). On the occasion of the plaza's reopening in January 2019, an online news article quoted a vendor's prediction of what would come: "Even without the plan, most of this will be gone in a generation. People will be buying what I sell in a department store instead of the market. . . . Soon, the tourists will have the place to themselves" (in Higgins 2019).

CHAPTER 6

Thinking about Endings

One of my intentions for this book was to spend a month or two in Ecuador in the summer of 2020 so I could write about the Venezuelan refugees in Cuenca. Since the acceleration of the political and economic unrest in Venezuela in 2015, Venezuelans have been leaving their country en masse. Many of them have worked their way to Cuenca, where they find a somewhat ambivalent welcome.[1] For several years I listened as Ecuadorians described their impressions of Venezuelans, and while some took real pity for their plight, others wanted nothing to do with them and wished that they would stop taxing the local capacities to serve the indigent and needy. Like most xenophobic stereotypes, I heard very contrary descriptions of Venezuelans. Some said they were uncouth and uncultured and prone to criminal activity; others said they were sure Venezuelans were arrogant and looked down their noses at their humble Ecuadorian hosts. My plan for 2020 was to look beyond these stereotypes and probe more deeply into the experiences of Venezuelans in Cuenca. I was especially interested in how their lives as refugees may contrast with those of North American expats. Then, of course, the Covid-19 pandemic struck the world, and my travel plans were suspended. Like so much else in life in 2020, my trip to Cuenca to do fieldwork was cancelled, and I had to figure out a different way to do my work.

When I started the first chapter of this book, years before the pandemic, I thought about the evolving nature of global communication and the ways technology has changed what I do. Until 2020, technology had mostly enhanced my in-person ethnography, keeping me up to date with people and events between visits to Cuenca or adding a textual dimension to the analytic work I might be doing. I found online resources particularly useful for understanding the expat experiences, as expats are so thoroughly engaged online. The internet is a vital part of their experiences with Cuenca and each other; it catalyzed expats' migration. However, I didn't see technology in any medium as the only means by which I might come to know about something important happening in the lives of the people I know. I have always valued personal contact. During the pandemic, the incremental shifts that we were all making to include different, digital, and technological ways of understanding our field sites suddenly became the only game in town.

As a nation, Ecuador received considerable press early in the pandemic, mostly because of the poor response to it in Guayaquil. Pictures of crowded hospitals, of dead bodies wrapped in plastic lying on the sidewalks, and of mass graves appeared in international news outlets. Cuenca, like most of the country, went into a quarantine, a stricter one than most American cities endured. Curfews limited the times people could be out of their homes to a few hours a day; cars could only be on the streets according to a scheduled rotation based on license plate numbers; fines were imposed for not wearing a mask; and schools, businesses, and all public transportation were closed down. As happened in many places around the world, the curve was flattened in a few weeks and the number of cases fell. Covid spread did not get as bad in Cuenca as it did in Guayaquil, the epicenter of the outbreak in Ecuador, and local hospitals were generally able to keep up with the caseloads as they waxed and waned over the course of the pandemic.[2] In contrast to the United States, Ecuadorians generally embraced the vaccines when they came, mostly from China, and about 80 percent of *cuencanos* were vaccinated by September 2021. The Delta variant that surged in parts of the United States did not take hold in vaccinated Ecuador, and by the fall of 2021, life was returning to normal.

It is hard to say what "normal" is now. The economic repercussions of Covid-19 have been brutal. Early in the pandemic, as the global economy ground to a halt, oil prices plummeted, depleting Ecuadorian government coffers. With little or no government assistance, businesses closed all over town, and some predict that a significant number will stay that way. Several private schools announced that they cannot reopen, no doubt further taxing the public school system. The tourist industry collapsed, and some hotels have been permanently shuttered. It might take some time before many travelers are confident enough to board airplanes and tourism returns to previous levels. Because of the economic fallout from the loss of tourism and the global economic downturn, the Ecuadorian government began a series of austerity measures a few weeks into the pandemic that remained in place for more than a year. Public hospitals and universities had their budgets slashed as the government tried to rein in spending. Alejandra wrote to me how upset she was when most of her coworkers at the hospital were fired or laid off. "There are parents with children to feed!" she lamented. University students and Indigenous groups protested the cuts, but to no avail. Crime rates have been rising, and tens of thousands of unemployed Ecuadorians made the decision to leave their country and head for the US-Mexico border. Long-term predictions for Ecuador are not optimistic, and the next few years will undoubtedly be difficult.

I kept in touch with those I know in Ecuador and New York during the pandemic through email, phone calls, WhatsApp, and videoconferencing. Not surprisingly, I found their experiences varied; some lost their jobs, some worked from home, and some were essential workers who put themselves at risk every day. Some got sick, but no one I know died. Financial hardship hit everyone; unemployed and underemployed migrants in New York stopped sending remittances, and in Cuenca, family members who were still employed found they were asked to share their earnings among a larger group of needy kin. I offer here two early Covid-19 stories, one from Will in New York and a much shorter email about life in Cuenca during lockdowns. The writer of the second is Rosa's youngest son, Billy, then twenty-seven years old.

Mapping the Pandemic

William: New York and Boston

On March 21, 2020, a Saturday, Will traveled by bus from his home in Manhattan to Boston to visit his brother and spend some quality time during the shutdown with his nieces and nephews. He is a doting uncle. New York State's stay-at-home order would go into effect the next day, March 22, and Will wanted to spend that time with his family, not alone in his Manhattan apartment. He thought the shutdown would last a couple of weeks at most. The bus ride was uneventful, and no one was wearing masks, yet. When he arrived in Boston, he spent the evening with his family, relaxing and playing with his nephews and niece. The next day, Sunday, the family was preparing to have a barbeque with a few friends, and Will was glad to be at his brother's house, surrounded by the warmth of his family. Will loves children; he is the fun uncle, the one who is up for all childish shenanigans.

Will was enjoying the day when around 4 p.m., out of nowhere, he began to feel ill. His head felt like it had been "cracked open," he said;

his body ached and he had a fever and felt incredibly weak. "One minute I was fine, and the next my head was exploding and I was sweating," he recalled. Worried that it was Covid-19, his brother took him that night to the hospital to be tested. This was still early in the pandemic when tests were scarce, and it took several days to get the results. Will was tested, told it was probable that he had Covid-19, was sent home with Tylenol to control the fever, and was told to quarantine himself. The next two days were hellish. He isolated himself in his nephew's bedroom, fearful to leave it for any reason. He urinated in a bottle that he took to the bathroom in the middle of the night when no one was around, wiping everything he touched. It still was not known that Covid-19 is not readily transmitted by touching surfaces. His family left food outside his door, but he had no appetite and ate very little. Even with the Tylenol, his fever raged continuously at 103; he vomited what little food he tried to eat, and then he started to have difficulties breathing. He felt a sharp pain in his lungs when he took a breath.

On Tuesday, Will's breathing was worse. He felt as if he couldn't catch his breath, and his brother took him back to the hospital. After hearing about the crowded conditions in the hospitals in New York, he was surprised to find this Boston hospital calm and the care attentive. He was placed on an IV for dehydration and nutrition and given a chest X-ray. He spent the whole day at the hospital, and in the early evening he was informed that he tested positive for Covid-19 and had pneumonia. No doubt concerned about keeping beds open for patients in more dire conditions, Will was given a course of antibiotics for the pneumonia and told to go home. The doctor warned him that if he did not improve with the antibiotics in six days, he probably would not recover, and he should prepare for his condition to get much worse. Will resisted going back to his brother's home; he did not want to infect anyone in the family, especially the children. He argued with the doctor, who insisted he be released only to his brother. He could not afford to go to a hotel for two weeks, and when he said he would return to New York by bus, the hospital staff threatened to call the police. He even considered going to a homeless shelter, but that was out of the question given the state of his health. He had no choice but to call his brother and return to his home. "I felt terrible going back to his house and putting everyone at risk," he said, but there was no other obvious option, and he was too sick to think.

The next days alone in his room were harrowing. His body ached from head to toe; he said he felt like he had "run a marathon for two weeks straight." He had intense migraine headaches and was unable to keep food and even some liquids down. His fever stayed between 102 and 103 degrees during the day and spiked higher at night. Night and day collapsed in a blur of fever, soaked sheets, chills, and bad dreams. All the while, Will had the doctor's words in mind. If he was still this sick after six days, would he die from this? The fifth day was the worst. His temperature soared to 104, his lungs ached with every breath, and he could not sleep or rest that night. At one point, he thought that he needed to go to the hospital, but he did not want to risk exposing his brother and his family again. He was feverish all night long, his bed a pool of sweat, his skin yellow and drained of life. Finally, around 10 a.m. of the sixth day, he fell asleep and slept until almost 5 p.m. When he awoke on the morning of the seventh day in his soaking-wet bed, he took his temperature. It was 98.6. "Gracias a Dios," he exclaimed. He started to feel better that day and ate a bit of soup his sister-in-law left outside his door. For three days he improved but then had a mild relapse. He was feverish but not nearly as badly as before, and he stayed in his room for another week until he felt stronger. He called his distraught mother every day to let her know he was improving, and he passed the time on his phone looking at videos and Facebook and talking to his young nephew through the door.

Altogether, Will spent more than three weeks in that room. By the end of the third week, he started to leave his room when everyone was asleep; he showered and found food, scurrying back to his room "like a mouse" to eat. He obsessively wiped every surface he touched. When he was strong enough, he packed his bag, cleaned his room with disinfectant, and left the house, waving to everyone peering out from the window. He took a bus back to New York. Thin to begin with, Will lost almost twenty-five pounds in three weeks. Months later, he still had daily headaches and kept a giant bottle of Tylenol on hand. Will was not charged at the hospital, and three months later, he still had not been sent a bill. He could not figure that one out, but he is not asking any questions, either.

In May and June, Will watched the Black Lives Matter protests outside of his apartment in Chelsea, feeling too weak and vulnerable to join the crowds in the street. He said he believes in the cause but was dismayed when he saw that a small, humble bodega like the kind he grew up around that sells soda and cigarettes was looted and damaged one night. Will went back to work in the restaurant, which was serving take-out only then, and was making enough to keep himself together until things returned to normal. He has been cooking at home, something he enjoys doing, trying new recipes and perfecting old ones. He went back on Facebook posting uplifting messages like "Stop complaining! Life is for the brave, not the cowardly" and "Whatever you do in life, make sure it makes you happy!" After his illness, these aphorisms seem even more touching. He was hoping his mother could come visit in 2021.

Billy: Cuenca

Billy is the youngest child in the Quitasaca family. He was the baby who was born on the apartment floor, with only twelve-year-old Alejandra in attendance. Billy is also the child whose infancy was imprinted by his mother's postpartum depression and withdrawal from him and everything else. By the time he was two years old, his oldest brother left for the United States, and when Billy was six, his father did too, creating a gaping emptiness in the household that remained unfilled for years. It was not long afterward, in 2002, that his mother became sick and began a long medical odyssey and frightful decline that culminated in the diagnosis of lupus. She was ill for almost a year and close to death on several occasions. Then, in 2004, when he was eleven years old, heart-wrenching tragedy struck the family when Cecilia, Billy's sixteen-year-old sister and most constant playmate growing up, was diagnosed with lupus and died from complications of the disease. She had stopped taking her medications, unbeknown to anyone in her family because she could not tolerate the side effects. The family was devastated by her death, and Rosa actively mourned her daughter for many years.

Billy grew up a quiet, introspective person, used to finding his own ways to fill time. Lost in the emotional turmoil of so many distressing family events, he mostly tried not to cause trouble to anyone. When he was a teenager I considered him the most inscrutable Quitasaca because it was difficult to keep up a conversation with him. It wasn't that he wasn't thoughtful; it was that he didn't think anyone was much interested in his thoughts. In college he studied a variety of subjects and was especially taken with language, literature, and history. Everyone worried about what sort of job he could get with a degree in those fields, and he let himself be swayed into studying college-level automotive mechanics instead. He did not especially like it, but his brother–in–law said he might be able to help Billy get a job, and that was of the utmost importance.

In reflecting on ethnographic responsibility, I have come to understand that what we think we might owe people could differ from what they might think we owe them. By "owe" I mean not only material objects or money but also care and even more intangibly, a kind of comprehension. A few years ago, Billy was occasionally snappish with me, recasting what I said in the coldest, not warmest light. I asked him about this, and he claimed that he just has a crude sense of humor and that I should not take anything he said to heart. I do, though. I can see reasons that he might resent me, even if he does not know he does. My family and I sweep into his life every couple of years, offering a glimpse of a different world but never fulfilling the promise of one. Especially when he was young, we took him to movies, out for pizza, and to soccer games. And then we left. Our mobility and affluence stood in stark contrast to his own life, which as a child was filled with such loss and sorrow. While it is nice to think we gave a grave little boy some fun memories, I also worry that in the end we left him more rather than less unsettled.

Billy is, however, doing all right. He graduated from college and was working until the pandemic, when he, like so many others, was laid off. He liked his job and has hopes of returning to it one day. In his free time, Billy has continued to be a student of the arts. When the internet is working at his house, when they have been able to pay the bill, he sits alone in his room listening to classical music on YouTube and dabbling in photography and short-story writing. He has a lovely girlfriend who is sharp and insightful and shares his interests in art. They enjoy taking photographs at dawn's first light when the city is still asleep. We share YouTube videos of music we especially like. He is by far the most politically astute Quitasaca, decrying Latin American dictatorships, global inequality, and mindless consumerism. He is, in short, an interested and interesting man of the world.

The Covid-19 pandemic made many of us think about time differently, at least for awhile. For me, it created a nostalgia for life before the pandemic, and it has made thinking about the future a dicey proposition. During lockdowns I noticed each day more, and the passage of time was simultaneously quickened and lengthened. We have learned to wait and defer activities and pleasures we were accustomed to taking on the spot, and it could very well be that aspects of our lives will be permanently reshaped. Early in the pandemic, Billy sent me an email that I found so evocative of what happened to time for so many of us in the early days of lockdown and other restrictions, a monotonous sameness of the days at home, punctuated with intermittent jolts of news of a deathly and chaotic reality.

April 3, 2020
Querida Anita,

It has been a long time since we talked and so much has happened; the life we are living now seems surreal. When I was small I hoped for something distinctive in my life and that I would not simply complete the irrevocable cycle. Today is now 16 days that we are in the house and everything is completely tranquil. The radio plays softly, the dog lies on the doormat, Doña Rosa looks after her plants, and to distract himself, my father hammers something. Our life seems stopped. Our life is far from all of the pain that is happening just a few kilometers away, inside our own borders. It doesn't matter that we have a family member on the front lines of the disaster, we are far from all of that.

At night, we watch the news and we see people crying, we worry that we are alone . . . but we feel this only at night. In the morning the dog returns to the mat, my mother returns to look at her plants, and the music softly plays, returning us to our tranquility. We are lucky. Each week my mother talks to my brother about herbs for pain and the dimensions of this tragedy and how it will end and the health of everyone in the family. Just like the week before.

I watch the news and listen to the hilarious Trump, but it loses all humor when he talks about how to deal with this disaster. What will happen to Vicente? What will happen to the other migrants like him? What will happen to Anita?

Working to an End

I always find writing endings for my ethnographic work difficult. Endings put a stop to something. In this case, a book, and intentionally or not, a book ending suggests that a story is complete. Does that mean that what continues does not matter? Is this really the end of the story? Of course, it is not. The place and people described here endure, and this ending, like most, is arbitrary. There will always be something else happening that I think I should watch unfold. Most ethnographers end their studies because they run out of money, or they think they have enough to contribute to the literature. Sometimes we run out of time, or as in this case, I do not think I can wait out time. Covid-19 may limit safe travel for some time yet, and while documenting Venezuelans in Cuenca, the long-term effects of the pandemic, or climate change is compelling, at a certain point one has to call "Time!" as I am doing now.

I have attempted here to be attentive to time and what accrues over time and what it means for the anthropological process, for what happens in the world and in people's lives. This has not been a straightforward story, arguing for clear losses or gains or even consistent patterns revealed through an examination of time's inexorable march. The story, like all honest ones, is more complicated, and the years mark and are marked in countless ways and configurations. Time is archived in our bodies, so I have shown how a young female fieldworker is vulnerable in ways that an older woman is not, how changing from two braids and a *pollera* to a ponytail and jeans destabilizes anthropological interpretations, calms a son's complaints, and contributes to the extinction of a cultural icon, and how youthful dreams are crushed under the weight of a present reality, as a middle-age man's belly expands while he fights loneliness and depression in a Long Island basement. Time resonates in our relationships that deepen and ease with the years as affection grows and memories accrue, but memories also weigh on the conscience. What might I have inadvertently or carelessly wrought by slipping in and out of people's lives? Time apart has separated couples and families; time studying created a physician out of a dark-skinned girl with an Indian name; and time passing has led to cultural shifts that allow a gay man to be returned to the heart center of his family.

We often track changes over time by talking about generations under the assumption that one age group differs from another in ideas, tendencies, and dispositions. The assumption is that larger social, cultural, economic, and political changes resonate with different age groups in different ways. I've done some of that here by watching lives unfold over generations and by suggesting that women who came of age in the 1990s are distinct from their mothers in some ways. I think younger women generally have more agency to make decisions for themselves than their mothers did. I am less confident in assigning the causes for this. Was it urban life in general? Better education and employment opportunities? Changes in the legal and political climate? Access to technology? The trickle-down effects of global and local cultural shifts? Transnational migration and forced separation? Of course, the answer is yes to all of these and more. Individual women have made bold choices for themselves and their families, but the changing times have allowed them options their mothers never had. And generations also influence one another. Blanca came around to accepting Will in part because her (grand)daughter would not have it any other way. Jessica might have followed through and had a child out of wedlock if her mother had not made it seem so impossible. It cuts both ways.

The accrual of time has chipped away at the entrenched race/class hierarchy in Cuenca in a slow and steady sort of way that makes conversations about ethnic or cultural difference more difficult. One thing builds on another until something budges. Elite families have a hard time finding maids these days, as poor girls from the city and country choose to go to school on the remittances their parents and brothers send. Rich children now rub elbows in school and college with those who might have, in an earlier generation, been mopping their families' kitchen floors. This limited but important de facto desegregation has altered some things. A well-educated colleague told me that the children of elites are now marrying non-elites whom they meet in school, much to the consternation of their parents. These are the calibrations that accrue over the course of lifetimes and that, taken as a whole and seen from a distance, have moved the needle some.

Lives unfold in complicated ways and are filled with losses and victories, hard work, missed opportunities, and maybe tragic mistakes. How does one account for what those individual experiences might mean in the bigger picture? So, yes, while the transnational migration and remittances of Ecuadorians has probably helped to shift the oppressive class dynamics in Cuenca a bit, that does not necessarily mean very much to the migrant men and women living in New York. Many have gone from being hopeful, future-oriented young people, excited about the possibilities of the unknown, to more subdued middle-age adults who squint at the future skeptically when they engage with it at all. To them, migration has meant adventure, separation, personal growth, liberation, relentless labor, and agonizing loneliness, but where their odysseys will end is not at all clear. Old age and undocumented status are not gentle companions, but the options are not good. It is one thing to admit to yourself that your youthful dreams went bust and quite another to take that reality back to your childhood hometown all these years later.

The time-space compression of globalization has led to all sorts of migrations in and out of Cuenca and sped up the pace of the flows of information and culture sharing. Yet so often we linger on frail and faulty notions of the past. Marta knows Ecuador has changed since she left more than twenty years ago; she sees pictures and talks to people, but in her day-to-day imagination, Cuenca is, for better or worse, exactly as it was the day she left. There is a fine line between memories and nostalgia, and most of us probably dabble in both. It is common to feel nostalgia, perhaps for family rituals, a particular time in life, or an idealized image of the past when things were somehow better. Nostalgia drives expats to Cuenca as they long for a different time, a simpler one they see reflected in the perceived slower pace and community values of Ecuadorians. These imaginaries are steeped in narratives that reveal a world that is redolent with uncontested white privilege. The elites of Cuenca share this vision with the expats. Both, it seems, have a sense that something important—cultural capital, social prestige, economic power—has been lost over the years, and they are in search of a recovery. The Virgin of Cajas narrative was an attempt to shape sentiments backward in 1989, and the UNESCO World Heritage Site designation, an elitist project if there ever was one, did so in 1999. The heritage designation was self-consciously retrospective, stopping the clock and pausing to linger nostalgically in the vestiges of colonialism to find a path to the future.

I have attempted to work with notes and remembrances and fought against slipping into nostalgia, that bittersweet longing for a romanticized real or imagined past. It hasn't always been easy, and when I do I find myself wafting into nostalgia, I usually encounter something instructive there. My nostalgic vision of Cuenca, for example, does not include the expats and the changes they brought. And no doubt many anthropologists have similar feelings about their field sites. David Berliner calls the intensity of ethnography a "cauldron of endonostalgia," a nostalgia that revolves around one's own experiences in the field (2020, 10). It is difficult to avoid endonostalgia, and I find myself cringing when Ecuadorians speak English to me in shops and restaurants, and I am concerned about the ways the gringo presence has contributed to gentrification. In pursuit of that lost "endo" time, I stubbornly go to the one remaining coffee shop in town that serves coffee made from a concentrated essence, as coffee was made in the old days. That coffee, by the way, is lousy. It always was.

This nostalgia for a less touristified Cuenca is not shared by most working-class and poor *cuencanos* I know. They express fond remembrances of earlier times and often wax eloquent about the foods they enjoyed—the eggs from the countryside or the fruit from the increasingly rare capuli cherry tree—and they also find the new stores, restaurants, and coffee shops exciting and elegant. They love them. Cuenca is now cosmopolitan, and by extension, they must be too. Indeed, the nostalgia that I or the expats or the elite have for the irretrievable past is, as Renato Rosaldo (1989) argues, a sentiment fabricated from relations of domination, as notions of our ideal replace consideration of the more painful and unsettled past of so many others. Alejandra may wish that she knew her grandmother better, and she has fond memories of going to her house as a youngster, yet she has no nostalgia for her own childhood and shudders at the life her grandmother endured. The past offers her no shelter from the present. For many Ecuadorians, thinking about the past, 1989, for example, means remembering a time when they likely were poorer, hungrier, and more marginalized.

Tourism and gentrification organized and packaged "others" in Cuenca so that what is allowed in the public space fits a particular iteration of refined history that the UNESCO designation aimed to preserve and market. The Plaza San Francisco market vendors compete with the Otavalan artisans for space and livelihood in a redesigned plaza meant to appeal to visitors and expats, with its outdoor cafés and open, clean appearance. Few who live in Cuenca might be interested in snapping their pictures in front of the giant letters spelling "CUENCA." That's clearly meant for tourists. The plaza's open space is reserved now for civic events that celebrate Cuenca and its history, while those whose lives depend upon using that space today are quite literally consigned to the margins. For decades, *curanderas*, ritual healers who cleanse people of illness using scented herbs, found their own spaces on the streets in and around the 9 de Octubre market. Today, they have been rounded up together in the Plaza Rotary, an obligatory stop not for local shoppers but rather for tourists. It is one thing to do your work in public, as they have always done, and quite another to work in front of tourists snapping photos of a tradition they do not understand. Tourists are interested in the authentic, a desire that comes with their nostalgic romanticism and naïve assumption that a trip to Ecuador is a trip back in time.

The arrival of expats in Cuenca has, moreover, provoked me to think about the discipline's, and my own, pretensions about expertise, authenticity, representation, and authority. I've come to realize that expats' engagements and entanglements with Cuenca are no less real than my own, and they are equally, albeit perhaps differently, fraught. We all operate in spheres of privilege despite our best intentions. And then, I also know that the same global processes and flows that brought the expats also suggested the openings for Ecuadorian women to have more choices to be educated, work, marry, or not marry, and they provided reinforcement to the work of feminists fighting for domestic violence laws. Are there possibilities for a world where we can have those latter things without the former?

While expats, tourists, and the elite so often look backward for meaning, many of the Ecuadorians I have met are focused on the here and now. Some people, like Alejandra and Pilar, have taken a more standard route to do something in life (*hacer algo en la vida*) such as pursuing an education and a profession, yet improvisation plays a role as well in people's lives and their responses to changing circumstances. Returned migrants have become facilitators for American expats who cannot navigate the formidable Ecuadorian bureaucracies, and even expats are in on it, hawking barbeque sauce to each other. There are fewer women, paid and unpaid, at home making lunches, and more employers are requiring 9 a.m. to 6 p.m. working hours to synchronize better with global business hours. The two-hour lunch break when the family gets together and eats the largest meal of the day is on the wane. Thirty years ago, Blanca was on the cutting edge of working with this particular time-space compression, serving full meals on the street at midday for market vendors and workers whose homes were often in the countryside. Today, her son-in-law has built a modern version of that. He wakes at dawn to make gourmet sandwiches to sell to workers in office buildings. I have never seen a *cuencana* carry her own lunch to work, by the way; it is just not something that is done. In the summer of 2019, when Alejandra visited us in Michigan, she was bemused and intrigued as she watched my husband pack his lunch every day for work. It seemed a sort of radical proposition to her. Seeing something that you hadn't before, as Alejandra did in our kitchen, creates moments of attentiveness and a recognition that things as one knows them are just that.

In presenting this portrait of life in a midsize Latin American city, I have aimed to be sensitive to how change unfolds in big and small ways over the long course. I have argued that the perspectives afforded by time can shift and alter understandings, that lives and what motivates them change over time, and that the meanings and experiences of change cannot be assumed. My focus has been on the city and those who live in it or have migrated from it and to it, and for the most part the dynamics I have described have unraveled over time. It is often their accrual over many years that makes the changes noteworthy or even recognizable.

I worry that conditions may change more radically in the near future because of ongoing vulnerabilities in the oil and tourist industries and perhaps even more ominously because of population growth and climate change. Traffic and smog in Cuenca are increasing, the weather is generally warmer than it has been in the past, and the rains are no longer as predictable as they once were. So far, I have heard only grumblings about the changes people are experiencing. Rural-to-urban migrants may complain of dying cherry trees in their hometowns, older women might disapprove of the revealing summery clothing younger women wear, and in a city known for its cool climate many residents complain about the rising temperatures. Few *cuencanos* seem to like the hot days that are becoming more common in January and February; some say the heat exhausts them and that it is hard to sleep on warm nights, without the accustomed security of heavy woolen blankets. As the effects of climate change continue to unravel and emerge and as knowledge and experience of those effects accrues, this is the next urgent story of change, not just of Cuenca but of the world.

Notes

Chapter 1: The Ethnography of Accrual

1. In the 2001 edition of *Saints, Scholars, and Schizophrenics: Mental Illness in Rural Ireland*, Nancy Scheper-Hughes describes returning to the Irish village where she did her fieldwork decades earlier to attempt a rapprochement with the community she had written about. Villagers read the first edition of the book and did not much like how she portrayed them. Her attempt at a reconciliation in 1999 was unsuccessful; she remained mostly unwelcome in the village, but she was able to document some of the changes in the village over the decades.
2. Some, like Richard Price and Sally Price, who worked in Suriname in the 1960s, were unable to return to their field sites because of endemic warfare.
3. "Gringo" and the feminine "gringa" are used by Ecuadorians for white foreigners. Most people claimed that the terms are not meant to be insulting, and I became used to people calling me "la gringita," the little gringa. There are many urban legends about the etymology of the word, but it is used ubiquitously in Latin America. Depending on context, location, and circumstances, the term can be more or less insulting.
4. *Humitas* are similar to tamales.
5. In 2020 Bucaram was implicated in a Covid corruption scheme to sell personal protection equipment. His home was raided; thousands of Covid-19 tests were found there.
6. The spelling is "Quechua" in Peru and Bolivia and "Quichua" in Ecuador.
7. In October 2019, protests against Moreno's government and policies erupted all over Ecuador. The protests began with Indigenous groups but spread to transportation workers who were angered by his decision to raise gasoline prices. In a kind of neoliberal déjà vu, Moreno had agreed to International Monetary Fund terms that loans would only be forthcoming if Ecuador reduced long-standing government subsidies for fuel. Protests turned violent, roads were blocked, and Moreno's government reacted aggressively and some say unconstitutionally to disband protesters.
8. In the summer of 2018, Ecuador legalized same-sex marriage.

9. Ulla Berg argues that during their interviews, applicants for US visas in Peru have to do a degree of culture work to convince US authorities that they intend to be visitors who will return to Peru and not become undocumented immigrants (2015). This culture work can include such behaviors as displaying ease and confidence with authorities.

Dateline 1990: Remembering and Forgetting

1. The rules of polite discourse are reflected in these letters. Note the standard greeting in each, the apologies for poor handwriting and so forth, and the underlying fear of being forgotten. These typify polite and humble manners for the poorer classes in Cuenca.
2. He was in the Amazon region working in the oil industry for most of 1988–1989.
3. This is the phone number of the property owner downstairs.
4. "Muy costeño" is an insulting reference to people who live on the coast of Ecuador and are stereotyped by those in the mountains as rude, impolite, and brusque. Rosa had a falling-out with this brother because she was in charge of his savings account in Cuenca, and instead of depositing his remittances, she spent them. It took years for the family to pay back the money and repair relations.

Chapter 2: Making a Cosmopolitan City

1. David Berliner (2020) argues that nostalgia, in various forms, is a "major force" in understandings of heritage, especially as it is conceived, organized, and administered by UNESCO.
2. Translations are mine unless otherwise indicated.
3. Also see Comaroff and Comaroff 2009; Dávila 2012, 3.
4. Perhaps less salient than it once was, Akhil Gupta and James Ferguson's 1997 essay suggests that not all field sites are held in equally high esteem by anthropologists. Gupta and Ferguson identify an implicit "hierarchy of purity" that differentially values locations that are more "not home" over places that are less so (13). The more exotic, hard to reach, and distant a place, the more authentic the culture and therefore the anthropologist who documents it. So it follows that in a field that has long romanticized the remote village study in which the anthropologist becomes integrated into everyday life of a small community, urban anthropology was once a bit suspect as being a lesser sort of field experience.
5. The 2009 Facebook post "Amo ser cuencana" was by María Rosa Crespo, at https://www.facebook.com/MORLAKAM/posts/340648272724002/.
6. The term *cholo boy* was used ubiquitously in the 1980s and 1990s to describe young men who migrated to New York. Jaime Astudillo and Claudio Cordero contend that the term was first used for young men of so-called good families who left the area after the fall of the Panama hatmaking industry. With no hat industry to manage and few prospects for the kind of work they wanted, these

young men, dubbed "parasites of the countryside" by Astudillo and Cordero, went to New York. Many of them returned *en seguida*, right away, when they realized they would have to work too hard in New York (1990, 11–12). Today the term refers almost exclusively to poor young men who migrate and implies that they are interested in making money and displaying a New York sensibility in clothing, musical tastes, and attitude.

7. This sense of loss that I and others might feel is surely what Renato Rosaldo (1989) identifies as "imperialist nostalgia," a longing for that which we destroyed. "We" here signifies not just the neocolonial endeavors of anthropologists generally but also the relentless imposition and pace of global capitalism. The point is that the feelings of nostalgia are themselves steeped in relations of power and domination.

Dateline 1988–1989: The Virgin of Cajas

1. The source is an undated, unsigned manuscript attributed to accounts by Pachi, *Guardiana de la Fe: Mensajes de la Santísima Virgen en El Cajas-Ecuador* (Quito: Librería Espiritual). Page numbers are cited in text, and translations are mine.

2. A video of Patricia's address at the October 2012 conference in Miami is posted by Servants of the Pierced Hearts of Jesus and Mary in "Our Lady Guardian of the Faith" on the Pierced Hearts website, at https://www.piercedhearts.org/hearts_jesus_mary/apparitions/guardian_faith.html.

Chapter 3: Single Women in the City

1. During Rafael Correa's presidency, 2007–2017, one of his projects was to reform the public schools. His administration improved upon infrastructure, repairing, renovating, and building schools, and worked to implement reforms to curriculum and monitoring of teacher performance. New school texts were written to promote critical thinking in very early grades, and teachers were held accountable for lesson plans and student achievement. Teachers were electronically tracked, when they arrived and when they left their school buildings, and they had to post their lesson plans daily online. Some teachers welcomed the changes, as they provided clear structure to all; others, especially those who worked the less prestigious night schools, chafed under the new regulatory regime that made them accountable for class time. Most people I spoke with lauded the educational changes under Correa, saying that public schools made great strides during this time.

2. In Latin America the movement from rural to urban areas has often meant, paradoxically, a decrease in women's status. In rural areas women often had access to the means of production as a source of social status; in urban areas, unskilled women are often excluded from wage earning and therefore more dependent on wage-earning men (Babb 1989; Chant 2002).

3. Contributions to production do not guarantee a voice in family decision making, although I have noticed, as others report, a shift toward more egalitarian

relations when women work for wages (Chant 2002; Deere and Twynman 2012).

4. This is a bit of a misleading number because the Ecuadorian census bureau considers girls twelve years of age and older in this statistic.

5. According to Ecuador's 2010 census, 40 percent of women over eighteen years in Azuay Province were married, 37.9 percent were single, 8.4 percent were in civil unions, 6.6 percent were widowed, and 6.9 percent were divorced or separated (INEC 2010).

   Because of transnational migration, the provincial population as a whole averaged 52.6 percent women and 47.4 percent men, with larger differences apparent in rural areas (Valle 2018, 90). The differential in males to females begins to widen in the 30–34 age range, in which the population reaches 54 percent female. That difference is maintained until old age, when it widens further (INEC 2018, 92).

6. Since Correa's administration, employers of domestic workers were required to contribute to the workers' social security account. Many have told me that this requirement is often circumvented by paying laborers cash under the table.

7. For critiques of resistance, see Abu-Lughod 1990; Ortner 1995.

Dateline 1988–2020: Alejandra

1. Birth order in the Andes and elsewhere in Latin America generally figures into how households manage labor and what opportunities are given to children. Older children often have fewer educational opportunities than do their younger siblings, and they are given heavier household workloads. Later, as the younger children grow, they often are freed from the responsibilities of household work that their older siblings are already doing. Traditionally, the youngest child was pressured to stay home with parents and care for them in their old age, but that is changing with time.

2. I wrote this detail about Alejandra's barrettes not from field notes but from looking at photographs I took that day in the countryside. When Alejandra read this chapter, she pointed out that I gave her those barrettes, something I do not recall.

3. The social security system in Ecuador is a semipublic subscriber system providing retirement benefits and health care to members and, depending on the plan, their families. Most members receive benefits through employer contributions, although an individual may pay a monthly fee, similar to an insurance premium, to access health care benefits. The José Carrasco Arteago hospital in Cuenca has a very good reputation, far above that of the public hospital.

Chapter 4: Ni de Aqui, Ni de Allá

1. Delgado Travel was founded in the 1980s to provide primarily the Ecuadorian community in the United States with money transfers and courier and other services as well as travel needs. In the 1990s Western Union did not have much of a presence in Ecuador, so Delgado Travel was the hub for sending money

and gifts back and forth. Delgado Travel also sold prepaid phone cards in the 1990s and provides customers with internet calling services today. Much of the transfer of remittances would not have happened if not for Delgado Travel, as the company has provided easy and inexpensive means for people to send money home. It has more than one hundred locations in US and Ecuadorian cities, all beginning from Delgado's first location in the United States on Roosevelt Avenue in Jackson Heights, Queens, at the heart of the Ecuadorian immigrant community.

2. "Yany" comes from "Yo amo Nueva York" (I [heart] New York), the iconic tourist slogan of New York that originated in the late 1970s (Klara 2017).

3. Brad Jokisch and Jason Pribilsky, in their 2002 article "The Panic to Leave," discuss migration mostly to Spain that took off in the late 1990s and early 2000s. That migration came primarily from Guayaquil and Quito, and some of it was legally documented. Beginning in 2008, a persistent downturn in Spain's economy led officials there to crack down on undocumented Ecuadorians and to offer incentives for migrants to return to Ecuador.

4. A UN study shows that in 2008, more women than men migrated from some areas of Ecuador, often to Europe, but 67 percent of migrants from Cuenca and elsewhere in Azuay Province were males mostly going to the United States. Migration from Guayaquil was nearly 56 percent female, and from Quito the proportions of men and women who migrated were about the same (UNFPA and FLACSO 2008, 17).

5. Patricio Belancázar Carpio has found that because of the historically small size of most rural landholdings in Azuay Province, there is a long history of money lending in its rural communities. Those wishing to go to the United States have tapped into an established cultural practice (Carpio 1992). David Kyle and Rachel Goldstein (2011) elaborate on the complex and often intimate networks that are tapped to find moneylenders.

6. In their 2014 national-level survey of Ecuadorian households with migrant family members who reported ever getting remittances, Simone Bertoli and Franchesca Marchetta report that 29 percent said they had not received remittances during the one-year study period (1075).

7. Ulla Berg describes in wonderful detail the "performance" that must be enacted to dispel suspicions by immigration authorities of a "mismatch" between "the paperwork and the embodied self" (2015, 93). She argues that the idea is to display a "natural ease" and an aura of "entitlement," all of which is practiced repeatedly.

8. This was when immigration policy was to reunite children traveling alone with their parents regardless of their immigration status.

Chapter 5: The Gringo Invasion

1. Hayes discusses *ILM* in greater detail, noting that its owners are motivated by a libertarian worldview that encourages individuals to take advantage of global inequalities to improve their own financial circumstances (2018, 56–57).

2. The Statons pitch their "Retirement Reimagined!" course on their website, at https://www.eddandcynthia.com/program.

3. Philip Sloane and Johana Silbersack report that real estate prices in Cuenca have risen in part because of expats but just as likely because of Ecuadorians returning from overseas migration and investing in real estate (2020, 56). In my conversations with expats, they universally denied they had influenced real estate prices, stating that they are less than 1 percent of the population and that is too small to make a difference. Sloane and Silbersack contend that expats compose closer to 2 percent of the population of Cuenca, and close to 75 percent of those who responded to their surveys rented rather than owned (44).

4. The comment was posted June 23, 2020, on Ecuador Expat Forum in a thread called "Expat Exodus from Ecuador: Real or Imaginary," at Expat Exchange, https://www.expatexchange.com/expatguide/202/3442879/Ecuador/Expats -Living-in-Ecuador/Exodus-from-Ecuador-Real-or-Imajinary.

Dateline 2015–2019: Soon the Tourists Will Have the Place to Themselves

1. Jason Antrosio and Rudi Colloredo Mansfeld define "artisan" slightly differently, finding that production is based in the household, where kinship and labor intersect. The authors liken artisanry to "cottage industries" in which, despite market pressures, the producers have some autonomy over their work and schedules (2015, 33). The merchant speaking at the 2016 forum was adding to this understanding by saying that production and sale should be located in the same place.

2. The local nature of much of the Otavalan craft sold in Cuenca is actually a bit dubious. In casual conversations I have had with those selling in the San Francisco market, several admitted that the goods they sell are produced elsewhere and that they are in essence vendors of the work of others. The familial dimension of artisan work does seem to matter, and some were quick to add that their family members produced the goods near Otavalo. Although the rhetoric of artisan production is about ancient skills and arts, it is clear that what artisans produce is heavily influenced by global trends and market evaluations. Antrosio and Colloredo Mansfeld (2015) point out that Otavalan weavers have adjusted their styles and technologies to cater to varying markets. In the years I have been visiting the San Francisco market, I also have seen a shift from thick handmade wool sweaters to machine-made synthetic or alpaca blends and from geometric designs in weavings to large floral ones resembling work from southern Mexico. Ecuadorian artisans watch market trends closely, and their nominally traditional goods shift in style and workmanship.

3. The review was posted January 26, 2020, on the Tripadvisor webpage "Plaza San Francisco," at https://www.tripadvisor.com/Attraction_Review-g294309 -d13108113-Reviews-Plaza_de_San_Francisco-Cuenca_Azuay_Province.html.

Chapter 6. Thinking about Endings

1. Gioconda Herrera (2019) writes about how race and ethnicity affect the welcome Ecuadorians give to different immigrant groups. Despite the 2008

constitution that promoted citizenship, darker-skinned immigrants from Haiti and Cuba have found it far more difficult to acquire legal working papers than immigrants from elsewhere.

2. Christian Arias-Reyes and colleagues (2020) in a study of Bolivia and Ecuador found decreased rates of Covid-19 infection at high altitudes. The authors argue that previous acclimatization to high altitude could provide some protection.

References

Abad, Bernardo
  1989   "Migración y esperanza: Tierra de las mujeres solas." *Vistazo*, July 20, 36–40.

Abbots, Emma-Jayne
  2014   "Embodying Country-City Relations: The Chola Cuencana in Highland Ecuador." In *Food between the Country and City: Ethnographies of a Changing Global Foodscape*, edited by Nuno Domingos, José Manuel Sobral, and Harry G. West, 41–56. New York: Bloomsbury.

Abu-Lughod, Lila
  1990   "The Romance of Resistance: Tracing Transformations of Power through Bedouin Women." *American Ethnologist* 17, no. 1: 41–55.

Albornoz, Victor Manuel
  1950   *Cuenca, ciudad para todos: Su cultura, belleza y laborosidad*. Cuenca, Ecuador: Municipalidad de Cuenca.

Allen, Catherine
  2002   *The Hold Life Has: Coca and Cultural Identity in the Andes*. 2d ed. Washington, DC: Smithsonian Institution Press.

Altimirano, Teófilo
  1984   *Presencia Andina en Lima metropolitana: Estudio sobre migrantes y clubes de provincianos*. Lima: Pontificia Universidad Católica del Perú.

Altimirano, Teófilo, and Lane Ryo Hirabayashi
  1997   "The Construction of Regional Identities in Urban Latin America." In *Migrants, Regional Identities and Latin American Cities*, edited by Altimirano and Hirabayashi, 7–21. Washington DC: American Anthropological Association.

Antrosio, Jason, and Rudi Colloredo-Mansfeld
  2015   *Fast, Easy and In-Cash: Artisan Hardship and Hope in the Global Economy*. Chicago: University of Chicago Press.

Arias-Reyes, Christian, Liliana Poma-Machicao, Fernanda Aliaga-Raduan, Favio Carvajal-Rodriguez, Mathias Dutschmann, Edith M. Schneider-Gasser, Gustavo Zubieta-Calleja, and Jorge Soliz

    2020   "Does the Pathogenesis of SARS-CoV-2 Virus Decrease at High-Altitude?" *Respiratory Physiology and Neurobiology* 277 (June): 103443. doi: 10.1016/j.resp.2020.103443.

Astudillo, Jaime, and Claudio Cordero E.

    1990   *Huayrapamushcas en USA*. Quito: Conejo.

Babb, Florence E.

    1989   *Between Field and Cooking Pot: The Political Economy of Market Women in Peru*. Austin: University of Texas Press.

    2018   *Women's Place in the Andes: Engaging Decolonial Feminist Anthropology*. Berkeley: University of California Press.

Banco Central del Ecuador

    2018   *Evolución de las remesas región austro*. Annual report. Quito: Banco Central.

Becker, Mark

    2011   "Correa, Indigenous Movements, and the Writing of a New Constitution in Ecuador." *Latin American Perspectives* 38, no. 1: 47–62.

Beckerman, Paul, and Andres Solimano

    2002   *Crisis and Dollarization in Ecuador: Stability, Growth, and Social Equity*. Washington, DC: Directions in Development, World Bank.

Benson, Michaela

    2011   *The British in Rural France*. Manchester, UK: Manchester University Press.

Benson, Michaela, and Karen O'Reilly

    2016   "From Lifestyle Migration to Lifestyle in Migration: Categories, Concepts, and Ways of Thinking." *Migration Studies* 4, no. 1: 20–37.

Berg, Ulla D.

    2015   *Mobile Selves: Race, Migration, and Belonging in Peru and the U.S.* New York: New York University Press.

Berliner, David

    2020   *Losing Culture: Nostalgia, Heritage, and Our Accelerated Times*. Translation by Dominic Horsfall. New Brunswick, NJ: Rutgers University Press.

Bertoli, Simone, and Francesca Marchetta

    2014   "Migration, Remittances and Poverty in Ecuador." *Journal of Development Studies* 50, no. 8: 1067–1089.

Bettwy, Sister Isabel

    1991   *I Am the Guardian of the Faith: Reported Apparitions of the Mother of God in Ecuador*. Steubenville, OH: Franciscan University Press.

Biles, James J.

    2009   "Informal Work in Latin America: Competing Perspectives and Recent Debates." *Geography Compass* 3, no. 1: 214–236.

Boccagni, Paolo
2011   "The Framing of Return from above and below in Ecuadorian Migration: A Project, a Myth, or a Political Device?" *Global Networks* 11, no. 4: 461–480.

Boccagni, Paolo, and Luis Eduardo Pérez Mucio
2021   "Fixed Places, Shifting Distances: Remittance Houses and Migrants' Negotiation of Home in Ecuador." *Migration Studies* 9, no. 1: 47–64.

Boira, Santiago, Elisa Chilet-Rosell, Sofía Jaramillo-Quiroz, and Jessica Reinoso
2017   "Sexismo, pensamientos distorsionados y violencia en las relaciones de pareja en estudiantes universitarios de Ecuador de áreas relacionadas con el bienestar y la salud." *Universitas Psychologica* 16, no. 4: 1–12.

Buechler, Hans, and Judith-Maria Buechler
1996   *The World of Sofia Velasquez: The Autobiography of a Bolivian Market Vendor*. New York: Columbia University.

Calvacho, Jorge
1989   "Lloran 4 imágenes divinas en casa de vidente de El Cajas." *El Universo*, February 3.

Cardoso, Fausto Martínez
2012   *Espacios de la Memoria en Cuenca*. Cuenca, Ecuador: Instituto Nacional de la Patrimonial Cultural.

Carpio, Patricio Belancázar
1992   *Entre pueblos y metropolis: La migración internacional en comunidades austro andinas en el Ecuador*. Quito: Abya-Yala.

Casanova, Erynn Masi de
2011   *Making Up the Difference: Women, Beauty, and Direct Selling in Ecuador*. Austin: University of Texas Press.

Chant, Sylvia
2002   "Researching Gender, Families, and Households in Latin America: From the 20th into the 21st Century." *Bulletin of Latin American Research* 21, no. 4: 545–575.
2006   "Female Household Headship, Privation, and Power: Challenging the 'Feminization of Poverty' Thesis." In *Out of the Shadows: Political Action and the Informal Economy in Latin America*, edited by Patricia Fernández-Kelly and Jon Scheper, 125–163. University Park: Pennsylvania State University Press.

Chioda, Laura
2016   *Work and Family: Latin American Women in Search of a New Balance*. Washington, DC: International Bank for Reconstruction and Development, World Bank.

CIDAP (Centro Interamericano de Artes Populares)
2016   "La Plaza San Francisco atesora una historia de personajes y formas de ocupación." Reprint from *El Tiempo*, July 18. Quito: CIDAP.

Colson, Elizabeth
 1984 "The Reordering of Experience: Anthropological Involvement with Time." *Journal of Anthropological Research* 40, no. 1: 1–13.

Comacho, Gloria Z.
 2014 *La violencia género contra las mujeres en el Ecuador: Análisis de los resultados de la encuesta nacional sobre relaciones familiares y violencia de género contra las mujeres.* Quito: Consejo Nacional para la Igualdad de Género.

Comaroff, John L., and Jean Comaroff
 2009 *Ethnicity, Inc.* Chicago: University of Chicago Press.

Cordero Espinoza, Claudio, Lucas Achig Subía, and Adrián Carrasco Vintimilla
 1989 "La region centro-sur." In *La sociedad azuayo-cañari: Pasado y presente*, edited by Leonardo Espinoza, 15–35. Quito: El Conejo.

Cordero Iñiguez, Juan
 2012 "Cuencanos y cuencanas el la transicíon del siglo XVIII al XIX." In *Historia del Azuay: Estudios de caso*, edited by Ana Luz Borrero Vega, 163–182. Cuenca, Ecuador: Encuentro Nacional de Historia de la Provincia del Azuay.

Crespo Toral, Hernán
 1998 "Cuenca de los Andes." In *Cuenca de los Andes*, edited by Rodrigo Aguilar Orejuela, 12–16. Cuenca, Ecuador: Municipalidad de Cuenca.

Croucher, Sheila
 2012 "Privileged Mobility in an Age of Globality." *Societies* 2, no. 1: 1–13.

Cuenca, Municipalidad de
 2018 *Diccionario de la real lengua morlaca.* http://www.cuenca.gob.ec/sites /default/files/diccionario.pdf.

Deere, Carmen Diana, and Jennifer Twyman
 2012 Asset Ownership and Egalitarian Decision Making in Dual-headed Household in Ecuador. *Review of Radical Political Economics* 44, no. 3: 313–320.

De León, Jason
 2015 *The Land of Open Graves: Living and Dying on the Migrant Trail.* Berkeley: University of California Press.

De Paepe, Pierre, Ramiro Echeverría Tapia, Edison Aguilar Santacruz, and Jean-Pierre Unger
 2012 "Ecuador's Silent Health Reform." *International Journal of Health Services* 42, no. 2: 219–233.

DiAngelo, Robin
 2019 *White Fragility: Why It's So Hard for White People to Talk about Racism.* New York: Penguin.

Dicks, Bella
 2007 *Culture on Display: The Production of Contemporary Visitability.* Maidenhead, UK: McGraw-Hill Education.

Dwyer, Dana
2019   "I Help Expats Find Affordable Housing in Cuenca." *International Living Magazine*, March 3. https://internationalliving.com/.

El Mercurio
2018   "Tarifa del tranvía será la menor possible." December 14. https://web.archive.org/web/20181214173856/https://ww2.elmercurio.com.ec/2018/12/14/ministro-del-mtop-hizo-recorrido-del-tranvia/.
2019   "Plaza San Francisco aún no recupera su comercio." September 14. https://web.archive.org/web/20190918024705/https://ww2.elmercurio.com.ec/2019/09/14/plaza-san-francisco-aun-no-recupera-su-comercio/
2020a   "Migración al exterior afectará a fuerza laboral." June 30. https://elmercurio.com.ec/2021/06/30/migracion-al-exterior-afectara-a-fuerza-laboral/.
2020b   "Los cuerpos de emigrantes que murieron al ir a EEUU por México ya están en el país." July 15. https://elmercurio.com.ec/2020/07/15/los-cuerpos-de-emigrantes-que-murieron-al-ir-a-eeuu-por-mexico-ya-estan-en-el-pais/.
2021a   "Registro Civil busca emitir más pasaportes." June 9. https://elmercurio.com.ec/2021/06/09/registro-civil-busca-emitir-mas-pasaportes/.
2021b   "Analizan impacto de la migracíon en lo laboral." June 30. https://elmercurio.com.ec/2021/06/30/portada-impresa-del-30-junio-2021/.
2021c   "Hay una pandemia de migración illegal." July 10. https://elmercurio.com.ec/2021/07/10/hay-una-pandemia-de-migracion-ilegal/.
2021d   "Denuncian secuestro de migrantes de Azuay y Gualaquiza." August 11. https://elmercurio.com.ec/?s=11+agosto+2021.

El Tiempo
2017   "Morlaquita 2017 espera por su soberana." March 18. https://web.archive.org/web/20170318094618/http://www.eltiempo.com.ec/noticias/entretenimiento/13/409432/morlaquita-2017-espera-por-su-soberana.

El Universo
2018   "Las mujeres de Ecuador trabajan más horas y ganan menos que los hombres." March 8. https://www.eluniverso.com/noticias/2018/03/08/nota/6657202/mujeres-ecuador-trabajan-mas-horas-ganan-menos-que-hombres/.

Fabiano, Johannes
2014   *Time and the Other: How Anthropology Makes Its Objects.* New York: Columbia University Press.

Ferreiro, Larrie D.
2013   *Measure of the Earth: The Enlightenment Expedition That Reshaped Our World.* New York: Basic Books.

Ferreiro Salazar, Cynthia, Karina García García, Leandra Macías Leiva, Alba Pérez Avellaneda, and Carlos Tomsich, eds.
N.d.   *Mujeres y hombres del Ecuador en Cifras III.* Quito: Instituto Nacional de Estadística y Censos.

Fretes-Ciblis, Vicente, Marcelo M. Giugale, and José Roberto López-Cálix
  2003   *Ecuador: An Economic and Social Agenda in the New Millennium.* Washington, DC: World Bank.

García Álvarez, Milton, Pablo Osorio Guerrero, and Luis Pasot Herrera
  2017   *Estudio sobre los impactos socio-económicos en Cuenca de la Migracíon residencial de norteamericanos y europeos: aportes para una convivencia armónica local. Informe final.* Cuenca, Ecuador: Municipalidad de Cuenca and UN Development Program.

Gee, Chuck Y., and Edward M. Coe
  1986   *Strategic Tourism Market Plan for Ecuador.* Prepared for USAID Quito. Washington, DC: International Science and Technology Institute.

Geertz, Clifford
  1973   *The Interpretation of Cultures: Selected Essays by Clifford Geertz.* New York: Basic Books.
  1988   *Works and Lives: The Anthropologist as Author.* Stanford, CA: Stanford University Press.

Gerlach, Allen
  2003   *Indians, Oil, and Politics: A Recent History of Ecuador.* Wilmington, DE: Scholarly Resources.

Glick Schiller, Nina, and Noel B. Salazar
  2013   "Regimes of Mobility across the Globe." *Journal of Ethnic and Migration Studies* 39, no. 2: 183–200.

Goslinga, Gillian, and Geyla Frank
  2007   "In the Shadows: Anthropological Encounters with Modernity." Foreword to *The Shadow Side of Fieldwork: Exploring the Blurred Borders between Ethnography and Life*, edited by Athena McLean and Anette Liebling, xi–xviii. Malden, MA: Blackwell.

Gupta, Akhil, and James Ferguson
  1997   "Discipline and Practice: The 'Field' as Site, Method, and Location in Anthropology." In *Anthropological Locations: Boundaries and Grounds of a Field Science*, edited by Akhil Gupta and James Ferguson, 1–46. Berkeley: University of California Press.

Hayes, Matthew
  2015   "'It Is Hard Being the Different One All the Time': Gringos and Racialized Identity in Lifestyle Migration to Ecuador." *Ethnic and Racial Studies* 38, no. 6: 943–958.
  2018   *Gringolandia: Lifestyle Migration under Late Capitalism.* Minneapolis: University of Minnesota Press.

Hermida, M. Augusta, Diego Hermida, Natasha Cabrera, and Cristian Calle
  2015   "La densidad urbana como variable de análisis de la ciudad: El caso de Cuenca, Ecuador." *EURE* 41, no. 124: 25–44.

Herrera, Gioconda
  2019   "From Immigration to Transit Migration: Race and Gender Entanglements in New Migration to Ecuador." In *New Migration Patterns in*

the Americas: Challenges for the 21st Century, edited by Andreas E. Feldman, Xóchtil Bada, and Stephanie Schütze, 285–315. New York: Palgrave-Macmillan.

Hidalgo-Capitán, Antonio Luis, and Ana Patricia Cubillo-Guevara
2014   "Seis debates abiertos sobre el Sumak Kawsay." *Íconos: Revista de Ciencias Sociales* 48: 25–40.

Higgins, Liam
2015   "Canadian Researcher Says That Despite Good Intentions, Cuenca Expats Help Sustain a Racist Class System That Oppresses Poorer Ecuadorians." *Cuenca Highlife*, July 2. https://cuencahighlife.com /article-claims-that-cuenca-expats-help-perpetuate-a-class-system -that-oppresses-poorer-ecuadorians-author-says-foreign-residents-are -racialized-white/.
2016   "San Francisco Plaza, a Focus of Cuenca Civic and Cultural Life for More than 450 Years, Reopens Today after 18-Month Renovation." *Cuenca Highlife*, January 29. https://cuencahighlife.com/san-francisco -plaza-years-intersection-urban-rural-life-frequently-focus-conflict/.

High, Holly
2011   "Melancholia and Anthropology." *American Ethnologist* 38, no. 2: 217–233.

Hirabayashi, Lane Ryo
1986   "The Migrant Village Association in Latin America: A Comparative Analysis." *Latin American Research Review* 21: 7–29.

Hirschkind, Lynn
1980   "On Conforming in Cuenca." PhD diss., University of Wisconsin.

Howell, Signe, and Aud Talle
2012   Introduction. In *Returns to the Field: Multitemporal Research and Contemporary Anthropology*, edited by Signe Howell and Aud Talle, 1–22. Bloomington: Indiana University Press.

Humboldt, Alexander von
2005   *Alexander von Humboldt: Diarios de viaje en la audiencia de Quito*. Edited by Segundo E. Moreno Yánez, translation by Christiana Borchat de Moreno.

Hurtado, Osvaldo
2002   *Deuda y desarrollo en el Ecuador contemporáneo*. Quito: Planeta.
2010   *Portrait of a Nation: Culture and Progress in Ecuador*. Translation by Barbra Sipe. Lanham, MD: Madison Books.

INEC (Ecuador, Instituto Nacional de Estadística y Censos)
2002   Provincia del Azuay: Difusión de resultados definitivos del VI Censo de Población y V de Vivienda 2001. Ecuador en Cifras, July. https:// www.ecuadorencifras.gob.ec/documentos/web-inec/Bibliotecas /Fasciculos_Provinciales/Fasciculo_Azuay.pdf.
2010   Resultados del Censo 2010: Fascículo provincial Azuay. Ecuador en Cifras. http://www.ecuadorencifras.gob.ec/wp-content/descargas /Manu-lateral/Resultados-provinciales/azuay.pdf.

2017a   "Los divorcios crecieron 83.45% en diez años en Ecuador." Ecuador en Cifras, June 2. https://www.ecuadorencifras.gob.ec/los-divorcios-crecieron-8345-en-diez-anos-en-ecuador/.

2017b   "Conozcamos a Cuenca a través de sus cifras." Ecuador en Cifras, November 1. https://www.ecuadorencifras.gob.ec/conozcamos-cuenca-a-traves-de-sus-cifras/.

2018   "En 27 años: Tasa de natalidad disminuyó en 13,4 nacidos vivos." Ecuador en Cifras, June 29. https://www.ecuadorencifras.gob.ec/en-27-anos-tasa-de-natalidad-disminuyo-en-134-nacidos-vivos/.

International Living Magazine

2009   "Colonial Cuenca: The World's Top Retirement Haven 2009." September 29, 16–17.

2020   "Cuenca, Ecuador." https://web.archive.org/web/20200921200011/https://internationalliving.com/countries/ecuador/cuenca/.

Jackson, John L., Jr.

2015   "Ethnography Is, Ethnography Ain't." In *Writing Culture and the Life of Anthropology*, edited by Orin Starn, 152–169. Durham, NC: Duke University Press.

Jackson, Michael

2017   "After the Fact: The Question of Fidelity in Ethnographic Writing. In *Crumpled Paper Boat: Experiments in Ethnographic Writing*, edited by Anand Pandian and Stuart J. McLean, 48–66. Durham, NC: Duke University Press.

Jacome H., Luis I.

2004   *The Late 1990s Financial Crisis in Ecuador: Institutional Weaknesses, Fiscal Rigidities, and Financial Dollarization at Work*. IMF Working Paper.

Jijón, Diego

1989   "Las apariciones de María." *Vistazo*, September 22, 1989, 70–75.

Jokisch, Brad, and Jason Pribilsky

2002   "The Panic to Leave: Economic Crisis and the 'New Emigration' from Ecuador." *International Migration* 40, no. 4: 75–102.

Klara, Robert

2017   "How the 'I Heart NY' Logo Transcended Marketing and Endures 4 Decades after Its Debut." *Adweek*, September 10, 2017. https://www.adweek.com/brand-marketing/how-the-i-heart-ny-logo-twice-transcended-marketing-and-endures-4-decades-after-its-debut/.

Klaufus, Christien

2006   *Bad Taste in Architecture: Discussion of the Popular in Residential Architecture in Southern Ecuador*. Utrecht, Netherlands: Department of Anthropology, Utrecht University.

2012   *Urban Residence: Housing and Social Transformations in Globalizing Ecuador*. New York: Berghahn.

Knauft, Bruce M.

2002   *Exchanging the Past: A Rainforest World of Before and After*. Chicago: University of Chicago Press.

Kyle, David
  2000   *Transnational Peasants: Migrations, Networks, and Ethnicity in Andean Ecuador.* Baltimore, MD: Johns Hopkins University Press.

Kyle, David J., and Rachel Goldstein
  2011   *Migration Industries: A Comparison of the Ecuador-US and Ecuador-Spain Cases.* Fiesole, Italy: European University Institute.

Leinaweaver, Jessaca
  2008   "Improving Oneself: Young People Getting Ahead in the Peruvian Andes." *Latin American Perspectives* 35, no. 4: 60–78.

Lind, Amy
  2003   "Gender and Neoliberal States: Feminists Remake the Nation in Ecuador." *Latin American Perspectives* 128, no. 3: 181–207.
  2012   "Revolution with a Woman's Face: Family Norms, Constitutional Reforms, and the Politics of Redistribution in Post-Neoliberal Ecuador." *Rethinking Marxism* 24, no. 4: 536–555.

Lobo, Susan
  1982   *A House of My Own: Social Organization in the Squatter Settlement.* Albuquerque: University of New Mexico Press.

Long, Colin, and Sophia Labadi
  2010   Introduction to *Heritage and Globalization*, edited by Sophia Labadi and Colin Long, 1–16. New York: Routledge.

López Monsalve, Rodrigo
  2003   *Cuenca patrimonial cultural de la humanidad.* Cuenca, Ecuador: Montsalve Moreno.

Malinowski, Bronislaw
  1961   *Argonauts of the Western Pacific.* New York: E. P. Dutton

Mancero Acosta, Mónica
  2012   *Nobles y cholos: Raza, género y clases en Cuenca 1995–2005.* Quito: Facultad Latinoamericana de Ciencias Sociales.

Márquez Tapia, Ricardo
  1995   *Cuenca colonial.* Biblioteca de Historia Ecuatoriana, volume 13. Quito: Nacional.

Mata-Codesal, Diana
  2013   "Towards a Gender-Sensitive Approach to Remittances in Ecuador." In *The International Handbook on Gender, Migration, and Transnationalism: Global and Development Perspectives*, edited by Laura Oso and Natalia Ribas, 361–375. Cheltenham, UK: Edward Elgar.

Melo, Ana C.
  2006   *Transnationalism in New York City: A Study of Remittance Sending by Ecuadorian Migrants.* Medford, MA: Fletcher School, Tufts University.

Metcalf, Peter
  2001   *They Lie, We Lie: Getting On with Anthropology.* New York: Routledge.

Middleton, DeWight R.
1981   "Ecuadorian Transformations: An Urban View." In *Cultural Transformations and Ethnicity in Modern Ecuador*, edited by Norman J. Whitten, 211–232. Urbana: University of Illinois Press.

Miles, Ann
2000   "Poor Adolescent Girls and Social Transformations in Cuenca, Ecuador." *Ethos* 28, no. 1: 54–74.
2004   *From Cuenca to Queens: An Anthropological Story of Transnational Migration*. Austin: University of Texas Press.
2013   *Living with Lupus: Women and Chronic Illness in Ecuador*. Austin: University of Texas Press.
2016   "*Sufrimiento* and Long-Term Ethnographic Engagement." In *Ethnographic Collaborations in Latin America: The Effects of Globalization*, edited by June C. Nash and Hans C. Buechler, 203–220. New York: Palgrave-Macmillan.

Mola, James
2011   "The Remembrances of Another Time Found in Cuenca." *Cuenca Perspectives by Jim*. Blog. April 3. http://cuencaperspectivesbyjim.blogspot.com/2011/04/.

Molstad, Gro Mathilde
1996   "*Guardiana de la Fe*": *Oposición religiosa y negociación de identidad, los nobles de Cuenca*. Quito: Abya-Yala.

ONU Mujeres
2015   *Mujeres ecuatorianas: Dos décadas de cambios 1995–2015*. Quito: United Nations.

Orejuela Aguilar, Rodrigo
2009   *Mercado, barrio y ciudad: Historia de "la Nueve."* Cuenca, Ecuador: Municipalidad de Cuenca.

Orlove, Ben
2002   *Lines in the Water: Nature and Culture at Lake Titicaca*. Berkeley: University of California Press.

Ormond, Meghann
2014   "Resorting to Plan J: Popular Perceptions of Singaporean Retirement Migration to Johor, Malaysia." *Asian and Pacific Migration Journal* 23, no. 1: 1–26.

Ortner, Sherry
1995   "Resistance and the Problem of Ethnographic Refusal." *Comparative Studies of Society and History* 37, no. 1: 173–193.

Pace, Richard
1998   *The Struggle for Amazon Town: Gurupá Revisited*. Boulder, CO: Lynne Rienner.

Paerregaard, Karsten
1997   *Linking Separate Worlds: Urban Migrants and Rural Lives in Peru*. Berg: New York.

Palacios Espinoza, Elvira, and Claudia Espinoza Molina
2014   "Contaminación del aire exterior: Cuenca-Ecuador 2009–2013; posibles efectos en la salud." *Revista de la Facultad de Ciencias Médicas Universidad de Cuenca* 32, 2: 6–17.

Parkin, David
2000   "Fieldwork Unfolding." In *Anthropologists in a Wider World*, edited by Paul Dresch, Wendy James, and David Parkin, 259–273. New York: Berghahn.

Pendelton, Wade
2002   "Katutura and Namibia: The People, the Place, and the Fieldwork." In *Chronicling Cultures: Long-Term Field Research in Anthropology*, edited by Robert V. Kemper and Anya Peterson Royce, 34–58. Walnut Creek, CA: Altamira.

Peoples Dispatch
2020   "University Students and Professors in Ecuador Protest against Budget Cuts." May 6. https://peoplesdispatch.org/2020/05/06 /university-students-and-professors-in-ecuador-protest-against -budget-cuts/.

Pribilsky, Jason
2007   *La Chulla Vida: Gender, Migration, and the Family in Andean Ecuador and New York City*. Syracuse, NY: Syracuse University Press.

Price, Richard, and Sally Price
2017   *Saamaka Dreaming*. Chapel Hill, NC: Duke University Press.

Radcliffe, Sarah, and Sallie Westwood
1996   *Remaking the Nation: Place, Identity, and Politics in Latin America*. London: Routledge.

Revista Avance
2016   "La Plaza de San Francisco al fin renovará su imagen." March 18. https://www.revistavance.com/component/content/article/18-marzo -de-2016/2749-la-plaza-de-san-francisco-al-fin-renovara-su-imagen .html?Itemid=101.

Rosaldo, Renato
1989   "Imperialist Nostalgia." *Representations* 26 (Spring): 107–122.

Ruales, Rebecca
2017   "Rafael Correa: The Ecuadorian Dream." *Harvard Political Review*, June 6. https://web.archive.org/web/20170606153337/http:// harvardpolitics.com/world/rafael-correa-the-ecuadorian-dream/.

Sanjek, Roger
1990   "A Vocabulary for Fieldnotes." In *Fieldnotes: The Making of Anthropology*, edited by Roger Sanjek, 92–121. Ithaca, NY: Cornell University Press.

Scarpaci, Joseph L.
2005   *Plazas and Barrios: Heritage Tourism and Globalization in the Latin American Centro Histórico*. Tucson: University of Arizona Press.

Scheper-Hughes, Nancy
2001　*Saints, Scholars, and Schizohrenics: Mental Illness in Rural Ireland.* Berkeley, CA: University of California.

Scott, Paul C.
1987　*Weapons of the Weak: Everyday Forms of Peasant Resistance.* New Haven, CT: Yale University Press.

Seligman, Linda J.
1989　"To Be in Between: The Cholas as Market Women." *Comparative Studies in Society and History* 31, no. 4: 694–721.
1993　"Between Worlds of Exchange: Ethnicity among Peruvian Market Women." *Cultural Anthropology* 8, no. 2: 187–213.

Sloane, Philip D., and Johanna Silbersack
2020　"Real Estate, Housing, and the Impact of Retirement Migration in Cuenca, Ecuador, and San Miguel de Allende, Mexico." In *Retirement Migration from the U.S. to Latin American Colonial Cities*, edited by Philip D. Sloane, Sheryl Zimmerman, and Johanna Silbersack, 41–66. Cham, Switzerland: Springer.

Trouillot, Michel-Rolph
2003　*Global Transformations: Anthropology and the Modern World.* New York: Palgrave Macmillan.

UNESCO
N.d.　"Historic Centre of Santa Ana de los Ríos de Cuenca." http://whc.unesco.org/en/list/863.

UNFPA and FLACSO (UN Population Fund and Facultad Latinoamericana de Ciencias Sociales)
2008　*Ecuador: La migración internacional en cifras.* Quito: UNFPA and FLACSO.

Urry, John
1990　*The Tourist Gaze: Leisure and Travel in Contemporary Societies.* London: Sage.

Valle, C.
2018　*Atlas de género.* Quito: Instituto Nacional de Estadistica y Censos.

Viteri, Maria Amelia
2015　"Cultural Imaginaries in the Residential Migration to Cotacachi." *Journal of Latin American Geography* 14, no. 1: 119–138.

Wang, Cheng-Tong Lir, and Evan Schofer
2018　"Coming Out of the Penumbras: World Culture and Cross-National Variation in Divorce Rates." *Social Forces* 97, no. 2 (December): 675–704.

Weismantel, Mary J.
1989　*Food, Gender, and Poverty in the Ecuadorian Andes.* Philadelphia: University of Pennsylvania Press.
2002　*Cholas and Pishtacos: Stories of Race and Sex in the Andes.* Chicago: University of Chicago Press.

Whitaker, Robert
 2004   *The Mapmaker's Wife: A True Tale of Love, Murder, and Survival in the Amazon*. New York: Basic Books.

World Bank
 N.d.   Fertility Rate, Total (Births per Woman)—Ecuador. https://data.worldbank.org/indicator/SP.DYN.TFRT.IN?locations=EC.

Wulf, Andrea
 2015   *The Invention of Nature: Alexander von Humboldt's New World*. New York: Knopf.

Index

social security: in Ecuador, 62,
68, 69, 70, 114, 178n3 (chap. 3),
178n6; in United States, 140,
141, 144
Staton, Ed and Cynthia, 143, 179n2
(chap. 5)
sufrimiento, 6, 81–83
Sumak Kawsay, 15, 45
superar, 62

Talbot, Patricia, 53–59
They Lie, We Lie (Metcalf), 136
tourism, 2, 16, 24, 30–32, 46
traffickers (*coyotes* or smugglers), 97,
98, 103, 111
trafficking, 48, 50, 135, 174;
pilgrimage and, 56, 57
transnational migration, 10, 18, 23,
24, 31, 171; demographic shifts
in, 178n5; effects on families of,
101–102; elite perceptions of, 43,
58; experiences of, 94–116; rates
of, 100
tranvía, 20, 36, 48–49, 50

ugly American, 136
UNESCO, 30–31, 36, 154;
description of Cuenca, 47
Universidad de Cuenca (University of
Cuenca), 39, 157
urban anthropology. *See* ethnography
US Border Patrol, 97, 100

US immigration policy, 100, 179n8
US–Mexico border, 96–98, 100, 105,
111, 116, 164

Venezuelan migrants, 19, 131, 139,
162
Vicente, 102–110; adolescence of,
85–89, 102; family relations of,
90; fieldwork observations of, 84,
85–86; future plans of, 113–115;
letters from, 25–29; remittances
from, 114; view of tourists by, 47
Virgin of Cajas, 52–59, 171
visas, US, 21, 97, 107, 115, 116, 176n9
Vistazo magazine, 55, 57, 95, 99
Viteri, Maria Amelia, 145

Wang, Cheng-Tong Lir, 67
Weismantel, Mary J., 32
Westwood, Sallie, 36
Whitaker, Robert, 40
William (Will), 110–115, 164–167
women: and adolescence 63, 90;
education of, 62, 68, 122; fertility
of, 66; rights of, 65; roles of,
65–67, 89, 117, 129; violence
against 65, 68, 79, 110, 173; virtue
of, 63, 90; and work, 64, 67–70,
121, 177n3
World Bank, 66
World Heritage Site designation,
30–31, 36, 47, 154